DECEPTION

The Untold Story of
East-West Espionage Today

EDWARD LUCAS

WALKER & COMPANY

NEW YORK

Published by Walker Publishing Company, Inc., New York
A Division of Bloomsbury Publishing

All papers used by Walker & Company are natural, recyclable products made
from wood grown in well-managed forests. The manufacturing processes conform
to the environmental regulations of the country of origin.

LIBRARY OF CONGRESS CATALOGING-IN-PUBLICATION DATA
Lucas, Edward, 1962–
Deception : the untold story of East-West espionage today / Edward Lucas. — 1st U.S. ed.
p. cm.
Includes bibliographical references and index.
ISBN 978-0-8027-1157-1
1. Western countries—Foreign relations—Russia (Federation) 2. Russia (Federation)—Foreign
relations—Western countries. 3. United States—Foreign relations—Russia (Federation)
4. Russia (Federation)—Foreign relations—United States.
5. Espionage, Russian—Western countries. 6. Espionage, Russian—United States.
7. Deception—Political aspects—Russia (Federation) I. Title.
D2025.5.R8L83 2012
327.12470182'1—dc23
2012005559

Visit Walker & Company's website at www.walkerbooks.com

First U.S. edition 2012

1 3 5 7 9 10 8 6 4 2

Typeset by Hewer Text UK Ltd, Edinburgh

Printed in the U.S.A. by Quad/Graphics, Fairfield, Pennsylvania

To My Parents

CONTENTS

INSET 2

R U S S I A

ABKHAZIA

Sukhumi

INGUSHETIA

Groźny

CHECHNYA

Black

SOUTH
OSSETIA

Tskhinvali

DAGESTAN

Sea Poti

Gori

G E O R G I A

Tbilisi

TURKEY

ARMENIA

AZERBAIJAN

0   100 miles

0   100 kilometres

Yerevan

R U S S I A

Moscow

K A Z A K H S T A N

Aral Sea

UZBEKISTAN

K R A I N E

Rostov

Caspian
Sea

TURKMENISTAN

Crimea

Ashgabat

SEE INSET 2

Baku

Black Sea

AZERBAIJAN

nbul

ARMENIA

Ankara

Tehran

T U R K E Y

I R A N

SYRIA

Baghdad

CYPRUS

I R A Q

LEBANON

KUWAIT

Introduction

The cold breath of the communist secret police state blighted countless lives behind the Iron Curtain. But it also touched my own childhood in 1970s Oxford. Olgica, our Yugoslav lodger, had an exciting secret: Uncle Dušan. The poet Matthew Arnold described Oxford as 'home of lost causes, and forsaken beliefs, and unpopular names, and impossible loyalties'. In Dušan's case, this was partly right: his surname (like those of most East European émigrés) if not exactly unpopular, was certainly baffling to British eyes and ears. I recall him as a glum, shadowy figure, with plenty to be glum about. His cause seemed irretrievably lost. He was a hero in his own twilight world, but in post-war Yugoslavia the authorities denounced anti-communists like him as criminals and traitors.* Many perished in mass graves or in the torture cells of the secret police. Dušan was one of the lucky ones. He had escaped to

---

* An official of the pre-war royalist government, his side had lost out to the communists in the internecine strife in wartime Yugoslavia. There (as in much of Eastern Europe) the Second World War had been a fight between not two sides, but three. The Nazis had battled with communist partisans and the royalist Chetniks, who loathed each other as much as they hated the invaders. When the Germans lost, the communists (who had enjoyed strong backing from Britain and America as well as from the Soviet Union) won their civil war against the much weaker royalists, and labelled them as fascist collaborators.

Britain, to a humble job as a mechanic and life in Crotch Crescent, a drab street in Oxford's outskirts — a sad comedown for someone who in pre-war Yugoslavia had been a high-flying young civil servant.

But in one respect, Dušan did not fit Arnold's dictum. Despite his disappointments, he had not forsaken his beliefs: communism was evil and the people who ruled his homeland were usurpers. In fact, Yugoslavia's independent-minded communists had become mild by comparison with the much tougher regimes of the Soviet bloc. But they were still ruthless in their treatment of dissenters, particularly those in contact with anti-communists abroad. Olgica's family maintained, at great risk, secret links with émigré relatives, flatly denying all knowledge of them under interrogation from the secret police. In Oxford, she visited her uncle each weekend. Had the authorities at home known that she was hobnobbing with a dangerous anti-communist émigré, her father's glittering medical career (which had even brought him, briefly, to Oxford) would end; her own future (she had stayed on to finish her schooling) would be jeopardised too. It could even be dangerous for her to return home, leaving her stranded in Britain as a teenage refugee.

My own childish preoccupations blundered into this grown-up world. Even before Olgica's arrival, my boyhood obsession had been Eastern Europe. I would spend hours looking at dusty atlases and reading about the vanished kingdoms and republics of the pre-communist era, with their long-forgotten politicians, quaint postage stamps and exotic languages. Now behind the Iron Curtain, they seemed as distant and unreal as Atlantis. In my early teens I needed an example of communist propaganda for a school history project and decided to write to the Yugoslav embassy in London, asking for an official statement of how their government saw their defeated royalist rivals. That would, I thought, sit nicely alongside the other exhibits I had already assembled, including a passage from Winston Churchill's history of the war, a poignant account of life in Cambridge by the exiled Yugoslav boy-king Peter, and a sizzling history of a British military mission to his doomed soldiers, the Chetniks.[1]

I proudly announced my plan. To my consternation, Olgica turned white. My mother took me aside: didn't I understand that the Yugoslav embassy in London would at once hand over this letter to the secret police? (With its sinister-sounding acronym UDBA, the *Uprava državne bezbednosti* or Department of State Security was the bane of the regime's critics at home and abroad). It would be obvious that my childish enquiry came from the very Oxford address at which the daughter of a top Yugoslav paediatrician was living while completing her A-levels. It was bad enough that the UDBA would instantly suspect her of propagandising about the royalist past – a crime in Yugoslavia. Worse, it would start checking up on her family history and might then discover her carefully concealed ties to the notorious inhabitant of Crotch Crescent. Her life could unravel in an instant.

This trivial episode taught me important lessons – albeit in politics not history. First, that the power of the communist state was based on the relentless, intrusive, bureaucratic reach of the security and intelligence services, and their capacity to ruin the lives of those who displeased them. Second that these agencies' reach extended far beyond their own grim dominions – even to the seemingly safe and secure world of an English university town. The extraordinary idea that my actions could put me under scrutiny by hostile foreign officials sparked an interest that has gripped me for decades. In the years that followed I devoured spy literature, from defectors' memoirs to John le Carré's novels. I tracked down retired spies and quizzed them. I also kept a beady eye on contemporaries who were offered jobs by MI6, as Britain's Secret Intelligence Service, SIS, is colloquially known.*

Even without knowing much about the intelligence world I was struck by the clumsiness of those approaches: on the same day a crop of identical government-issue buff envelopes would arrive in student pigeonholes. Some recipients ignored the strictures to keep silent. A friend even framed the letter and put it in his lavatory, so his friends could appreciate the unconvincing letterhead and the strangulated wording of the offer: 'From time to time opportunities arise in government service overseas of a specialised and confidential nature.' For those who did apply, the clumsy efforts of the vetting officers (also accompanied by dire warnings about secrecy) were similarly corrosive of confidence in the spooks' world-view. Did it really matter in the struggle against the Soviet empire, I wondered, if Tom had gay flings, if Dick smoked dope or if Harriet had a boyfriend in the Socialist Workers' Party?

I reckoned I could do more good on the outside, and searched for any East European cause that would accept my help. Inspired by my father, who smuggled books to fellow-philosophers persecuted in Czechoslovakia, I helped organise a student campaign to support Poland's Solidarity movement, crushed by martial law in December 1981. I waved placards outside embassies and wrote letters of protest on behalf of political prisoners. I studied unfashionable languages such as Polish, and practised them by befriending bitter old émigrés in the dusty clubs and offices of west London – the world of le Carré's Estonian 'General' in *Smiley's People*.[2] Like the spy author's fictional émigrés, these real-life ones had been

---

* Based since 1995 in a green-glazed ziggurat on the southern bank of the Thames, the Secret Intelligence Service is informally called MI6; semi-official names include 'the Friends' or more formally 'Other Whitehall Agencies'. Its employees usually refer to 'the Office'; outside contacts may coyly call it 'the Firm'.

sponsored by Britain's spooks, then betrayed and dumped. I did not know then the full extent of the fiasco of Operation Jungle, which I detail in chapter 9.

This book is the result of my twin interests, espionage and Eastern Europe. I would occasionally take the number 12 bus down Westminster Bridge Road in Lambeth, past the headquarters of Britain's MI6. The location was in those days, supposedly, a closely guarded official secret, though the bus conductor was prone to announce jovially 'Century House – all spies alight here'. I never went inside. But I would gaze up at the grubby concrete structure, with a petrol station incongruously sited in its forecourt. Was this really our answer to the fearsome Soviet Lubyanka in Moscow? The imposing classical façade of the KGB citadel (originally an insurance company headquarters) would have suited the grandest streets in central London. But the MI6 building looked liked a scruffy Soviet tower block.

Spies, whether paid agents, idealistic volunteers, or professional intelligence officers, were foot soldiers in the struggle between East and West that shaped the lives of all post-war generations, including mine. They intrigued me as a student, activist and journalist, first in London and later behind the Iron Curtain. In the 1980s I rubbed shoulders and clinked glasses with spooks on both sides, dodging their blandishments while swapping jokes, jibes, arguments and ideas. For a brief while, the collapse of communism looked set to doom the whole business. Now that the Soviet Union was gone, and with it the danger of the Cold War turning hot, what was left to spy on? But the champagne corks that spooks popped in Britain and America in August 1991 were as premature as the gloom in the Lubyanka as the statue of Felix Dzerzhinsky, Lenin's secret-police chief, was hauled away by a crane to the cheers of exuberant Muscovites. MI6, the CIA and their partner services rejigged their budgets and turned to new targets: rogue arms dealers, terrorists, gangsters and cyber-criminals. But new crime and old espionage soon proved to be easy bedfellows; the spivs and crooks in the foreground were sometimes new, but in the background lurked, more often than not, the wily and ruthless figures of the old Soviet-block intelligence world.

They were the dark partners in the new order. Far from being swept into the dustbin of history with the rubble of the old system, the communist-era spooks have evolved to match the new conditions. Some figures from the old days stayed undercover, gaining trusted roles in the new state structures. One of them was the Estonian Herman Simm, whose activities are the subject of chapter 11. Others turned to business, where their foreign languages and knowledge of the outside world gave them a flying start in the new game. All across the former Soviet empire, assets of the Communist Party and its front organisations speedily melted away, often ending up in the hands of the wily and well connected. So too did the operational funds of the KGB and its allied agencies. Estimates of the money squirrelled away abroad during the collapse of the Soviet Union are in the tens of billions of dollars; a crop of still-unexplained suicides in the old system's dying days disposed of those in a position to blab.[3] These caches of illicitly acquired cash were a financial springboard for the fleet-footed members of the old elite in their new business careers. In effect they turned their power into wealth, and then back into power.

In Russia itself Soviet-era spies, chief among them Vladimir Putin, a former KGB officer, now run the country. They are known as the *Siloviki* or 'men of power'.* The old KGB was

---

* An untranslatable Russian word derived from *sila* (force). It could be rendered as 'men of power' or more colloquially as 'the hard men'. It chiefly refers to the veterans of the Soviet-era KGB and members of its successor organisations. But it also includes those with a background in the armed forces and in the quasi-military Interior Ministry (MVD) as well as prosecutors and other agencies with the powers to snoop, bug and punish.

decapitated in 1991 amid the Soviet collapse, but not uprooted. Instead it renamed itself, just as so often in the past. (Under Vladimir Lenin it was the Cheka; later it became the OGPU, then the NKVD and finally the KGB.) It is now split into two: the FSB, which has inherited the repressive domestic apparatus of the old system, and the SVR, which is the heir to the Soviet foreign intelligence service; alongside both works the separate GRU military intelligence agency.[4]

Part of this book, therefore, deals with this deception: the story of how the ex-spooks and their friends, in effect in a criminal conspiracy, took over one of the world's largest countries, hugely enriching themselves and duping the West. Their modus operandi fuses organised crime, big business, conventional diplomacy – and intelligence. I show that Russia's spymasters are now using not only old tools against us, but also new ones of which their Soviet-era predecessors could only have dreamed.

Their most potent weapon is ordinariness. Just as Russian politicians and officials seem at first sight to hail from the same besuited and unremarkable caste as their counterparts in other industrialised countries, the spies I describe in this book appear neither glamorous nor sinister. They lead normal lives and work in normal jobs, moving effortlessly and inconspicuously among us. They are the kind of people you might meet at the school gates, work alongside in an office, bump into on a business trip, or see mowing the lawn next door. Yet their real job is to penetrate our society, to influence it for their own ends, and to steal our secrets.

The best known of this new generation of Russian spies was Anna Chapman, the young redhead who was made a global superstar by her arrest and deportation in June 2010. She has become an intimate friend of Mr Putin's, a prized asset of his political machine, a prominent figure in Russian finance, and a television celebrity. But as I show in chapter 7, her main talents in working abroad were not the highly honed skills of spy-school legend. She started her life here in the humdrum London suburb of Stoke Newington, to the outside eye just another hard-partying, quick-witted young Russian woman with an English husband and an eye for the main chance, enjoying the safety and comfort of life in Britain. But her ordinariness was deceptive. She was well placed to carry out her espionage assignments precisely because she seemed so inconspicuous. Her later transformation into a trophy superspy adds another dimension. It is proof of the skills of her *imidzhmekeri* (image-makers) and casts a revealing light on Russia itself.

The spy scandal that made Ms Chapman famous was part of a larger picture. She was one of ten people arrested in the United States in June 2010, all of whom lived unremarkable middle-class lives, seemingly far away from traditional espionage targets such as the Pentagon or State Department. She and another Russian lived there under their own names. Seven others had fraudu-lently obtained identities – American, British, Canadian, Irish and Uruguayan (the tenth was the latter's Peruvian spouse). One more suspect, a Russian called Pavel Kapustin, working under the alias of Christopher Metsos, was arrested in Cyprus but allowed to escape by the authorities there – an episode, never satisfacto-rily explained, which still arouses fury in American officialdom.[5] (In a related case, a Russian who once worked at Microsoft was deported on immigration grounds in mid-July of that year).

Some people reacted with derision to the idea that Russia would send spies to suburbia, others with surprise. Both reactions were mistaken. This was not a new or foolish initiative by the Kremlin's spymasters, but the latest twist in an old and sinister one. Only two years previously, in 2008, the case of Herman Simm had highlighted Russia's penetration of NATO. A portly Estonian ex-policeman who had become that country's top national-secu-rity official, he was exposed as a Russian agent after some able work by Western spycatchers. His case officer – the career spy in charge of his activities – was unmasked too. This was 'Antonio': a Russian masquerading as a Portuguese businessman, under an elaborately constructed illegal identity. But the media furore over that case soon died down, leaving most people unaware of the effort that Russia, like the Soviet Union before it, still puts into deception, infiltration and subversion. After much lobbying and argument, I was able to persuade the Estonian authorities to allow me to interview Simm; the results of that investigation are in chapter 11.

The international media frenzy surrounding Ms Chapman trivialised espionage as a branch of show business. The mistake was easily made: pouting and haughty, the Russian firecracker could easily be a fictional character, not a real one. She would fit in neatly as the sultry sidekick to the arch-villain in a Bond movie – 007's relationship with '90-60-90' (Ms Chapman's Russian nickname, which comes from her shapely figure*) would provide appropriately cheesy sexual tension. The lurid and seemingly pointless affair invited ridicule. *New York* magazine's headline was 'Russian Spies Too Useless, Sexy to Prosecute'. In London, the *Guardian* said confidently that 'none of the 10 Russians had culled any secrets from their hideouts in US suburbia'. A grand old man of Anglo-American journalism opined that the Russian illegals' operation was marked by 'complete futility'.[6] As the detainees were swapped in Vienna for four people jailed in Russia for spying, David Cornwell, who under the pseudonym John le Carré so ably captured the dark intrigues of Cold War espionage, even suggested that out-of-control 'rightists' in America's intelligence agencies were trying to jinx the improvement in Russian–American relations. He asked: 'As we watch live in glorious Technicolor the

* In inches she would be 35–24–35

greatest spy-swap of the twenty-first century, and hear in our memories the zither twanging out the Harry Lime theme, do the spies expect us to go scurrying back to our cold war shelters? Is that the cunning plan?'[7]

With respect to Britain's greatest spy writer, and with rather less to other commentators, that is an oddly complacent approach. Spies need to seem as boring and inconspicuous as possible, to develop the capabilities that their real jobs require. If they are to be humble errand-runners, ferrying money, false documents and other wherewithal to more glamorous operatives, then they need jobs that allow them to travel. George Smiley, le Carré's best-known character, spent the war years working undercover as an official (supposedly Swiss) of a Swedish shipping company – the perfect background for someone needing a regular excuse to visit Hamburg or other German ports.[8] For some the task is to gain jobs, hobbies or lifestyles that give access to secret information. If the mission is identifying potential sources and the weaknesses that will enable their recruitment, they should be good networkers. If they are case officers, who recruit, direct, motivate and check the agents, they need a lifestyle in which meeting a wide range of people arouses no suspicion. If they are moles, aiming to penetrate the other side's security or intelligence services, they need educational and career paths that will make them credible candidates for recruitment there.

Charles Crawford, a British diplomat in the region for many years, explains it well on his blog.[9] Espionage means finding out where highly sensitive and useful information is stored or circulated, then using the human or physical weaknesses in its protection to copy the information in an undetectable way. All this must be done without anyone noticing or suspecting, and repeated many times over. In such work invisibility is a prime advantage. Spycatchers can watch the every waking and sleeping hour of a

diplomat suspected of spying. They can comb through visa applications to spot foreign visitors who may be more or less than they
seem. They can put suspects on their own side under surveillance
to see if they are having odd meetings with strange people. Such
techniques may be effective in catching a spook disguised as a
diplomat, or a careless traitor. But they have almost no chance of
catching a properly trained and targeted 'illegal' – someone working under an acquired or stolen identity.

As I show in chapter 6, such a person is an asset that can be
used whenever, however and wherever it is needed. That Russia
is running such agents in America, Britain and Europe (and elsewhere) should be cause for alarm. Imagine that someone who
loathes you has a key to your front door. It will be little comfort
if he has not yet got round to burning your house down, stealing
your valuables, or planting drugs. The worry is that he could.

Russians do not trivialise or ridicule espionage. They take it
rather seriously, both as a threat from abroad and as something
that their country excels in. Admittedly, people everywhere find
fictional spies glamorous. America has the amnesiac but inde-
structible Jason Bourne:[10] Commander Bond's high jinks sprinkle
stardust over the reputation of SIS. But real-life spies in Western
countries have only modest privileges compared to their counterparts elsewhere. In Britain, for example, they retire at 55, earlier
than the diplomatic colleagues whose cover they use. They have
rather larger and more loosely scrutinised expense accounts than
other officials, but on the whole enjoy the same lifestyle as any
other middle-class professional.

The Soviet legacy, however, has left a distinctive aura around
espionage in Russia. For officers of the KGB (such as Ms
Chapman's father Vasily, or Mr Putin and hundreds of thousands
like them) life was markedly nicer than for fellow inmates of the
workers' paradise. Housed in the KGB's special accommodation,

its officers had access to shops stocked with otherwise unavailable products. They holidayed at KGB resorts and were spared some of the system's petty restrictions on daily life. Those in the elite foreign-espionage division, the First Chief Directorate, and some colleagues in cryptography and counter-intelligence, could even be sent to work abroad – perhaps even a posting to the fabled Western cornucopia that the class warriors both despised and envied.

Privileges aside, the KGB also enjoyed a mystique that still lingers over its successor organisations. People saw it (rather inaccurately) as efficient, knowledgeable and incorruptible. Its officers had a job that mattered, in an organisation that worked, and were well rewarded for it. Few in the claustrophobic, ill-run and bribe-plagued Soviet Union could boast as much. Like the space programme and sporting heroes, the KGB also touched another emotional chord: patriotism. Though its ultimate loyalty was to the Communist Party, not to the Soviet state (it described itself as the Party's 'sword and shield'), it basked in the reflected glory of the defeat of Nazi Germany. Rather as the Battle of Britain provides Britain's 'finest hour', as the Resistance epitomises France's national myth, and as the Normandy beaches exemplify America's commitment to the freedom of Europe, the Great Patriotic War (as the Second World War is known in Russia) was the central plank in the Soviet Union's self-image – and plays the same role in Russian identity today.

For all the heroism displayed by Soviet soldiers in defeating the Nazi invaders, the real role of the secret police in those years was a despicable mix of war crimes against the foe, ruthless pacification of 'liberated' territories and persecution of real or imagined waverers on its own side.[11] Yet Soviet wartime history mostly comes across in a quite different light: on the television screens later adorned by Ms Chapman's lightweight programme on unsolved mysteries,[12] viewers used to watch the exploits of the best-known Soviet fictional spy, Max Otto von Stirlitz (to give him his German cover name). His wartime mission was to penetrate the Nazi high command. Unlike Bond, Stirlitz shuns gadgets, guns and girls. His weapon is his mind, fuelled not by communist ideology but a plangent patriotism. Though implausible, books and films featuring his exploits were compelling and sympathetic by the hackneyed standards of Soviet propaganda.[13] They so captivated a tough teenager in the backstreets of 1970s Leningrad that he took the unusual step of walking into the city's KGB headquarters and volunteering his services. But the young Vladimir Putin was told that the organisation did not accept walk-ins; he should get an education first and wait to be approached.*

The Soviet Union is gone, but the links between Russia's spies today and their dark and bloody past are real enough. Of course the old and new are not identical. Ms Chapman's Soviet-era predecessors wore ill-fitting grey suits and sought the shadows. She likes leather catsuits and the spotlight. They served a totalitarian superpower. She serves post-Soviet Russia, a country that is undeniably capitalist and claims to be democratic. But a lasting connection is privilege. The dispensations enjoyed by Russia's spooks now mean that they lead a life apart, just as KGB officers did in the Soviet era. The difference is not only in salary and access to consumer goods, but in the privilege of living above and outside the law. The results range from the trivial to the monstrous. An officer of the FSB can drive while drunk (and mow down pedestrians) with impunity. A flash of his ID badge will intimidate any lesser official; he can triumph in any private legal or commercial dispute; he can ignore planning regulations when he builds his

---

* Putin studied international law at Leningrad State University. He graduated in 1975 and joined the KGB immediately afterwards.

house in the country. As I show in chapter 1, he can ruin the lives – literally – of those who displease him.

Ms Chapman does not just hit the old Soviet buttons in the Russian psyche. She tickles its modern neuroses too. Her brand is based not on the steely puritanism of the wartime Soviet military but on the sleazy glitz of modern Russia. Her role was to spy not on the hated Nazis of long ago, but on a new bugbear: Western countries such as Britain and America, which the Russian regime sees as duplicitous, arrogant and greedy. Though the elite likes to shop, bank, frolic and school their children in and around London, many of its members despise Britain, just as they resent what they see as American hegemony and the bossiness of the European Union.

This hostility stems in part from an inferiority complex: for all the West's ills, its inhabitants enjoy a quality of life that is missing in Russia. This is despite what many Russians see as its baffling weakness and indolence (I have heard Russians complain in the same breath, quite unselfconsciously, about the feeble levels of maths education in the West and the flabby unfemininity of British and American women). Another reason is that Russians object to what they see as the West's political interference – for example by sponsoring media-freedom and pro-democracy causes, and sheltering fugitives from Russia, who claim to be persecuted for their political beliefs, but are seen (at least by the authorities in Moscow) as mere swindlers and terrorists.

Many people dismiss even the existence of this enmity, let alone its seriousness. For them, the era of East–West confrontation ended with Mikhail Gorbachev's *perestroika* (reform) and *glasnost* (openness). The fall of the Berlin Wall in 1989 and the collapse of the Soviet Union two years later buried it. The eastwards expansion of NATO laid its ghost and it became completely irrelevant after the 'reset' of American relations with Russia in 2009 under the presidency of Barack Obama. Launched on 6 March 2009, this involved the handing over by the American secretary of state Hillary Clinton to her Russian opposite number, the foreign minister Sergei Lavrov, of a large symbolic button marked *Peregruzka – Reset*.* The aim was to separate issues on which the United States and the Russian authorities were bound to disagree (such as human rights, and the security of the countries of the former Soviet empire) with those where agreement was possible and even pressingly needed, such as Afghanistan, arms control, a legal regime in space, etc. Supporters say it helped speed transit of military matériel to Afghanistan, in curbing (a little) Iran's nuclear programme, and in a new treaty on strategic nuclear arms. The administration's other foreign-policy initiatives, in the Middle East, China, Eastern Europe, Iran and North Korea have been marked by a notable lack of success and infirmity of purpose, but at least to its fans the 'reset' has been a success, simply by improving the rhetoric (if not the reality) of the relationship. The European Union is if anything even more eager to avoid confrontation, partly in order not to jeopardise the continent's gas supplies (a quarter of which still come from Russia). Moreover, many Eurocrats see bad relations as the product of insufficiently skilful diplomacy, not the necessary result of clashing values and objectives. That makes it hard to take a tough line with Russia.

From this viewpoint, worries about the silencing of critics in Russia, or the remaining wrangles over the future of faraway countries such as Georgia and Ukraine, are trivial. Nothing need disturb the safety and comfort of Western public opinion. Such complacency happily coincides with financial interests. For many bankers, oilmen, lawyers and others, their fortunes depend on

---

* Unfortunately the Russian word on the button means 'overload'; the correct term for 'reset' would have been *Perezagruzka*.

good relations with Russia. The sweet smell of money triumphs over the stench from below. Economic woes in the West only heighten the temptation.

I disagree with this approach and in 2007 wrote *The New Cold War* to explain why.[14] That book highlighted Russia's use of cash, energy and divide-and-rule diplomacy to undermine the Atlantic Alliance, to weaken the European Union and NATO, and to sow distrust between their 'old' and ex-communist members. I highlighted Russia's bullying of neighbours such as Estonia and Georgia; and the penetration of Europe through corruption of politicians, businessmen and others. Since 2007 the once-controversial notion that Russia is run by xenophobic kleptocrats (a portmanteau word from 'kleptocracy' or 'rule by thieves') has become commonplace. This new book unveils the hidden side of Russia's dealings with the West: the use of espionage for knowledge, for influence and ultimately for power. The outcome of these manoeuvres will determine whether the West brings Russia towards its standards of liberty, legality and cooperation, or whether it will be the other way round, as we accommodate (or even adopt) the authoritarian crony-capitalism that is the Moscow regime's hallmark.*

Few cases highlight this corruption and brutality better than the one I begin with: the torture and death in 2009 of Sergei Magnitsky, a Russian lawyer working for a British investor. He exposed a $230m fraud by a criminal group led by the FSB and backed at the highest level in the regime.[15] He paid for this

---

* The 'West' is a wobbly concept that defies precise description. It includes Anglosphere countries such as Australia and New Zealand (and in many cases Japan), which are not 'western' in any geographical sense. In this book I use it broadly to mean in economic and political terms the thirty-four member countries of the Paris-based Organisation for Economic Cooperation and Development, a rich-country club that promotes good governance. In a security context I use it to mean NATO and its allies, which would include, for these purposes, Sweden and Finland.

discovery with his life; since his death the authorities have tried to cover up his murder, and their fraud, with a mixture of bombast, lies, bullying and evasion. The scandal exemplifies the overlap between gangsterdom and power in Russia, the abuse of the legal system, and the bravery of those Russians willing to defend the rule of law. The tentacles of FSB power stretch to the West too, not least because Russian officials have snooped on and intimidated Mr Magnitsky's colleagues and defenders in London and elsewhere. As I show in subsequent chapters, the ruling regime represents not just a tragedy for Russia: it is a direct threat to our own well-being and safety.

In the annals of Western intelligence history, victories feature more than defeats. Many know of the triumphant exfiltration – spy parlance for a secret rescue – in 1985 of the brave and brilliant Oleg Gordievsky, for years Britain's top spy in the KGB. The defection in 1992 of Vasily Mitrokhin, a senior archivist in Russia's espionage service, is also rightly celebrated.[16] The KGB laboured under big disadvantages: the increasingly apparent failures of the planned economy, the climate of fear that impeded sensible decision-making, and the burden of political interference. Yet the West's ultimate victory in the Cold War does not mean its intelligence services were winners all the time. The comforting account of a past studded with triumphs is misleading and leads to complacency. In chapters 8 and 9 I highlight some little-known stories of the previous decades in East–West spy wars, and their mostly dismal results for British and American intelligence. Our services were crippled by conflicting objectives: whether to spy on the Soviet block or to try to topple it. They repeatedly fell victim to Soviet deception operations. They were penetrated by traitors such as Kim Philby, and paralysed by the fear that more such moles remained undiscovered.

The episodes I have chosen to illustrate these problems are linked to the Baltic states of Estonia, Latvia and Lithuania. These have been vulnerable and contested territory on the East–West frontline for a hundred years. Even today, they stand most to gain if we win – and most to lose if we are defeated. I make no secret of my sympathy for their cause. I lived there in 1990–94 when they wriggled out of the Kremlin's clutches. I witnessed their growing prosperity and rejoiced over what seemed like their safe landing in NATO in 2004. I have also seen how Russia systematically tries to undermine their sovereignty and subvert their security. The tales of the spy wars there include torture and treachery, deep deceptions and cynical double-dealing. They feature tragedy and triumph, brilliance and bungling, heroism, sacrifice, betrayal – and deception.

The first episode comes in the months after the Russian revolution of 1917, when outside governments, chiefly Britain, France and the United States, believed that they could snuff out the communist experiment before it took root and spread to other countries. The British envoy in Moscow, Robert Bruce Lockhart, fell for a brilliant deception operation personally masterminded by the Bolshevik leader, Vladimir Lenin. Lockhart believed Lenin's bodyguards – a crack force of Latvian riflemen – would switch sides in return for the offer of an independent Latvian state, backed by the Western powers. But having failed to check properly the credentials of his supposed Latvian allies, Lockhart was hooked by Lenin's ruse. The British agent's naivety and carelessness not only landed him in jail. It also confirmed Russian suspicions about Western meddling, and fuelled Lenin's propaganda machine, which was warning Russians of foreign meddling and menaces. Catching a British spy red-handed trying to mount a putsch was the best possible proof of that.

Despite that humiliating lesson, Western intelligence in the region then fell victim to a far greater deception: the 'Trust'. British spymasters' gullibility and recklessness in the early 1920s

allowed the Cheka, the forerunner of the KGB, to pretend that
a huge underground organisation in Soviet Russia was eager to
receive outside help. Nothing of the kind existed: the Trust was
an invention. Scores of anti-communist Russians went to their
deaths on botched operations planned by Western spy chiefs who
believed triumph was just around the corner. This fiasco also cost
the life of Britain's reckless 'ace of spies', Sidney Reilly. His successors proved to be the epitome of the secretive incompetence that
plagues the world of espionage. They proved unwilling or unable
to learn from their mistakes, making a similar blunder only twenty
years later when they backed bogus anti-Soviet resistance group-
ings in Estonia, Latvia and Lithuania. British, American and other
Western spymasters saw these countries as ideal springboards for
both spying and subversion: the Soviet-occupied Baltic states were
easily accessible by plane or boat, with ardently anti-communist
populations that were already fighting a guerrilla war against their
new Soviet rulers. But the result was a catastrophe. The brave
men that we sent to help this cause ended up in the clutches of
the KGB.

I have tracked down perhaps the last survivor of those days.
He is living peacefully in southern England, cherishing medals
awarded by a country he thought would not be free in his lifetime, and a statuette given in belated gratitude by SIS. I have also
found a previously unpublicised example of a successful mission in
the Soviet Union by a star British spy and traces of others. But the
balance sheet is still grim. The spy chiefs' deluded belief in partisan warfare in the Baltic cost hundreds of lives and ruined thousands. It squandered money, prestige and credibility on a cause
that brought no gain and great pain.

The latest blunder came when the Baltic states regained independence in 1991, and Western intelligence piled back in to its old
stamping ground. Again, the Russians were waiting and again the

West was caught in a deception. Herman Simm, the most trusted official in the most trusted of all the ex-communist countries, Estonia, was a linchpin between its defence ministry and foreign allies. He gained plaudits for his efficiency and helpfulness, and top Estonian and NATO security clearances. The people who administered these systems somehow failed to spot that the avuncular ex-policeman was a long-standing KGB agent. To Estonia's lasting credit, it did not try to hush up the catastrophe: Simm was caught, prosecuted and jailed. Not only that, the Estonian authorities gave me exclusive and repeated access to him. One reason for Estonian sensitivity is a startling and little-known aspect of the story. Simm was not spying only for the Russians.

Simm was an exception because he was caught. So too were Ms Chapman and the spies in America. But their story reveals the long-term efforts Russia makes and the vulnerabilities it exploits. How many other 'illegals' are living unnoticed in Britain, Europe or America? And how many agents have they recruited? Raising the alarm over this is a central aim of this book. The West has largely let down its guard. The CIA's counter-espionage officers and their counter-intelligence colleagues* at the FBI still devote time and money to catching Russian spies. But this is the exception, not the rule. Since 11 September 2001, priorities have shifted. Britain's Security Service, usually known by its acronym MI5, claims to devote only 4 per cent of its resources to counter-intelligence – the overwhelming majority goes to counter-terrorism.[17] In Belgium a mere handful of local spycatchers, ill-paid and lacking political backing, have to keep track of the hundreds of

---

* An arcane distinction is sometimes drawn between counter-espionage (active and offensive measures, such as distracting, impeding, expelling or recruiting the officers of a hostile foreign service) and counter-intelligence (more general preventative measures such as screening and surveillance, aimed at finding leaks and plugging them).

Russians aiming to penetrate the European Union, the NATO headquarters in Brussels and other tempting targets.

The passage of time and other priorities have eroded the expertise and institutional memory that in Cold War days helped spycatchers keep track of Soviet penetration attempts. Concerns for privacy have made vetting procedures flimsy. Officials can make money on the side, take lucrative jobs on retirement, take unexplained foreign trips, copy documents onto memory sticks from supposedly secure laptops and carry an array of electronic gadgets that never come under scrutiny. I also highlight the mistaken complacency that has surrounded the expansion of NATO to the ex-communist countries. It was right to enlarge the alliance (chiefly because of Russia's neo-imperialist sabre-rattling) but intelligence and security services have grossly underestimated the Soviet-era shadow that still lies over the region. The liberation of 1989–91 was intoxicating, but its effects were only skin-deep. Replacing the planned economy with free markets, state censorship with free media, and one-party rule with free elections were hugely important changes. But the transformation of the political and economic systems could not be matched by an instant change in the human beings that inhabit them. Millions of people in the region have grown up under communism and collaborated with it. The toxic legacy of secret police files, with the shabby compromises and sordid secrets they contain, still taints public life. It provides plenty of scope for blackmailing the guilty – and smearing the innocent. Even those seen in the West as heroes, such as Poland's former president Lech Wałęsa, have come under a cloud of suspicion about past collaboration.[18] Although not everything in the secret police files is true, and many true things are not in the files, the dirty secrets of the past, many of them spirited away to Russia in the dying days of the old regimes, create great possibilities for pressurising anyone born before, roughly, 1970.

In short, the collapse of communism left a series of human time-bombs all over the former empire – with the Kremlin in charge of the remote controls.

Neither the Simm case, nor the exposure of Ms Chapman and her colleagues, have properly woken up public opinion and officialdom. This book presents bluntly and independently a message that officials find hard to articulate openly, and that the public seems so unwilling to hear. It is this: Russian spies' activities are not just a lingering spasm of old Soviet institutions, twitching like the tail of a dying dinosaur. They are part of a wider effort to penetrate and manipulate, which targets the weakest parts of our system: its open and trusting approach to outsiders and newcomers. Because this threat is underestimated or outright ignored, it is especially potent. It is part of a world, espionage, of which outsiders mostly know little and understand less.

Drawing together the threads of the past and the present, this book will show how the old KGB techniques of deception and subversion are now deployed in the service of new aims. The battle lines were more clearly drawn in the days of the Cold War, when the threat was of communist victory. The corrupt autocracy that rules Russia now is playing by capitalist rules – and the threat is even more corrosive. Yet some things are the same. Russia's new spies, like their Soviet predecessors, engage in the subversion, manipulation and penetration of the West. They also defend a regime that, as I show in the following chapters, is tyrannical, criminal and murderous.

I

Looting and Murder

Life in Moscow can seem remarkably normal. Middle-class professionals wear the same clothes, drive the same cars, take the same holidays, eat the same food and do the same jobs as millions of their counterparts in cities all round the world. This is especially so in the field of finance. Shares and profits rise on the back of Russia's oil and gas boom, and the consumption it pays for. Financiers invest; their lawyers handle the details and deal with problems. Serving them is a growing Russian middle class of articulate, confident English-speaking professionals who could easily do the same jobs in New York, London, Frankfurt or Dubai. For many people, especially those who believe Russia is on the right track, the growth of the financial and legal system in Moscow is one of the great grounds for optimism. Other parts of life in Russia, from traffic-clogged big-city streets and corrupt officialdom to terrorism and bubbling civil war along the country's southern fringe, may be depressing, chaotic, dark and even dangerous, but that world seldom touches the bright, snazzily furnished offices of central Moscow.

In the case of Sergei Magnitsky, however, it did. His name is not well known, though it deserves to be. His story provides a moral and human backdrop to the subsequent chapters on the wiles and ways of Russia's spies. Aged only 37 when he died in 2009, Mr

Magnitsky was part of the first generation of Russians for nearly a century whose lives were unclouded by fear. When Soviet controls over speech, belief and travel withered, he was a teenager. He was well-educated in a way that previous cohorts of Russian students could only dream of. His mind was not shaped by forced study of the perverse doctrines of Marxism–Leninism but by adherence to the crystalline principles of the law. Neither brutalised by Soviet-era conscription nor burdened by compromises of adult life under totalitarianism, he enjoyed the middle-class comforts and certainties that are taken for granted in the West and had been unimaginable in the Soviet Union. He had able colleagues, stimulating challenges and a happy home. His dream, like the half-successful reformers of the Tsarist era a century earlier, was for Russia to be a law-governed state. He was the sort of person who made even sceptics feel that Russia's long-term future was bright.

Polished and polyglot, Mr Magnitsky was the kind of Russian that readers of this book could easily encounter. You might have a drink with him on a foreign holiday, hear him at a seminar, or find him sitting across the table at a business meeting. In that sense, he is rather like the other Russians covered in this book: the undercover spies in the West. It is easy to imagine him sipping a cocktail in London with Ms Chapman, or strolling the streets of Boston in conversation with Donald Heathfield – her superspy colleague who worked as a management consultant in America. But while these people were pursuing their clandestine missions on behalf of Russia's spymasters, Mr Magnitsky was involved in another story.[1] It involves colossal sums of money, extraordinary cruelty and impunity for wrongdoers. The cast includes senior members of the FSB, working hand in hand with organised crime and senior state officials.

I will begin by introducing the man who unwittingly brought Mr Magnitsky to his doom, and since then has campaigned

untiringly for his cause. William ('Bill') Browder is an American-
born financier, now with British nationality, who used to be one
of the best-known Western investors in Russia. He is an abrasive,
mercurial figure, bursting with nervous energy, capable of
charm and fury in quick succession. He has a fascinating family
background: his grandfather Earl Browder was a leader of the
American Communist Party. But it was capitalism not communism that entranced the grandson. He spotted in the 1990s that
many outsiders were overestimating the risks of doing business
in Russia. Admittedly, the dangers were great: the rule of law
was weak, property rights flimsy, political stability uncertain, the
economy rocky, and crime and corruption pervasive. But daunting does not mean impossible. The companies and shares on sale
were not valueless, just cheap. If the situation improved just a little
(or if even perceptions of it did) then the gains to be made were
potentially huge. Suppose, for example, that investors reckoned
that an ill-run Russian oil company, instead of being worth a mere
1 per cent of a comparable foreign one, was instead worth 10 per
cent. That would raise the value of its shares tenfold – meaning
a colossal profit for someone who bought before the perception
changed.

   Mr Browder's investment company, Hermitage Capital
Management, therefore pursued a threefold strategy. First,
it bought shares in companies that owned an underlying asset,
such as oil, gas or minerals. Second, he talked up Russia as an
investment destination, insisting that it was merely 'bad' instead
of outright 'horrible'.* His third tactic was to highlight abuses of

* As well as highlighting the potential, some felt he was downplaying the
dangers. A notable occasion was in early 2005 at the Davos World Economic
Forum, when opinion was already turning sharply against the evident cronyism
and incompetence of the Putin regime. Mr Browder was one of a handful of
prominent Westerners to express a strong contrary opinion.

shareholder rights. His sharp-eyed team of analysts pored over company accounts and other documents, looking for evidence of fraud and waste. When they found them, Mr Browder would launch lawsuits, media campaigns and other stunts to seek redress.[2]

This was well timed. Some Russian companies were already realising that in order to make the most of their stock-exchange listings, they had to pay at least a semblance of attention to outside investors' interests. From 2000 onwards, Mr Browder's efforts also coincided with a push from the Kremlin, which disliked the way over-mighty 'oligarchs' (politically powerful tycoons) were running the country's biggest companies in their private interests. The coincidence of interest was short-lived. The Putin regime's longer-term aim was not to promote good corporate governance and shareholder value, but to seize money and power for itself. But that was for later. For nearly a decade, Mr Browder and Hermitage flourished mightily. Their campaigns brought some quick victories, some slower ones, and sometimes failed altogether, but the hard work and high profile at least helped justify the hefty management charges the investors paid. The 'Hermitage effect',[3] as the company terms it, received the ultimate accolade in 2002: it was the subject of a Harvard Business School case study.[4] During the period between Mr Putin's arrival in office in 2000 and the fund's moving to London in 2005, the value of Hermitage's investments rose eightfold; during the whole period of its existence, the increase was thirty-fivefold. Few in the history of finance can boast such a record.

I did not always get on with Mr Browder during my time in Moscow as bureau chief for the *Economist* from 1998 to 2002. Our disputes may look like ancient history now but they were sharp at the time. In particular, although I admired his energy and brains, I disliked his backing for Mr Putin's regime. The new government had in my view brought superficial stability, but at far too high a price. Moreover I was unmoved by the plight of foreign investors who had knowingly put their money into companies run by crooks, nincompoops and political cronies, and were then surprised to find that those businesses were run badly. If you buy shares in Russia, you should expect to be defrauded, rather as if you go mud-wrestling you expect to get dirty.

Our sharpest disagreement came in 2003 after I left Russia, when we took opposite sides over the defining issue of the early Putin era. Mr Browder endorsed the arrest of Mikhail Khodorkovsky, then Russia's richest man, who had defied Mr Putin, not least by turning up tieless to a meeting in the Kremlin – a huge snub in protocol-conscious Russia. Mr Khodorkovsky, an energy tycoon, had also put a large number of parliamentarians on the payroll to bolster his political clout and was planning a deal with a big American oil company in defiance of Kremlin guidelines. He was certainly an obstacle to Mr Putin's plan to seize the commanding heights of power in Russia. Some thought he might even want to displace Mr Putin from the top job (in his first years in office, the Russian president had seemed a grey and somewhat unimpressive figure). Mr Putin's vengeance was decisive and ruthless. Mr Khodorkovsky was jailed on flimsy charges and his company Yukos (which had many foreign shareholders) was bankrupted, with its assets disposed of in a dodgy auction where Kremlin cronies bought them cheaply.[5] I agreed with Mr Browder that Mr Khodorkovsky had in previous years abused the rights of his minority shareholders, and I did not see him simply as a martyr to repression. But I reckoned that the balance between the tycoon's past misdeeds and later virtues mattered less than the authorities' flagrant abuse of the courts in a political vendetta.

Mr Browder could afford to discount my criticism. He was making millions. But he was also making more powerful enemies elsewhere: every dollar not stolen as a result of his efforts to stop corporate sleaze dented the income of some corrupt and powerful person. In November 2005 border guards turned him back from Moscow's Sheremetyevo airport, citing undisclosed national security grounds.[6] Returning to London, he stayed bullish on Russia, lobbying to overturn the authorities' decision and insisting that his plight was a mere misunderstanding. But at a summit meeting in St Petersburg in July 2006* a journalist raised Mr Browder's case at a press conference. Mr Putin replied that he had never heard of Mr Browder (which was implausible) but that he could 'imagine that this person had broken the laws of our country'[7]. At that point, Mr Browder says, he gave up trying to return to Russia: the signal of deep official displeasure was unambiguous and he did not want to share Mr Khodorkovsky's fate. Behind the scenes he had already begun liquidating his holdings and pulling out his staff. With Mr Browder no longer at the helm in Moscow, investors were asking for their money back; other emerging markets looked more attractive. As it happened, the move was not just prescient but profitable. Shortly afterwards, the world financial crisis broke, and Russian share and bond prices plunged. Mr Browder's investors escaped without a scratch.

At this stage, the story was just one of many such tales in Russia: the country's recent history is littered with investors who cross swords with the authorities and lose. The lucky ones negotiate a deal; the unlucky ones are glad to leave the country alive. But in Mr Browder's case, his enforced absence was just the prologue to a tragedy worthy of Dostoevsky. It involved a mammoth fraud,

---

* Russia was chairing the G-8 (a group of countries that in those days tried to run the world economy). The original G-6, convened in 1975, comprised Britain, France, Germany, Italy, Japan and the United States and then added Canada as a member. As a sop to Mr Yeltsin, Russia was invited to join in 1997. Since 2009, the G-20, which includes the big emerging economies, has largely taken the G-8's place.

in which officials stole three companies owned by Mr Browder's fund and used them to swindle the citizens of Russia. The perpetrators of this crime were not some rogue bunch of junior officials. On the contrary, they were the unit of the Interior Ministry charged with safeguarding their taxpayers' interests. They worked in cahoots with senior officers of the FSB's K Directorate, which is supposed to deal with 'economic crimes'.

Readers may find the term 'economic crimes' unfamiliar: in other criminal justice systems it could be rendered as 'white-collar crime'. But in a Russian context it is redolent of the Soviet era, in which the same KGB department persecuted the black market – the now-forgotten trade in everything from purloined state property to foreign currency, antiques, second-hand goods or sexual services. Even in Soviet days, persecution was mixed with profit. Pay-offs, particularly from the Brezhnev era onwards, were rife. Confiscated goods had a habit of ending up in the dachas of senior officers. Prostitutes found they could stay in business by offering their services free of charge to the right person, or collaborating in entrapment schemes. The difference under capitalism is that the sums involved in corruption now are greater and the means more sophisticated.

An agency such as K Directorate in a Western country would deal with corporate fraud, excise scams, money-laundering and high-level corruption, and all other overlaps between organised criminality and the financial system. Not in Russia. Unfair though this judgement may be to those of its officers who genuinely want to serve the public interest, it has become in most cases a unit for perpetrating economic crime, not fighting it. In late January 2007 Mr Browder seized on a chance personal meeting with Dmitry Medvedev, then the leading presidential candidate, and received a promise of help with his visa. But the actual reaction was a kind of 'help' normally seen in gangster movies. In mid February 2007 a senior figure from the Interior Ministry tax-crimes department, Lieutenant Colonel Artyom Kuznetsov, telephoned the head of research at Hermitage in Moscow, requesting an 'informal meeting' for a report he said he was writing on Mr Browder's visa. Depending on how Hermitage 'behaved', the visa could be issued, he said: 'The sooner we meet and you provide what is necessary, the sooner your problems will disappear.' The company rejected what it (reasonably in a Russian context) reckoned was an extortion attempt. In retrospect, it was probably even more sinister: a ruse to get hold of the company's documents, as the first stage in a planned looting spree.

This involved the illegal expropriation of Mr Browder's companies, the theft of $230m from the Russian taxpayer, and the death of Mr Magnitsky, the man who uncovered it. It started on 22 May 2007 when Viktor Voronin, head of K Directorate, and his subordinate Aleksandr Kuvaldin, issued a finding that a company associated with Hermitage called Kameya had underpaid its dividend withholding tax.

This sounds both complicated and trivial, and on the surface it is. Outsiders are ill placed to judge the merits of arguments over corporate taxation, especially when one side declines to present its case in public. Though I find Hermitage's case convincing, a layman's view cannot be conclusive and I would not want it given any particular weight. The Russian authorities may have powerful arguments, though they have for whatever reason not produced them. But the facts as presented by Hermitage are these: Kameya, a relatively small company, had paid $135m in taxes in 2006, at a time when Aeroflot, the country's largest airline, paid $130m, and the best-known brewery paid $131m.* It was scarcely shirking its duties as a corporate citizen. Indeed, it was the hefty taxes that

---

* Kameya also paid more than the combined taxes paid by the largest retailer (XS, which paid $57m) and the largest dairy and juice company (Wimm Bill Dann, which paid $42m). Hermitage's other companies paid a further $272m.

Hermitage's associated companies had paid in past years which had probably marked it as a target for the scam originally.

Regardless of the merits of the dispute itself, what seems to me quite clear is that the FSB's involvement in a tax dispute was beyond its remit and that its subsequent behaviour, along with that of other state agencies, was a shocking abuse of the system. In a country that claims to abide by the rule of law, the authorities do not automatically triumph in the courts. On paper, Russia's procedures in contested business tax matters do not seem unusual. The tax authority first queries a payment, then waits for the company's response; if unconvinced it reissues a tax demand; if the money is still unpaid it turns to the Interior Ministry to enforce it. At that point the taxpayer has the right to a fair hearing and legal representation. In practice (as in so many parts of life in Russia) things are very different. In this case no tax claims were made and none of these procedures was followed. Indeed, on 12 May 2009, in a bizarre coda to the obliteration of Hermitage's presence in Russia, Kameya received a final tax audit from the federal tax service inspectorate stating that all taxes had been paid in full and none was owed.

On 4 June 2007 a group of twenty-five Interior Ministry officers, led by Lieutenant Colonel Kuznetsov, raided the Hermitage offices in Moscow, with a warrant relating only to Kameya, and seized documents, computers and other materials involving three quite unrelated Hermitage companies: Makhaon, Parfenion and Rilend. On the same day Kuznetsov, also without a warrant, raided an American-owned law firm, Firestone Duncan, which specialises in legal paperwork. He confiscated the statutory documents and seals of the three Hermitage subsidiary companies – in all two vanloads of materials. That was outrageous enough. What was worse was the way the officials behaved during the raid. When a lawyer at Firestone Duncan protested, the visitors beat

and arrested him. After paying a 15,000 rouble (roughly $500) fine
he was released, and spent two weeks in hospital. His name is still
available in news reports of the incident, but I am omitting it at the
request of friends who say he fears for his safety.

This was no coincidence. According to Hermitage, all the
lawyers associated with the company suffered robberies or break-
ins in the two-week period around the raid. By the brusque standards of Russian law enforcement, the raids were not in themselves unusual. The unannounced arrival of masked men toting
machine guns, who remove documents and computers from your
office, is a run-of-the-mill business risk in Russia, no more unusual
than, say, having British health and safety inspectors demanding
that you fit new fire doors, or America's Internal Revenue Service
quibbling over allowable business expenses in a tax return. The
twist in Russia is that such searches and seizures are often carried
out by state officials on behalf of a third party, such as a business
rival to the victim. Having identified the source of the persecution, the victim starts negotiating – or if he has good connections
himself, considers counter-measures.

Mr Browder, from his exile in London's Mayfair financial
district, was puzzled. Clearly the problem had, as he put it to
me, 'metastasised'. But why? The raid could be revenge by one
of the politically influential companies he had chivvied for bad
management and impenetrable finances. Or the aim could be
simply to derail his campaign to return to Russia. At any rate, he
reckoned, it was a headache not a nightmare, particularly as he had
largely wound down his operations there anyway. This was a big
misjudgement: far from being the vengeance of some disgruntled
subject of Mr Browder's campaigns, the raid was carried out by his
erstwhile ally, the Russian state itself. Despite multiple requests and
complaints, the authorities did not return the confiscated items.
Nor did they explain on what grounds they were holding them.

Hermitage then received a troubling phone call. A bailiff from the St Petersburg Arbitration Court was seeking to enforce judgements to the tune of several hundred million dollars arising out of lawsuits against Hermitage companies. But Hermitage had never heard of these cases. A baffled Mr Browder commissioned Mr Magnitsky, head of the tax and audit department at Firestone Duncan, to investigate. A notable figure in the field of tax law, Mr Magnitsky was an ideal choice. He immediately found that no fewer than ten cases had been lodged in St Petersburg. While a colleague set off for Russia's second city to find out more about these mysterious lawsuits, Mr Magnitsky began scouring official registries for clues. In October 2007 he made his first breakthrough. While the documents and seals of his client had been supposedly in the custody of Kuznetsov and a colleague, Major Pavel Karpov, they in fact had been used to re-register the companies.

Such chicanery may seem puzzling to outsiders who live in a world where courts offer redress, the media highlights official wrongdoing, and elected representatives are able to take up grievances. A Western policeman who steals a company document risks losing his job and would probably face prosecution. Anyone trying to use the stolen document would be guilty of attempted fraud and face criminal charges too. But for all its outward signs of normality, Russia offers none of these routes to justice, which is why crimes involving stolen corporate documents are common. Possession is nine-tenths of the law – or all of it. The result is corporate raiding, Russian style. In the West, this technique involves brainy and ruthless investment bankers who swoop on a company to dislodge a dozy management team. The Russian equivalent involves a powerful bit of the state machinery stealing a company from its owners. This often starts with a raid in which company documents are confiscated by officials, and then end up in the hands of the raiders who use them to change the company's ownership. The victims may negotiate a settlement where they stay on as managers. At worst they are lucky to escape with their lives. Something on these lines seemed to be happening, although the motive was puzzling. The perpetrators had gone to some lengths to loot a pestilential foreigner's assets, presumably in the belief that the effect would be lucrative or at least punitive. But it was neither. With its investments wound down, Hermitage thought it had little to lose, and needed care little for the wrath of Russian officialdom.

While Mr Browder and his colleagues pondered this puzzle Mr Magnitsky prepared criminal complaints implicating Kuznetsov and Karpov. He also discovered a new twist: the new owner of the Hermitage companies was a previously unknown firm called Pluton, registered in the provincial republic of Tatarstan. It was not the sort of outfit that would normally engage in high finance. The owner was a former sawmill employee called Victor Markelov who had served a jail sentence for manslaughter. His fellow directors were two other ex-convicts.* All three had been released from jail early. Though odd by Western standards, such developments are not unusual in Russia, where ex-convicts, as well as drunks and tramps, often feature in corporate frauds. For a modest financial or liquid consideration, they will sign whatever papers are required, providing a fig leaf of disguise for the perpetrators at modest cost.

By this stage Hermitage had lost its companies, but the fraudsters had not gained anything except to drive Mr Browder out of Russia. But the next stage of the swindle was to change that. It involved a lawsuit, based on forged backdated contracts purporting to show that the Hermitage companies had promised to sell a large quantity of Gazprom shares. Claiming that the companies

---

* They were: Valery Kurochkin, a convicted thief, and Vyacheslav Khlebnikov, a convicted burglar. The three companies were called Instar, Logos Plus and Grand Active.

had then reneged on the deal, the claimants (three previously unknown firms) sued for a startling $1.3bn in damages for fore-gone profits. The supposedly broken contracts could hardly have been flimsier. They were littered with inaccuracies. They referred to bank accounts that were opened only subsequently. They used inaccurate addresses. A power of attorney – a document rarely used in the West but an essential part of any business transaction in Russia – was dated four months before the company concerned had come into existence. One of the claimants identified himself using a passport that later turned out to be stolen. In evidence, they presented a mixture of forged documents and copies of materials seized in the raids. In any legal system worthy of the name, the investigators who took custody of these documents should have safeguarded them, not let them fall into the hands of fraudsters.

With proper legal representation, these ludicrous cases would have been easy to win. But the stolen Hermitage companies did not have proper lawyers. In a complaint to the Russian chief pros-ecutor, Yuri Chaika, Hermitage says of its supposed representa-tives that it:

Had no prior knowledge of, or acquaintance with, these lawyers . . . never hired or appointed them and . . . never authorised or ratified their appointment as attorneys or agents of any kind.[8]

Instead of defending their clients against the preposterous alle-gations of non-existent breaches of bogus contracts, backed by palpably phoney evidence, the lawyers simply accepted full liabil-ity. The judges in the cases showed a striking lack of curiosity about the proceedings. For example: if the two parties agreed, why had it been necessary to go to court at all? Rather than ask such uncomfortable questions, they immediately ruled that the compa-nies had to pay the damages sought. Having gained his victory,

Lieutenant Colonel Kuznetsov then approached some of the biggest banks in Moscow. He produced a narrowly drafted warrant giving him the power to locate any assets belonging to Kameya – but demanded details of all assets belonging to Hermitage. Some complied either fully or in part, prompting furious complaints from Hermitage. Only the Duch bank ING, to its credit, bluntly declined, pointing out that the warrant bore no relation to the information sought.

At any rate, the assets were phantom and the search for them a sideshow. The real victim, the Russian taxpayer, was moving into sight. The fraudsters' henchmen, now posing as the legal owners of the company, used the judgment to argue that its past profits were now illusory, and the tax paid on them must be refunded. On 24 December 2007 they filed amended tax returns for 2006. These argued that as the new court judgments had wiped out the Hermitage companies' taxable profits in that year, they were there-fore entitled to a refund of the $230m in capital gains taxes these companies had paid. This was a striking and substantial claim that in any normal tax system would have been subject to thorough and lengthy scrutiny. Making the Russian tax authorities disgorge even the smallest and simplest refund is mind-bendingly slow and difficult. But thanks to the patronage of the FSB and other powerful institutions (the Interior Ministry and the upper reaches of government), the claimants won agreement for their refund – thought to be the largest single such payment in Russian financial history – from the two tax authorities concerned in a single day.[*]

---

[*] The 5.4bn roubles was paid out within two days via a newly created account at Universal Savings Bank. This was a curious institution. Two nominee share-holders in the bank were also shareholders in the three obscure companies that became the owners of the stolen Hermitage companies. The main beneficial shareholder is a convicted criminal called Dmitri Klyuev, who has past links to other questionable FSB-related transactions. In the summer of 2008, once Hermitage started firing its legal salvos, the bank filed for voluntary liquidation.

The payment was premature: one of the court judgments did not even come into effect until 11 January. Even the simplest checks by the tax authorities would have shown that the transaction was fraudulent. Although two officials of the tax authorities gave sworn statements that they had made all possible and necessary checks before authorising the transactions, it is hard to square this with reality. Russian bureaucrats are known for many things, but not for a happy-go-lucky attitude to paperwork, nor for working extremely quickly. If the statements from the officials are to be believed, they made a series of extensive and complex checks with other state agencies, and received completely satisfactory replies, all in the space of a few hours in late December when Russia is shutting down for its lengthy New Year festivities.

It may be illustrative to imagine what would have happened if such a fraud were attempted in a Western country. Mr Browder would have immediately secured a court order preventing the fraudsters using the property they had acquired. Even a whiff of official involvement in a crime of this scale would alert the media (and the blogosphere). Lawmakers would ask questions; bodies that represent business would make complaints too; and anti-corruption agencies would take a hard look at the behaviour of the officials concerned. None of these mechanisms works properly in Russia. On paper, the state is accountable in all these ways, but in practice using them is mostly useless – and in some cases actually dangerous.

Between 3 and 11 December 2007 Hermitage had submitted no fewer than six lengthy complaints detailing the theft of the companies. Two went to the chief prosecutor – who promptly passed them to Major Karpov. Unsurprisingly, no action followed. Two went to the department of the Interior Ministry that deals with internal corruption issues. It declined to take action, with the Kafkaesque justification: 'We are unable to open an inquiry into an investigator when such an inquiry is requested by the target of the investigator's current work.' One went to the St Petersburg branch of the Russian State Investigative Committee, which replied that it could find nothing amiss. The sixth went to the same body's federal offices, which opened a low-level inquiry on 5 February. That delay cost the Russian taxpayer $230m.

The robbers now had their loot. But they were still at risk of being found out. The fraud was not an elegant one. Whether from carelessness or complacency, the phoney documentation was littered with mistakes. Moreover Hermitage was firing salvoes of official complaints inside Russia, and was running an effective PR campaign abroad. It was time for a criminal case against the pesky foreigners to scare them into silence.

The authorities had to try to prove that Hermitage had done something wrong. If the evidence did not exist, it must be invented. On 26 February, Karpov, Kuvaldin and two of Kuznetsov's other subordinates flew to the provincial city of Elista, capital of Kalmykia. This republic is one of the poorest and oddest places in Russia, Buddhist by religion and long ruled by a chess-mad despot called Kirsan Ilyumzhinov. Like many investors in Russia, for tax purposes Hermitage had established its investment subsidiaries there.* As a 'Free Economic Zone' – one of eleven in Russia – the republic was an onshore tax haven, with an 11 per cent tax rate on corporate profits, against 35 per cent in Moscow. Hermitage also used another tax break aimed at promoting the employment of disabled people. In 1996 it had hired four such staff, nominated by the Kalmykian authorities, for the undemanding task of sending press clippings on a monthly basis.[9] Investigators in Elista

---

* The federal authorities abolished this loophole in 2002. In 2006 they ended another quirk, a two-tier market in Gazprom shares. This had created a lucrative opportunity for investors (including Hermitage) to buy locally listed ones for foreign clients at a large and legal discount.

had on several occasions, most recently in 2004, started looking at Hermitage's tax affairs, each time ruling that no crime had taken place. The law offered little scope for further pursuit: the deadline for collecting tax debts had expired. But in 2008 the visitors from Moscow had little difficulty in persuading their Elista colleagues to reopen a case and to transfer the investigation to the Russian capital. They summoned a local investigating officer back from vacation. Witnesses interviewed in the FSB office in Elista readily agreed to change their story, saying that Hermitage had never actually paid them. (Hermitage has produced payment orders to support its position.)

Whether or not Hermitage's conduct in all this was flawless, average, or questionable is not the point here. Nothing in its activities, in any legal system imaginable, would carry sanctions including the criminal prosecution, arbitrary imprisonment, or physical abuse leading to death of one of its lawyers. Yet that is just what happened. On 5 May 2008 Kuznetsov initiated a criminal case against not Hermitage itself, but its lawyers, claiming they did not have genuine powers of attorney to represent their client: in effect, he was saying that the only person who could legally represent the company was the person who stole it. That marked a grim step to lawlessness. A lawyer is an officer of the court, bound to do his professional best to make his client's case clearly and convincingly. It is a sure sign of a rotten legal and political system when lawyers are punished for the crime of representing their clients. When I tried to explain this case to a friend, he asked in innocent puzzlement: 'Why didn't they call the police?' That question highlights the gulf between the way Russia works and the standards expected in the West. In this case, the criminals were the police, as Mr Magnitsky discovered when he tried to find out what had happened to his complaints against Kuznetsov and Karpov. Far from being independently investigated, these had been forwarded to the men themselves. On attending the Investigative Committee offices in Moscow to give a deposition, he was surprised to see Kuznetsov there – officials explained this by saying that he was 'assisting' them.

Meanwhile Hermitage lawyers filed fifteen more complaints, with every relevant law enforcement and regulatory agency. Mr Browder and his colleagues were sure that the episode would be dealt with properly once higher authorities became aware of it. As ardent advocates of the rule of law in Russia, Prime Minister Putin and President Dmitri Medvedev surely could not ignore evidence that their officials had defrauded taxpayers of $230m? But Mr Magnitsky's work had the opposite effect. Having already threatened Hermitage lawyers with criminal charges in May, in August 2008 the fraudsters ordered a police raid on the offices of four law firms working for Hermitage.* The lawyers at the firms also received summonses, in violation of a Russian law that specifically prohibits lawyers being subject to questioning by the criminal justice authorities for anything relating to their dealings with clients. Undeterred, Mr Magnitsky in October 2008 filed a comprehensive dossier to the State Investigative Committee. If Mr Putin's claim to have created a 'dictatorship of law' in Russia

* A farcical but revealing element in this came with the discovery of 'stolen' documents brought from Russia to London and then sent back to Moscow from the DHL office in Lambeth, by two men of Slavic appearance (captured on CCTV), falsely giving the address of the Hermitage office in London. Barely forty-five minutes after the package was delivered to a law office in Moscow, the police arrived in search of the documents and confiscated the package, in what looks like a clumsy attempt to frame Mr Khairetdinov, another of the Hermitage lawyers. It is unclear what the package contained. A police protocol lists obviously forged documents, such as a power of attorney issued in the name of a non-existent person (using a surname that had featured in previous lawsuits against Hermitage), official files that would normally be in the custody of the authorities, and 'documents in foreign language' with 'stamps of Belize'.

counted for anything, it should make it possible to challenge abuses such as this. But the truth is that the law in Russia is a trap for the brave, not a weapon for the weak. By challenging the authorities in court, you leave yourself open to their retribution. The idealistic Mr Magnitsky was about to learn this the hard way.

The next stage of intimidation came when the authorities opened criminal cases against the two Hermitage Fund lawyers who had reported the police involvement in the $230m theft. These men, Eduard Khairetdinov and Vladimir Pastukhov, and some colleagues, promptly went abroad. Had Mr Magnitsky followed suit he would be alive today. On 12 November 2008 Kuznetsov and his three subordinates were instructed to investigate possible criminal conduct by Hermitage's lawyers. On 24 November 2008 four law enforcement officers came to Mr Magnitsky's home and arrested him in front of his wife and two children. All applications for bail were peremptorily turned down. Russian media have reported that he was planning to go abroad, citing plane tickets to Kiev reserved in his name. But these were booked only by phone, by an unidentified male voice, and never collected. Booking bogus tickets is a tactic commonly used by Russian criminal justice authorities wanting to plant 'evidence' that a suspect is planning to flee. The FSB statement said Mr Magnitsky had applied for a visa for the UK. The British consulate in Moscow denies that any such application was made.

The denial of bail meant that Mr Magnitsky never saw his children again; indeed he never heard their voices, as telephone calls to his family were denied. His contact with his loved ones was limited to snatched glimpses at brief and farcically unfair court hearings. Only once, a month before his death, was he allowed a brief meeting with his wife and mother. He died in jail just under a year after he was arrested, eight days before the expiry of the maximum limit for pre-trial detention.

The initial reason given was 'rupture to the abdominal membrane', which was later replaced with 'heart failure'. A fairer assessment would have been death by torture. Mr Magnitsky had been kept in abominable conditions.[10] The authorities ignored his complaints and repeatedly denied him medical attention, even when he was in great pain with life-threatening ailments. His body showed signs of direct physical abuse in the final hours of his life. Squeamish readers may wish to skip what follows.[11]

Mr Magnitsky was initially locked up in a detention centre, in an unheated cell with an unglazed window, and with just four beds for the eight prisoners. The lights burned round the clock. He was shifted from cell to cell sixteen times, with his belongings often going 'missing' amid the move. Here he describes life after court hearings for those in custody:

> Prisoners [arriving back] are not taken to their cells immediately and are instead held in a prison box for 3–3.5 hours. Not once have I been returned to my cell earlier than 23:00. This prison box is 20–22 m², it has no windows or ventilation and may hold up to seventy people at the same time and this means that there is neither any room to sit nor even to stand. Many of the prisoners smoke in the prison box and this makes it very difficult to breathe . . . the time in between hot meals can be up to 38 hours (from 18:00 the day before the visit to court when a prisoner receives a hot meal to 8:00 when breakfast is served on the day after the visit to court).

This is a standard tactic in the Russian (and before that the Soviet) jail system, to weaken a prisoner's resistance. Later he was put in a cell that was flooded with sewage – this extract is from his prison diary on 9 September 2009:

At about midday, in the cell, sewage started to rise from the drain under the sink, and half of the cell floor was flooded straight away. We asked for a plumber to be called, but he only arrived at 22:00 and could not repair the fault. We requested to be transferred to a different cell but were told that we had to stay put until the next morning. On the morning of the following day the plumber did not arrive and by the evening the whole floor was covered in a layer of sewage. It was impossible to walk on the floor and we were forced to move around the cell by climbing on the beds like monkeys.

Throughout his ordeal, Mr Magnitsky made complaints and requests – over 450 in total – on everything from the denial of hot water for washing to demands to meet his family, phone his children, and have medical attention. That is more than one for each day of his imprisonment. They, and his jail diary, make poignant reading.

The reason for the ill-treatment was simple. The authorities wanted Mr Magnitsky to switch sides. If he would retract his testimony against the police officers, and instead give evidence confessing that he was responsible for the fraud and implicating Mr Browder, he could go free. Such tactics were familiar in the Soviet era, when political prisoners were told that they would never see their families again, or that their children would be sent to orphanages, if they did not incriminate their fellow-dissidents. It is shocking to find the same approach in 2009 in a country that is a signatory to the European Convention on Human Rights and is a member of the Council of Europe.

Each time Mr Magnitsky refused to cooperate, the authorities worsened his conditions. By June he had lost 40lb (18kg). He began to experience severe abdominal pain. After an initial stay in an overcrowded and squalid detention centre, Mr Magnitsky had been transferred to the 'Sailor's Rest' prison (*Matrosskaya tishina* in Russian) where conditions were marginally less bad, with a mere three prisoners to a 16m² cell. Medical services were better there too. On 1 July an ultrasound examination diagnosed 'calculous cholecystitis', an illness caused by untreated gallstones (choleliths, in medical terminology). The symptoms include pain, anorexia, nausea, vomiting and fever. The prison doctors prescribed a further examination and surgery in a month's time. But a week before that treatment, Mr Magnitsky was transferred to the notorious Butyrka prison, which has no ultrasound machine and none of the surgical or medical facilities required for his treatment. The ostensible reason for his move was renovation works, though an independent investigation later established that these never took place. In any case it is unclear why Mr Magnitsky, already seriously ill, should be one of the handful of inmates needing to be moved. Questioned later by independent investigators, the prison director, Ivan Prokopenko, said he did not consider Magnitsky sick, remarking: 'Prisoners often try to pass themselves off as sick in order to get better conditions. We are all sick. I, for instance, have osteochondrosis.'[12]

On 9 August Mr Magnitsky demanded a meeting with Mr Prokopenko, complaining that his health was at risk because of ill treatment. On 11 August he followed it up with a second complaint demanding immediate medical attention. On 19 August his lawyers complained again, both to Mr Prokopenko and to the chief investigator in the case, Oleg Silchenko, demanding an ultrasound examination. On 25 August, after Mr Magnitsky had spent a sleepless night in agony, the lawyers made an urgent complaint demanding a medical examination and surgery for cholecystitis and pancreatitis – the latter disease resulting from lack of treatment of the former. Following a meeting with Silchenko, on 13 October 2009, Mr Magnitsky wrote the following witness statement:

I believe that [Interior Ministry Lieutenant Colonel Artyom] Kuznetsov and other law enforcement officers in conspiracy with him could be involved in the theft of Rilend, Makhaon, Parfenion and the subsequent theft of 5.4bn roubles from the State Treasury and were extremely interested in suppressing my activity relating to assisting my client in investigating the circumstances connected with these criminal offences. This was the reason for my unlawful criminal prosecution being carried out by investigator Silchenko. I believe that with Silchenko's participation or with his tacit approval, inhuman conditions were created for me in the detention centre, which humiliate human dignity. While in custody, I have been transferred five times to four different detention centres. I am tired of counting the cells to which I have been transferred innumerable times. I am denied medical assistance. On many occasions, for artificial and unjustifiable reasons, my mother's and wife's visits were prohibited, as well as telephone conversations with my little children. While in custody, situations have been created for me where I was deprived of the right to have a weekly shower, to watch television, to use a refrigerator, and simply to live under normal conditions, to the extent they can be 'normal' in a detention centre. I am convinced that such intolerable conditions are being created for me with my investigators' full knowledge. I am convinced that the only possibility to stop this humiliating treatment is for me to accept false accusations, to incriminate myself and other persons.*

Far from being intimidated by his treatment, on 16 October 2009 Mr Magnitsky reiterated his allegations in greater detail. That sealed his fate. On 12 November another farcical pre-trial hearing

---

* Mr Magnitsky's lawyer, Dmitri Kharitonov, also says that on repeated occasions Silchenko offered to release him if he would incriminate Mr Browder.

brought a curt dismissal of his appeal for bail, on the grounds that
the time to file it had elapsed. This was a big psychological blow,
perhaps aggravating his physical woes. By 13 November he was
vomiting constantly, with a visibly swollen stomach. Even at that
stage, a simple medical intervention could have saved his life. On
16 November Mr Magnitsky was transferred from Butyrka to the
'Sailor's Rest' for 'emergency medical treatment'. But the doctor
there prescribed only a painkiller. When that failed, he had Mr
Magnitsky put in a straitjacket and referred him for psychiatric
evaluation. Eight guards from a special disciplinary squad arrived.
They handcuffed the dying man, beat him with rubber batons and
took him to an isolation cell, where he lay handcuffed on the floor
by the side of a bed. He was found dead an hour and a half later by
a doctor and nurse who had been kept waiting outside his cell for
one hour and eighteen minutes.

Around this time, Mr Browder's staff in London started receiving terse, threatening text messages in Russian on their mobile
phones. Copies they have supplied to me make chilling reading.
One read: 'What is more frightening, I don't know . . . death
or prison?' A later one used a quote from The Godfather to try
to intimidate the recipient: 'If history tells us anything, it is that
anyone can be killed. Michael Corleone.' One after his death said
mockingly: 'A lawyer dies in investigative detention, in the framework of an interesting criminal case. An emblematic case. Paid-for
articles won't work. Extradition etc.'

Even in Russia, where public opinion is hardened to news of
official misconduct, Mr Magnitsky's death caused a public outcry.
He was not some marginal figure from the political opposition,
nor an investigative journalist who had clearly been asking for
trouble, neither was he from the country's troubled and violent
southern fringe, where many Russians think tough treatment
by the authorities offers the only hope of quelling terrorist

insurgencies by violent Islamist extremists. Mr Magnitsky fell into none of these categories: he was just a middle-class Russian lawyer trying to do his job. Belatedly, some of the wheels in the system began to turn. Pressure groups and official watchdogs made the first moves. Within weeks an independent group, the Moscow Public Oversight Commission, blamed his death on 'psychological and physical pressure'. One member termed it 'premeditated murder.'[13] The Moscow Helsinki Group, headed by Lyudmila Alekseyeva, the doyenne of the Soviet dissident movement, submitted a powerfully argued criminal complaint. It said that the death

did not occur accidentally. It did not occur merely through the oversight or negligence of some particular prison officials. Sergei Magnitsky died from torture that was wilfully inflicted upon him.

As pressure grew, Mr Medvedev ordered an official investigation. He signed a law prohibiting the detention of suspects in tax crime cases. Though twenty prison officials, including the deputy head of the federal prison service, were fired, nineteen of them had nothing to do with the Magnitsky case. The only figure directly involved in the case was Major-General Anatoli Mikhalkin, who had headed the Interior Ministry's tax crimes department in Moscow, and had been named by Mr Magnitsky in one of his complaints. The official reason for his dismissal was 'retirement'. On 25 June 2010 the internal security department of the MVD started an investigation into Kuznetsov, following an appeal by Mrs Clinton. It has brought no result. On the contrary, several of the people directly involved in the case have received medals and promotions. Kuznetsov moved from the Moscow City tax crimes office to a job in the federal economic-security division of the MVD. Karpov also moved to a job at the federal level. An official inquiry by the Investigative Committee exonerated Silchenko, the investigator ultimately responsible for Mr Magnitsky's death, of all wrongdoing. One week before the anniversary of his death, the MVD held an annual awards ceremony recognising the thirty 'best investigators' among its million-plus officers. Five of the awards went to people directly involved in the Magnitsky case, including Silchenko and Karpov. Growing international condemnation of the case has brought largely ineffective and token responses in Russia. A commission set up by Mr Medvedev's Human Rights Council said that Silchenko 'bears serious responsibility for [Mr] Magnitsky's death' and that he might have died as a result of a beating by medical orderlies.[14] A report by the State Investigative Committee in July 2011 accepted that Mr Magnitsky died because of failures in his medical care. But the Interior Ministry said it saw 'no reason' to investigate the action of its officials. Instead Russian prosecutors said they would reopen the case against Mr Magnitsky (oddly, cases against dead people can be tried in Russia). They even summoned his mother as a witness.

Meanwhile, the perpetrators were getting rich. Official Russian documents show that cars and real estate worth $3m were registered to Kuznetsov, his wife and his pensioner parents in the period between the raid on Firestone Duncan and Mr Magnitsky's death. An investigation by Hermitage claims that Olga Stepanova, a senior official in the Moscow tax inspectorate, her subordinates and their families suddenly gained $43m in offshore property and other assets following the phoney tax refund.[15] Nobody has established so far that this has anything to do with the Magnitsky case. But there would be those who would find the coincidence striking. Nor is it proved where the bulk of the money stolen from the Russian taxpayer went. Mr Browder's investigators believe that the finger points to the higher reaches of the FSB, and still more senior figures in the Interior Ministry, in the tax authorities and in the prosecutors' office.

Had they known five years ago the result of their scheming, the perpetrators would surely have decided to pick another target. It is hard to see now what will stop Mr Browder's formidable campaign against the sixty people he accuses of benefiting from the fraud, or of complicity in Mr Magnitsky's death.[16] The European Parliament has voted to ban them from the European Union; Canada's parliament has proposed a similar resolution and it has passed in the Netherlands. More than twenty American senators have backed legislation banning these individuals from the United States, provoking a furious response from the Russian authorities.

While Mr Browder has shed his reputation as a grandstanding wheeler-dealer for that of an inspirational leader of a moral crusade, the Russian authorities' response to the case has been a textbook study in how not to handle a tricky issue. As in so many episodes, from the mysterious apartment-block bombings in 1999[17] to the looting of Yukos, they have made their case spectacularly poorly, with a mixture of paranoid silence, bluster and deceit. The best place to test all these claims would be in court, with proper lawyers on both sides and a fair judge in the middle. That does not seem likely to happen. Overall, while some officials have condemned Mr Magnitsky's treatment, others have implied that he deserved it, and others still have made counter-allegations. When, prompted by Mr Browder's researchers, the Swiss authorities opened a money-laundering investigation into accounts at Credit Suisse, the bank that handled many of the transfers benefiting those implicated in the case, the Russian authorities launched a clumsy attempt to summons Mr Browder for questioning in Moscow (understandably, he has declined to go). Credit Suisse says it is co-operating with the investigation.

The genesis, course and aftermath of this case exemplify the weakness of the bits of the Russian system that should constrain the powerful and protect the innocent. Appeals to politicians either went unanswered or brought ineffective responses. Russian voters clearly care about the case and believe that an injustice was done. But the political system offers no way to resolve their concern. Attempts to use the parts of the state machinery that offer redress to wronged citizens got nowhere. Civil-society organisations tried to raise the case, but without success. The media barked – bravely in some cases – but could not bite. Only external pressure, belatedly, has inconvenienced the people behind the fraud and murder, who are now (in some cases) unable to travel freely to the West.

The case is a concentrated episode in a much wider story: the ex-KGB's abuse of power, including murder and looting. The FSB – its main successor organisation – has tried and trusted tools for intimidating individuals and for misusing the instruments of state power to create an alternative reality, in which the innocent are the guilty and justice serves the state's interest, not the public one. The FSB acts as the Russian regime's enforcers, punishing the brave and bullying the cowardly in order to head off any credible political or economic challenge. In return, it has a licence to loot, using both the tools of espionage and a veneer of legality in which criminal actions have the force of law. It has placed its trusted officers in parts of the state apparatus that are supposedly independent: public, governmental, or judicial bodies. Hermitage researchers are convinced, for example, that Kuznetsov, nominally an official of the Interior Ministry, is in fact an FSB officer, making sure that his masters' interests are served there; also in the FSB, they believe, are the people in the Moscow city tax department who supervised the bogus refund (which was by no means the first of its kind). The ultimate blame for Mr Magnitsky's death reaches even higher than those named here. At the head of the scam, says Hermitage, were top Russian officials including a government minister with a close friend who is a senior official. An analogy comes from the real-estate business: the most senior official is the 'landowner'; he cuts in a 'property developer' to construct the scam, who then buys in whatever brain and muscle-power is needed. The profits from this 'project' pay off any troublesome outsiders.

The system that perpetrated the crimes described in this chapter is the epitome of the Russian state machine today. The story of Sergei Magnitsky is not just a human tragedy; it is a political parable. His fate may help calibrate the reader's moral compass in the pages ahead, which deal with events past and present outside Russia. The people responsible for his death in prison are the heirs of the Soviet KGB, and colleagues of Russia's present-day spymasters.

Many find it easy to be blasé about Russian spies. Espionage is a grubby business always and everywhere. Spies' political masters in many countries deploy them for bad reasons as well as high ones. Why are the Kremlin's lot worse than anyone else's? For all its undoubted flaws, Russia today is not a totalitarian superpower with ambitions for world domination. Its intelligence agencies are decades away from the mass murderers of the old KGB. Even the Cold War did not deserve the moral clarity that some of its Western protagonists liked to maintain. Indeed, as I myself show in later chapters, cynicism and incompetence blot the record of British and American intelligence in Eastern Europe. For all these reasons, many would argue, it is surely time to grow up, and keep the tiresome but ultimately anachronistic phenomenon of Russian espionage in proper proportion?

A proportionate response is indeed merited. But it should be tougher, not softer, than the West's current stance. As Sergei Magnitsky's story shows, the dark threads of murder and mayhem that started with Lenin's Red Terror after the Bolshevik revolution in 1917 continue to the present day in the heart of Russia's bureaucracy, with officials swindling their own taxpayers out of a fortune, and then killing the man who tried to expose their misdeeds. The next chapters explain the origins of the corrupt autocracy that rules Russia's mafia state, its aims, and then its activities in our midst.

2

The Pirate State

The story of Sergei Magnitsky should be a wake-up call to the outside world, revealing the true nature of the regime in Russia. But outsiders have systematically (and in some cases wilfully) misread events since 1999, when the chaotic but pluralist era of Boris Yeltsin gave way to the corrupt and authoritarian rule of the ex-KGB hard men – the *Siloviki*. Telling the real story of these men's doings is hard and even dangerous. For Russia's self-censoring mainstream media, no-go areas include Mr Putin's private wealth, his sexual preferences, and the mysterious 'terrorist' bombings of autumn 1999 that stoked public anxiety, making the unknown stopgap prime minister a shoo-in for the presidency. It is often forgotten that Mr Putin arrived on the national stage as a political cipher: a quiet, grey, timid-looking man, blinking nervously in the unaccustomed limelight. He was the fifth prime minister in the space of twelve months: many at the time thought, wrongly, that his stint in office would be equally brief (as we will see later in the book, the outward appearance of mediocrity can be dangerously deceptive). Now the media admiringly portray Mr Putin and his colleagues as chaste, brave (and in his case virile) guardians of the national interest, not brutes or swindlers. Privately, few Russians believe these political arrangements are fair or efficient. But they see no way of changing them.

That reflects the contradiction at the heart of Russian public life. The twelve years of the ex-KGB regime has brought not the promised transformation to order and modernity, but only a sleazy stability. Corruption and incompetence mean that public services are still dire, despite the billions squandered on them. The result is demoralising and tiresome. Many of the brightest and best Russians yearn to live and work abroad. But at home, few see any alternative to Mr Putin and his colleagues. Whatever their shortcomings, in the view of many Russians, they are the least bad option – certainly better than the uncertainties and humiliations of the 1990s.

The harshest fate awaits those who try active opposition. Demonstrators for causes that displease the Kremlin risk arrest. A stark example of this is the protestors who gather on the 31st of the month (when it happens) to defend Article 31 of the Russian constitution, which guarantees freedom of assembly. Apparently oblivious to the irony, police haul them away: punishing those demonstrating for the right to demonstrate. The FSB and other organs of state power have closed down independent public life in Russia. They have intimidated journalists (and even bloggers); they bully trade unionists; they infiltrate and disrupt opposition parties. The threat of Soviet-style coercive psychiatric treatment is in the background (and sometimes even the foreground) during interrogations. All critics of the regime count as potential 'extremists', and 'extremism' is a criminal offence, punishable in some cases by the death penalty. In July 2010 the FSB gained new rights to issue warnings to individuals, organisations, and media outlets to stop activities it considers actually or potentially extremist.

A full account of the misrule that results would take a whole book, with full chapters, rather than just fleeting mentions, for subjects such as the mistreatment of the country's millions of migrant workers.* Most of the worst abuses happen in the republics of the North Caucasus, such as Chechnya, Ingushetia and Dagestan, where the authorities are struggling to maintain control amid a growing insurgency from Islamist groups and others infuriated by their corrupt and incompetent rulers. But the noxious cocktail there poisons public life in Moscow too. A signal example of this came with the murder in January 2009 of Stanislav Markelov, a leading human rights lawyer who had represented many victims of abuse in Chechnya. The men who gunned him down in the middle of Moscow in broad daylight also killed a young journalist, Anastasia Baburova. So hardened is international public opinion to the regime's habitual use of violence against its opponents that other cases barely attract attention. In March 2009 Lev Ponamarov, a leading human-rights activist, was severely beaten. This appears to have been a snub to a visiting European human-rights representative, Sabine Leutheusser-Schnarrenberger, whom he had just met. In July, Albert Pchelintsev, an anti-corruption activist, was shot with a stun gun, by attackers who told him that it was to 'shut him up'. Natalya Estemirova, the leading campaigner and researcher in Chechnya for Memorial, the oldest and best-known Russian human-rights organisation, was abducted and murdered in July 2009. The Chechen president Ramzan Kadyrov said callously that he would not have bothered to murder a woman 'devoid of honour, merit and conscience'. Oleg Orlov, chairman of Memorial, accused Mr Kadyrov of 'political responsibility' for the killing and was then prosecuted for criminal slander (he was acquitted in June 2011).[1] The investigative journalist Oleg Kashin received a crippling beating in November 2010.

* Mostly from other bits of the former Soviet Union, they are habitually cheated, abused and on occasion murdered, by their employers, or by the police, or by thuggish political extremists.

These killings, assaults and other forms of intimidation often bear the FSB's fingerprints. It makes no difference when other Russian authorities condemn the lawlessness. Mr Medvedev, for example, repeatedly denounced corruption and what he memorably termed 'legal nihilism'. Yet for the most part, the Russian president was part of the problem, not of the solution. It was he, for example, who in August 2010 signed into law the FSB's new powers to issue intimidatory warnings. Human Rights Watch states in its most recent report that the climate remains 'deeply negative', with only rhetorical commitments to human rights and the rule of law.[2]

Those who seek the secrets of the regime are at even greater danger. Russian journalists who turn over such stones risk violent attacks or death. Foreign journalistic inquiry too has become far harder over the past ten years as the regime and its business cronies have discovered England's tough and far-reaching libel law. Finding source material is tricky. The paper trail often goes cold in places such as the British Virgin Islands, which blocks outsiders from finding the ultimate beneficial ownership of the companies registered there. But the greed and cynicism of supposedly more reputable countries in dealing with dubious but tempting customers is if anything worse.[3]

Even in America, Britain and Continental European countries that claim to shun crime and corruption, officials are unwilling to speak out publicly about the sea of dirty Russian money that swills through property markets, banking systems, financial exchanges and (increasingly) politics. In the course of an important investigation I appealed to a well-placed Western official to help me see some crucial documents. He responded: 'We would love to help you, but however discreetly we do it, the Russians will find out. And they will take it as a declaration of war.' A Finnish official, faced with a specific request that could have cast a damning light on a senior Russian figure's behaviour, answered: 'Good luck. But we can't help you. That's why we're still here'. Such coyness stems only partly from prudence. Some officials have personal financial reasons for going easy on Russia: a lucrative directorship may be awaiting them when they leave government service. Others fear more generally that moral grandstanding will be bad for business; some feel that criticism of Russia is selective and even hypocriti- cal, given the corruption and misrule in other countries, not least in the West.

These perceptions are changing, albeit slowly. Russia's reputa- tion as a promising emerging market looks increasingly hollow, as other competitors for foreign trade and investment do better. Russia's place in the BRIC group – Brazil, Russia, India and China – is now largely nominal, as the other three countries forge ahead. Closer to home, the smaller but more advanced states of Central Europe have outstripped Russia in importance. The Czech Republic, with a population of only 10m people, buys more German exports than Russia with 140m people. Even including oil and gas, Poland is now a substantially bigger trading partner for Germany than Russia.[4]

Yet declining importance does not mean irrelevance, and few European leaders are willing to contemplate a real confrontation. They argue that many places are worse run than Russia, which does not look like a rogue state, or even a particularly threaten- ing one. They also note that Russia, for its part, does not want a confrontation either. Having indulged in Soviet symbolism and nostalgia at the start of his time in power (when he described the USSR's collapse as the 'geopolitical catastrophe' of the last century, and reinstated the tune of the Soviet national anthem) Mr Putin switched tack. Russia has mended fences with neighbours such as Poland, expressing sympathy for the victims of Soviet-era crimes such as the Hitler–Stalin Pact and the wartime Katyń massacre

of captured Polish officers, and in some cases explicitly repudiat-
ing the lies surrounding those crimes, which had only lately been
making a revolting comeback.

Russia has also in large part signed up to the rules of the international game (though it may not always obey them). It has negotiated with seeming sincerity to join outfits such as the Organisation
for Economic Cooperation and Development (a rich-world think-
tank in Paris) and the World Trade Organisation, which regu-
lates global trade. Many leading members of Russia's government,
especially those dealing with financial and economic policy, look
no worse and in some ways rather better than their counterparts in
other ex-communist countries. As Daniel Treisman, an American
academic, argues, Russia is no more messily ruled than other
middle-income countries such as Mexico or Turkey.[5] Rigged
elections, manipulated media, high-level corruption and abuse of
state power are unpleasant phenomena, but sadly not rare ones.
Russia's legal system sometimes works – especially in cases that,
unlike Mr Magnitsky's, do not involve the interests of the rich and
powerful. Charities and pressure groups can function with only
mild difficulties so long as they stay away from taboo areas such as
Chechnya. Elections in the provinces sometimes yield surprising
results that annoy the country's leaders. It has a degree of media
freedom (chiefly on the internet and in small-circulation publica-
tions). Emigration provides an important safety valve: unlike in
the Soviet era, if you don't like it, you can leave. The state expects
little of its citizens, and vice versa.

Given that Russia emerged from communist dictatorship only
twenty-one years ago, the right response, its advocates argue, is to
be impressed that the country is so normal, rather than depressed
that it is not better. Such special pleading makes it easy for foreigners to conclude that Russia, once you get used to it, is just another
roughly hewn emerging market, more a source of opportunity

than danger. In any case, Russia does not take much notice of outside strictures, so the best thing is to shut up. Critics of Russia's domestic and foreign policy certainly need to be careful not to exaggerate their case. Some aspects of politics may be reminiscent of fascism, such as the personality cult of Mr Putin, the overlap between business and politics, and thuggish youth movements (as I note later, one of these now boasts Ms Chapman as a senior figure). But Russia is not a totalitarian country, or even a fully autocratic one. Vladislav Inozemtsev, an economics professor highly critical of the regime, concedes:

Contemporary Russia is not a candidate to become a Soviet Union 2.0. It is a country in which citizens have unrestricted access to information, own property, leave and return to the country freely, and develop private businesses of all kinds.[6]

After an era where Russia resembled Weimar Germany in some respects, nothing like the Nazi Party or Hitlerian ideology is in sight.

The temptation among many Westerners, therefore, is to accept the superficial image of normality and cooperation, without digging too deeply into the violent, thieving and distorted mind-set and personalities behind it, or their pervasive incompetence and penchant for risky short cuts. A glimpse behind this veil of official timidity and self-interest came with the WikiLeaks revelations that started in November 2010. They exposed the almost panicky concern of American diplomats about the level of corruption in Russia, about the fusion between crime, business and government, and about its spillover into the West. America's then Secretary of Defence Robert Gates observed in a secret cable that Russia was 'an oligarchy run by the security services'.[7] Britain's Michael Davenport, a seasoned Russia-watcher in the

Foreign Office, termed it a 'corrupt autocracy' when talking to his American colleagues.[8] But that was mild by the standards of a more extensive analysis compiled in mid November 2009 by the American embassy in Moscow. Classified 'secret' (but now available at the click of a mouse on the WikiLeaks website), it was to prepare the director of the FBI, Robert Mueller, for a two-day visit to Moscow. It highlighted the real nature of his *Siloviki* interlocutors, the FSB director Aleksandr Bortnikov, the SVR director Mikhail Fradkov, and the Interior Minister Rashid Nurgaliyev. It described them as:

Putin protégés who believe a strong state exercising effective political and economic control is the answer to most problems. They advocate tightening the screws against domestic opposition and their alleged external supporters – principally the US and its Western allies.[9]

The diplomats went on to note that although the FSB and MVD* (as the Interior Ministry is known) nominally share the FBI's responsibilities – criminal prosecution, organised crime, and counter-terrorism – they are also fully immersed in Russia's political battles:

Russian security service leaders play a far more open political role than their counterparts in the West. Your three interlocutors accrue political power in the Russian system by using the legal system against political enemies – turning the courts into weapons of political warfare rather than independent arbiters. They control large numbers of men and resources – the MVD alone has more than 190,000 soldiers in its internal security divisions. Despite their

* *Ministerstvo Vnutrennykh Del* (Ministry of Internal Affairs).

similar outlook and background, they are often competitors for influence against each other – with shadowy conflicts occasionally bubbling to the surface.

It also revealed the security services' role in pushing back against perceived outside interference:

After the 'colour' revolutions in Georgia and Ukraine, Russian security services stepped up their efforts against the US and other Western powers, which they blame for inciting the protests and overthrowing the governments in Tbilisi and Kyiv [Kiev]. Their officers maintain constant vigilance against the US government representatives through active surveillance and they have sought to stifle US humanitarian programs in the North Caucasus. MVD forces harass and intimidate political opposition protests while 'investigations' against Western-supported NGOs [on] trumped up charges (like using pirated software) have hindered the work that those organisations seek to accomplish.

Concern about potential social unrest associated with the recent economic crisis provided justification for the security services' push earlier this year to eliminate jury trials and to broaden the definition of 'treason' to include the organisation of protests against the government.

After linking Russian law-enforcement to organised crime, the cable concluded with a sharp indictment of the role played by the FSB in demoralising and persecuting American government employees in Russia:

While portions of the FSB are working cooperatively with US law enforcement, some sections, particularly those dealing with counter-intelligence, are not. Harassing activity against all embassy personnel has spiked in the past several months to a level not seen in many years. Embassy personnel have suffered personally slanderous and falsely prurient attacks in the media. Family members have been the victims of psychologically terrifying assertions that their USG [United States Government] employee spouses had met accidental deaths. Home intrusions have become far more commonplace and bold, and activity against our locally engaged Russian staff continues at a record pace. We have no doubt that this activity originates in the FSB.

This in itself is a kind of deception. American taxpayers foot the bill for these diplomats and analysts, for their allowances, salaries and expense accounts. But they do not get the truth. At the time that these telegrams were drafted, American officials were playing down the problems in relations with Russia, and trying to make a success of the so-called 'reset' in relations. Yet privately – as we can now read – they took a far more pessimistic (and realistic) view. Another leaked telegram painted a hair-raising picture of the corruption inside the Moscow city administration: it spoke of a 'three-tiered structure in Moscow's criminal world' headed by Yuri Luzhkov (the then mayor, who denies any wrongdoing). 'The FSB, MVD, and militia are at the second level. Finally, ordinary criminals and corrupt inspectors are at the lowest level,' it claimed.[10] The tone of such telegrams is far closer to the writings of outsiders such as Amy Knight, a top American analyst of the KGB's lasting influence in modern Russia. She pointed out in 2011 that the FSB is not only an instrument of power; it determines who holds it.[11]

Another deception was the earlier attempt to portray Russia in the 1990s as a democratic country, even though it was in that era that the current authoritarian system has its roots. As Mr Inozemtsev points out:

The quasi-authoritarian 'superpresidential' Russian political style arose in the 'democratic' period of the mid-1990s, when then-President Boris Yeltsin forcibly dissolved the legitimate Parliament and pushed through a new constitution under which the powers of the President were not balanced by any restraints. Indeed, his status resembled that of the Führer of the German nation, as . . . determined by the *Ermächtigungsgesetz* (Enabling Act) of 23 March 1933. Later, Yeltsin's inner circle orchestrated his victory in the 1996 presidential elections. This derailed the country from the natural path of alternating power between liberal and socialist politicians that, however improbably, led Eastern Europe to its often anxious but successful development in the 1990s and 2000s. From that time on, the idea that 'there is no alternative' to the current leader or to his chosen successor has become a vital part of Russian politics.

It is true that Yeltsin's inner circle turned deplorably to election-rigging and the use of illicit money in politics as its popularity waned. They created the system, at least in embryo, that Mr Putin and his friends were later to develop and exploit. The continuity between the Yeltsin years and the Putin era that followed is no coincidence. It was a last desperate throw of the dice by Mr Yeltsin's family in 1999, when impeachment (and possibly jail) was looming, to turn to the ex-KGB for help. But for all his own faults (and the much worse ones of his family members and hangers-on), Mr Yeltsin, Russia's first democratically elected president, had strong principles. He was determined not to muzzle the media or lock up the opposition. He distrusted the intelligence and security services and encouraged competition between them. By contrast Mr Putin has given the FSB a near-monopoly.

Just after the collapse of the Soviet system, the Russian reformers' plan was quite different. The FSB was intended to be a kind of beefed up FBI, responsible for fighting organised crime and for counter-terrorism, plus spy-catching as required (in that era many Russians saw Western countries, and their spy agencies, as friendly partners, not rivals). Those times are long gone. The FSB is now a sprawling empire, with capabilities ranging from electronic intelligence-gathering to controlling Russia's borders and operations beyond them. Its instincts are xenophobic and authoritarian, with heavy doses of paranoia, ignorance, religiosity and nostalgia for the Soviet past. As a result, it now is like no other spy service in the developed world. The best analysis of its role comes from a hard-working (and brave) Moscow-based husband-and-wife team, Andrei Soldatov and Irina Borogan.[12] They liken the FSB to the *Mukhabarat* religious police of Saudi Arabia and other Muslim countries: impenetrable, ruthless and brutal. They argue: 'The intelligence bureaucracy considers itself above criticism, impervious to the demands of democracy.'[13] In their arbitrary power and incompetence, the officials of the FSB and its sister agencies epitomise the lawlessness and corruption that plague Russia and menace the outside world. But those inside the agency see themselves rather differently, as the ultimate guardians of Russia's national security, thoroughly deserving of the rich rewards they reap. Nikolai Patrushev, who succeeded Mr Putin as the agency's director in 2000, characterised his colleagues in startling terms:

Our best colleagues, the honour and pride of the FSB, don't do their work for the money. When I give government awards to our people, I scrutinise their faces. There are the highbrow intellectual analysts, the broad-shouldered, weather-beaten Special Forces men, the taciturn explosives specialists, exacting investigators and the discreet counter-espionage operational officers. They all look different, but there is one very special characteristic that unites all these people, and it is a very important quality. It is their sense of service. They are, if you like, our new nobility.[14]

That is true in one sense: the old nobility in Russia were mostly capricious, extravagant, incompetent and cruel. They set the scene for the Bolshevik revolution that brought them exile, death, destitution and imprisonment. But presumably Mr Patrushev did not have that in mind.

It would be wrong to term the FSB and its sister agencies simply as rebranded versions of the old KGB. Despite a narrower scope, they enjoy a far freer rein. The tactics are less brutal, certainly compared to the years of totalitarian terror under Stalin. They do not practise mass murder (and resort to assassination only on rare occasions). Russia is not a police state, in which the KGB, acting on behalf of (and tightly controlled by) the Communist Party, exercises rigid control over everything from foreign travel to people's sex lives. Nor is Russia a closed society, in which every foreigner is suspect, and every trip abroad a potential security risk. The old KGB spent a lot of time worrying about currency speculation (the rouble's official exchange rate was grotesquely overvalued). It vetted every application for foreign travel, and devoted vast resources to monitoring mail. The new regime is different, and not only because the Party is over. Instead of steaming open letters, the FSB uses powerful computers to scan emails. Instead of forcing all foreign visitors to stay in a handful of closely monitored hotels under the watchful eyes of Intourist guides, it focuses only on outsiders acting suspiciously.

To say that the regime in Moscow is suffused with the unpleasant ideology, values, habits, attitudes and behaviour of the Soviet era does not mean that it harbours communist or collectivist sympathies. Even its most diehard figures do not hanker after the planned economy or the one-party state, or for the costly and brittle apparatus of bureaucracy and control that went with them. They mourn the Soviet Union's power, not its politics. They recall growing up in a great country – a superpower – defined by the size of its nuclear arsenal, its global reach, and its wartime sacrifice. In their lifetime, all that disappeared. The Soviet system became the butt of jokes – for the senility of its gerontocratic leadership, for the poor quality of its consumer goods and for the omnipresent shortages. What came next was worse: the humiliating retreat from the old empire, the acceptance of German reunification on the West's terms, and playing second fiddle to America in global politics.

All of these things are associated in Russian minds with the 1990s. But what they disliked about that era was the weakness and chaos, not the capitalism. Many in Russia think, wrongly, that outsiders exploited the political disintegration to push through NATO expansion (of which more later) and to buy up Russia's natural resources cheaply. Their driving concern now is to restore Russia's standing in the world, and to prevent the West from ever again exploiting its weakness. The agenda is of stark competition for resources, status and power, against a background of perceived injustice and humiliation.

Opinions about the past are not monolithic. Few if any would defend Stalin outright. Some, particularly in the human-rights council set up by Mr Medvedev, actively argued for a radical break with the whole murderous and criminal system that the dictator inherited, developed and bequeathed.[15] They want memorials to his victims, and to rename streets called after communist heroes, paving the way to reconciliation with the European Union and a strategic alliance against China. Such nuances are a welcome contrast to the early Putin years, when any criticism of Stalin or Soviet power brought a knee-jerk and allergic response. But it would be premature to say that any real shift is under way. Polls show that the majority of Russians do not want 'de-Stalinisation'.[16] Mr Putin, set for twelve years more as Russian president, dislikes the whole idea. Unknotting the threads of pride and shame will take many years. The regime remains ready to use the pomp of the Soviet past when it suits it, even if some privately find the associated jargon, ideology and priorities anachronistic and perhaps outright distasteful. What does define it unambiguously is an enthusiastic adoption of the crudest forms of private enterprise. Russia's spookocrats like the new system not out of any close reading of Friedrich von Hayek or Adam Smith, but because it works for them. Whereas in the Soviet era the rewards of leadership were at best access to foreign goods and a luxurious dacha, the spoils of office now are colossal. No longer cloistered in the pretend austerity of Party discipline, they can enjoy the best the world has to offer, when, how and where they want it.

Greed is a defining characteristic of this new elite, but not the only one. Despite its good fortune (and great fortunes) the regime's world view is harsh and pessimistic. The prison-yard mentality has spread to those who run the state: show weakness, and you suffer. What counts is intense loyalty to friends, ruthless rivalry with everyone else, and vengeance on those who betray you. Andrei Illarionov, a former top Kremlin aide in the early years of the Putin era, when the Russian leader was still championing economic reform, has now fallen out with the regime and criticises it in the harshest terms. He is now a fellow at the free-market Cato Institute in Washington, DC and has written a powerful denunciation of the twenty-two agencies that he estimates make up the ruling power structure.

The members of 'Siloviki Incorporated' (SI) share a strong sense of allegiance to the group; an attitude of relative flexibility regarding short- and medium-term goals; and rather strict codes of conduct and honour, including the ideas of 'always taking care of one's own' and not violating the custom of omertà (silence). As one

might expect in a group with roots in the secret-police and intelligence services, members place great emphasis on obeying superiors, showing strong loyalty to one another, and preserving strict
discipline. There are both formal and informal means of enforcing
these norms. Those who violate the code are subject to the harshest forms of punishment, including death . . . Their training instils
in them a feeling of being superior to the rest of the populace, of
being the rightful 'bosses' of everyone else. For those who remain
on active duty, their perquisites of office include two items that
confer real power in today's Russia: the right to carry and use
weapons, and an FSB credential (known as a *vezdekhod*) that acts as
a carte blanche giving its owner the right to enter any place, office,
building, or territory whatsoever, public or private.[17]

He continues:

Speaking at the Lubyanka – the Moscow headquarters building
that the FSB inherited from the KGB – on 'Security Organs Day'
(known as 'Chekist Day') in December 1999, Putin said that 'the
mission of the group of FSB officers sent undercover to work in
the government is being accomplished successfully'. With the state
as their base, the *Siloviki* have taken over key business and media
organisations as well. There are now few areas of Russian life
where the SI's long arm fails to reach.

It is important not to glamorise the result. As Mr Inozemtsev
points out, the prime characteristic of Russia's rulers is 'ignorance, intricately if poorly disguised beneath a veneer of scientific
degrees'. But incompetent thuggishness is no more pleasant than
the competent kind. And as the economist Mr Inozemtsev himself
admits, the security and (mislabelled) 'law enforcement' organs
have mushroomed:

More than 200,000 professional military officers in the country
[are] on active duty. Around 1.1m soldiers serve on the staff of the
Interior Ministry; more than 300,000 serve inside the FSB; around
200,000 work in prosecutors' offices; and another 150,000 in different investigative committees. Close to the same number work
for the tax police; and more than 100,000 serve in the Customs
Committee and in the Federal Migration Service. We won't
mention smaller organisations like the Anti-Drug Administration
and many others. In total, more than 3.4m people – close to 12 per
cent of the active male workforce – are employed in organisations
that hew to the principles of vertical organisation, unquestioning
obedience and deeply rooted corruption.[18]

The FSB in particular is under no kind of constitutional, legal or
democratic oversight. It is a state within a state; a law unto itself.
Its counterparts in Western countries make mistakes, exceed their
power and on occasion misuse their privileges for self-enrichment
or to serve domestic political ends. But they are ultimately under
legal and political control. Some such agencies even have internal
ombudsmen and offer protection for whistle-blowers. In Russia
the parliamentary committees that are meant to supervise the
spooks are ciphers. The FSB is responsible only to its director – a
close ally of Mr Putin.

Mr Putin's arrival in power in 1999, say Soldatov and Borogan,
gave the secret services the right, for the first time in Russia's
history, to 'define their own political agenda'.[19] Top of that agenda
is stability, drawing on both the KGB's repression of dissidents
and the Tsarist secret-police punishment of political extremism.
Both the old and new secret police are based on the quasi-mystical
regard for the interests of the state, coupled with a mixture of
contempt and fear for its individual subjects. Both used, or use, a
similar palette of tactics – ranging from crude intimidation to subtle

deception. They were and are legalistic yet unconstrained by any concern for justice. In the FSB's own eyes, their role is to 'serve and protect'. But the idea of public service in this context is very different from the Western concept, where the voters' wishes, channelled by politicians and constrained by the rule of law, provide the framework in which public officials operate. In Russia, 'service' is first and foremost self-service: helping oneself to the fruits of office, be they bureaucratic rents from corruption or the spoils of the country's mineral wealth. Only after that comes public service. This is not service to the rules or processes of the state, but to a more abstract and transcendental idea of the national interest. Russia must be strong – in its use of military, financial and diplomatic power. If it cannot be strong it must be feared, or at least respected. The task of the public servant is to make that so.

A further component of the FSB mind-set is religiosity, in some cases with an admixture of mysticism. As Soldatov and Borogan note, the FSB has strengthened its ties with the Russian Orthodox Church – once the chief target of KGB persecution. In 2002 the then Patriarch of the Russian Orthodox Church, Aleksei II, blessed the reopening of the restored Cathedral of St Sophia of God's Wisdom on Lubyanka Square, near the FSB headquarters. The then FSB chief Nikolai Patrushev attended the ceremony. This reflects the increasing search among Russia's new leaders for old roots. Ideas of Russian uniqueness fit well with the rejection of foreign ideas such as political competition. They also chime with the notion – deeply held if bizarre to outsiders – that following the fall of ancient Rome and Constantinople, Moscow is the 'Third Rome', besieged by enemies who must be resisted at all costs. Indeed, the seemingly arcane subject of Byzantine history has become oddly popular among the FSB and in like-minded political circles. In January 2008 Russian state television broadcast a remarkable documentary called 'The Fall of an Empire: The Lesson of Byzantium'.[20] Echoing the regime's view of the 1990s, it blamed the end of the Byzantine empire on the intrigues of local 'oligarchs' and Western crusaders. The idea of a global conspiracy against Russia is central to the curriculum of the FSB Academy, which is fostering a new generation of *Siloviki*.

Unfortunately these ideas fall on fertile ground. Though Soviet-era education in the hard sciences was excellent, the tradition of study in the humanities was repressed and distorted. A real discussion of history and philosophy would have been corrosive for Marxism–Leninism. Only carefully vetted academics were allowed to teach and study such sensitive subjects. This legacy weakens Russia's resistance to batty and paranoid theories. And the surviving cadres of Soviet-trained academics have in many cases found it easy to switch from the intricacies of dialectical materialism to exploring hidden international machinations against Russia. A truly startling example of the overlap between paranoia and mysticism is the theory of *Mertvaya voda* or 'dead water', a miraculous substance that (in Russian folklore) can revive the dead and heal wounds. To see it cropping up in the FSB academy syllabus and in the mainstream discussion of geopolitics is surprising: rather as if the FBI training camp at Quantico instructed its special agents in Hopi chanting or astral projection.[21]

Soviet-style fanaticism and ideology has for the most part given way to mere prejudice and paranoia. But the surplus nervous energy goes into personal self-interest. At least in their own eyes, the 'Chekists' were selfless public servants, devoted to the cause of communism and the greater glory of the state, and among them corruption was severely constrained and usually ruthlessly punished. Their successors' capacity for self-enrichment is colossal. Soldatov and Borogan lift just one corner of the carpet. They highlight senior FSB officers' abuse of power to build millionaires' mansions on plots of land, gained at knock-down prices, in Moscow's most desirable suburb, the area around the Rublevo-Uspenskoye highway to the west of the city.

That looks like petty corruption compared with the colossal sums that can be earned by diverting financial flows in energy and other businesses. Under the new system, the men who run Russia, by and large, also own it. The dividing line between public and private interests is hopelessly blurred. People who are government ministers or senior public officials in the morning are the chairmen or chief executive officers of commercial enterprises in the afternoon. Although these entities have products, managers, audited accounts, respectable bankers, shareholders and even listings on reputable foreign stock exchanges, they are not real companies in a Western sense: their managers' aim is not to add value, raise profitability, reward shareholders and invest for the future. Instead their role is to siphon off money to insiders' private schemes and to promote Russia's foreign-policy agenda. The clearest example of this is in energy, where Gazprom and other natural resource companies trample on their shareholders' interests as they pursue dubious and grandiose schemes. These companies have hugely inflated costs; they sell their oil and gas through murky intermediaries; they loot their subsidiaries (the treatment of the Gazprom pension fund is a particular scandal[22]). A few brave campaigners such as Aleksei Navalny, a blogger, and the former government ministers Boris Nemtsov and Vladimir Milov, try to keep track of the looting and raise public concern against it.[23] But they face intimidating lawsuits and other threats; the public seems to accept that though its interests (both Rosneft and Gazprom are partly state-owned) are being abused by the country's elite, nothing much can be done about it.

In some respects, this landscape of power does not differ greatly from that of other corrupt, autocratically run, resentful countries with big intelligence services such as China or Iran. But in these countries the spooks are the servants of the state. In Russia, they have for the past ten years largely run it. Mr Putin, the country's undisputed leader, spent his formative years in the KGB. His right-hand man, Igor Sechin, a deputy prime minister and tycoon in the oil and shipbuilding industries, worked in military intelligence. Another ex-spook is the head of Russian railways, Vladimir Yakunin (who is also a string-puller in intrigues involving the Baltic states). So is the head of the Defence-Industrial Commission, which oversees Russia's arms industry, Sergei Ivanov. So is Viktor Ivanov (no relation), who heads the powerful anti-drug agency. So are numerous others at the heights of political and economic life in Russia.

In numerical terms the *Siloviki* are a diminishing force. Olga Kryshtanovskaya, a sociologist who specialises in monitoring their role, reckons that they comprised nearly half the top 1,000 people in the country when Mr Medvedev came to power but fell to just under a quarter by late 2010.[24] Nor are they monolithic. Fights between *Siloviki* clans are formidable and sometimes public. In one instance a senior ex-KGB man, Viktor Cherkesov, publicly appealed in a newspaper article for a truce in a fight with a rival clan.[25] In another rumble in the same row, a financier called Oleg Shvartsman gave lurid details of the way in which his fund-management company handled the $3.2bn assets of senior officials in the SVR foreign-intelligence service and FSB.[26] He explained that this gave him political clout in enabling a kind of corporate raiding, in which owners could be persuaded to sell their firms for knock-down prices – these are also the tactics used to punish Mr Browder. Corruption hits the effectiveness of the security and intelligence agencies, as it does every other bit of Russian officialdom. Junior officers detest the fact that their bosses' snouts are bigger, and deeper in the trough. Yet to focus on numbers, positions and squabbles misses the point. As Russia decays under the crushing weight of economic and social failure, the ideas the FSB stands for are becoming more powerful, not less.

From the outside, it is easy to conclude that this political arrangement cannot last. The infrastructure is crumbling, the demographic collapse accelerating and the economy is becoming obsolete. Russia is running out of people. The old cadre-factories of the Soviet Union are no longer forging the steely spooks of the Cold War. Even those minted in the later Soviet period, such as Mr Putin, are far less impressive, intellectually and operationally, than their predecessors. The great game of geopolitical competition with the West required idealism, brains and determination. Serving the Soviet Union in its declining years did not arouse the same loyalty or attract the same talents. The main motivator for those joining government service now is greed, mixed with resentment or a touch of Russian chauvinism. So it is tempting to imagine that the spookocracy will fade away with time, to the point that it will be dislodged by the growing Russian middle class, with its aspirations to live in a normal country. But the economist Mr Inozemtsev does not believe much will change. He argues:

> The elite's most important goal is the preservation of a system that enables incompetents to control the country's wealth. Hoping that change will come when the current ruling class retires and newcomers replace them is forlorn.

He concludes that the Russian elite has 'piratised' one of the world's richest countries, creating a neo-feudal system that is more stable than outsiders, plagued by wishful thinking, are willing to realise.

A big test of government is in the results it yields versus its costs. A benign autocracy may in some cases be better than a chaotic winner-takes-all political competition that leads to chaos and mob rule. It would be a mistake to dismiss the present Russian arrangement out of hand, especially at a time when political systems in Europe and America have signally failed to make the farsighted and sensible decisions that fans of parliamentary democracy believe it produces. It is easy to argue that Russia needs strong government in its transition from seven decades of totalitarianism. Western-style multiparty democracy may not suit all countries. Corruption, and an overlap with business and politics, is not confined to Russia (think of Italy under Silvio Berlusconi). As far as the role of the ex-spooks is concerned, the KGB employed some of the country's brightest and most knowledgeable people. It would not necessarily be stupid or evil for Russia to draw on their talents now.

But in this case, such considerations do not affect the verdict: the experiment has been a spectacular failure. The regime has presided over an orgy of greed and waste, but with more than a trillion dollars of extra oil and gas revenues flooding into the country between 2000 and 2010, pitifully little has been built or repaired. The visitor may be impressed by the sleek black limousines that clog the Moscow streets, by the high-rise luxury apartments and by the glitzy shopping malls, but he will search in vain for a network of high-speed rail lines, for new world-class universities, or even for a proper arterial road linking Russia with its distant provinces on the Pacific coast. Outside Moscow and a handful of other big cities, Russia is rotting. Only the rise in bribes is impressive – by one estimate more than 164bn roubles ($6bn) is paid in kickbacks in Russia every year.[27] Others would see that as a wild under-estimate. A common unscientific assumption in Russia is that roughly half the 4 trillion roubles ($140bn) in public spending is purloined.

The power relations among the self-proclaimed new nobility in Russia are shrouded in mystery. Even the most expert insiders disagree about whether Mr Putin brought in his old colleagues in order to hold on to the power he so unexpectedly gained in 1999, or whether those colleagues put him there in the first place. He certainly cut a remarkably unimpressive figure in his early months as prime minister and then president, prompting ribald jokes about his inexperience and indecisiveness that seem bizarrely misplaced in retrospect. Perhaps his grey unprepossessing demeanour was part of his KGB training in covert operations: it certainly fitted the textbook instructions for infiltration, which are to respond to scrutiny by seeming unthreatening and inconspicuous. That disarmed critics and encouraged rivals to over-reach themselves (signal examples include oligarchs such as Mr Khodorkovsky of Yukos: in retrospect, he should have challenged the president a lot earlier, or not at all). Now Mr Putin is not only the unchallenged leader of Russia. He is also (according to estimates by the CIA) one of the richest men in the world. But he does not rule alone.

A detailed explanation of the ruling circles in Russia involves weighing the importance of figures that even sophisticated observers have barely heard of, such as Mr Putin's cousin Igor, the brothers Yuri and Mikhail Kovalchuk, or the oil-trading magnate Gennady Timchenko. Some are members of *Ozero* (Lake), a cooperative that built dachas in a complex on the Komsomolskoye lake near St Petersburg. A prominent member of that group is Mr Yakunin, the railways chief. Another is Viktor Zubkov, now First Deputy Prime Minister. Mr Treisman, the American academic, who is a largely sympathetic observer of Russia under Mr Putin, gives in his book some tantalising hints of the Russian leader's business past, including the troubling and unexplained question of his membership of the advisory board of the German-registered St Petersburg Real Estate Holding Company (known by its abbreviation SPAG). In 2003 German police raided offices and homes associated with the company in an investigation about the laundering of 'tens of millions of euros' for a St Petersburg crime syndicate involved in 'numerous crimes, including vehicle smuggling, human trafficking, alcohol smuggling, extortion and confidence trickstering'.

No arrests were made and the investigation fizzled out. A banker who worked with SPAG said he had no knowledge of the company's alleged links with organised crime and had agreed to take on the company as a client because of Mr Putin's presence on its board. Mr Putin stepped down from SPAG's board when he became president in 2000. He has consistently denied any wrongdoing. Another SPAG advisory board member, a Liechtenstein-based financier called Rudolf Ritter, was acquitted on charges of laundering more than $1m for the Colombian Cali drug cartel, but convicted on a charge of illegally trading the company's shares. Reports in *Newsweek*[28] and *Le Monde* in 2001 and 2000 highlighted German official concerns about SPAG. Mr Putin had a close friendship with Vladimir Smirnov, head of SPAG's St Petersburg affiliate, a company called Znamenskaya. He also was deeply involved in the lucrative municipal fuel business. Shortly after Mr Putin became president Mr Smirnov moved to Moscow, working first in the Kremlin property department, which administers the vast inheritance of the old Soviet Communist Party. He later moved to an agency that exports enriched uranium. The German journalist Jürgen Roth, in a book on this and related issues called *Die Gangster aus dem Osten* (*The Gangsters from the East*), alleges a systematic attempt to cover tracks and deter investigators.[29]

The best explanation of how Russia really works that I have encountered is an unpublished one, compiled by the corporate intelligence service of a big Western company that has extensive dealings with Russia. These corporate spy services have many similarities to government agencies: they often employ retired spooks, are able to trade information and insights with those still inside the secret world, and are sometimes less constrained by the legal and bureaucratic restrictions that hamper public officials. This company's analysts may have come closer than most (and certainly closer than some governments) to unravelling the truth.

According to their theory, Russia operates with two layers of governance. Mr Putin is chair of an 'executive board' comprising officials in public view such as Mr Sechin. But he is also a member of a shadowy 'supervisory board', a cabal of ex-spooks and other associates from St Petersburg days, probably only four in number. At least one of them (whose name for legal reasons I cannot mention in print) does not live in Russia. His nickname is 'cashier'. Other members of the putative 'four' are even more obscure. They include a former colleague of Mr Putin from his days as a KGB officer in Dresden, and an antique dealer from St Petersburg with close ties to that city's underworld. The four plus one are never seen in public together, though Western intelligence agencies have picked up some traces of coordination: Mr Putin and one of the four were in Sochi in 2007 just as the then Russian president fired his prime minister and appointed the unknown Mr Zubkov. Another foreign intelligence agency believes that Mr Putin made a seven-hour flight to Russia's far east in the summer of 2008 with a member of his supervisory board on the presidential plane. An executive jet belonging to one member of the supervisory board appears to act as an air taxi for other members. In March 2008, for example, this aircraft flew to Prague to pick up Alina Kabayeva, a gymnast whose name has been linked to Mr Putin in the Russian tabloid press. It flew her to the holiday resort of Sochi in time to meet the Russian leader who arrived there on the same day.

Some theorise that the real story of Mr Putin's rise to power is the fusion between wilier elements of organised crime in St Petersburg, such as the Tambov mafia, with the remains of the KGB in that city, and the transplantation of that formidable hybrid to power in Moscow. It is also tempting to see crime, business and intelligence as the three pillars of power in Russia. Yet such explanations are too elegant and too simple. Gangsterdom, spook-dom and officialdom are intertwined, to the point that they are really just one pillar with three sides: a kind of unholy trinity.

Making sense of these swirling allegations and theories is tricky, not least because of the ever-present threats of violence and lawsuits.[30] But whether by accident or design, our view of Russia is clouded by misinformation and wishful thinking; in some cases clear evidence exists of intimidation and deception. Skewed perceptions are one reason why the West's response has been so weak to the subject of the next chapter: the regime's activities abroad.

3

Deadly Games and Useful Idiots

Many reading this grim account may still feel that greedy, lawless and incompetent spooks are chiefly a problem for Russians. It may all be a great pity, but why should outsiders actually mind what happens inside the Kremlin's realms? But as I will show in this chapter, the toxic combination of chauvinism and criminality is a problem for the rest of the world too. In no other country have gangster-dom and state power overlapped to such a threatening extent. The most powerful drug cartels may have high-tech communications equipment or the ability to penetrate a law-enforcement agency, or have some politicians on the payroll. But they have nothing that (yet) matches Russia's ruling criminal syndicate's capabilities. It has almost limitless money, global geographical scope and the full armoury of state technical and logistical resources, from spy satellites to submarines, giving unprecedented capabilities in snoop-ing and manipulation. Russia's world-class hackers, for example, work sometimes in government, sometimes under official protec-tion and sometimes entirely in their own criminal interest.[1] Russian dirty money and underhand business practices taint and corrode the financial systems, business cultures and politics of the countries they touch. As Don Jensen, a stalwart American critic of the regime, points out, Russia's main export is not oil and gas. It is corruption.[2]

Though officials do not speak about this much in public, they worry a lot about it in private. A cable from the American embassy in Madrid in August 2010 (now available on WikiLeaks) termed Russia a 'virtual mafia state'.[3] It stated baldly that Russian intelligence agencies were using mafia bosses to carry out criminal operations such as arms trafficking. It highlighted the secret support and protection that Russian intelligence in Spain provides for gangsters, who in return work 'as a complement to state structures' to carry out tasks that the Russian government could not be publicly linked to. The cable cited gun-running to Kurdish separatists in Turkey and also the mysterious case of the *Arctic Sea* cargo ship, hijacked in 2009 in a complex tale that probably involved smuggling elements of Russia's S-300 air defence system to Iran.[4]

The source of the allegations was José Grinda González, nicknamed 'Pepe', a senior Spanish prosecutor who has spent a decade investigating the Russian mafia. His record in fighting Russian organised crime leaves other European countries looking feeble and ineffective. He was responsible for the investigation of Zakhar Kalashov, the most senior 'Russian mafia' figure (he has Georgian nationality) to be jailed in Europe. Mr González was involved in two big anti-mafia operations in recent years, 'Avispa' (2005–07) and 'Troika' (2008–09), which resulted in the arrest of more than sixty suspects.

In January 2010 Mr González gave a frank briefing to a US–Spanish working group. He not only described Russia and Belarus as 'mafia states' where 'one cannot differentiate between the activities of the government and OC [organised crime] groups.'* He also endorsed the sensational claims made by Aleksandr Litvinenko, a Russian political exile poisoned by a polonium isotope in London in 2009. (Mr Litvinenko, a former FSB officer, claimed in two

---

* He also put Georgia in this category and said that Ukraine was heading there.

books, both banned in Russia, that the former KGB was involved in assassinations and drug smuggling, and staged terrorist outrages for political purposes.)

Among other insights, Mr González said the Liberal Democratic Party of Russia was created by the intelligence services and was closely tied to the mafia (run by the clownish Vladimir Zhirinovsky, it adopts extreme political positions but its deputies in the Duma dependably vote the Kremlin line). The FSB, he said, had the upper hand in the state's symbiotic relationship with criminality. Crime bosses who do not toe the line risk being killed or jailed. Perhaps most worryingly of all, he appeared pessimistic about the Spanish state's ability to deal with the Russian mafia. Attempts to 'decapitate it' had failed, he said. And its senior bosses were fighting back, with a 'systematic campaign' to manipulate the Spanish legal system.

Mr González's views are striking, but they are not extreme. Other officials say much the same thing in unattributable briefings. What is unusual is that, thanks to WikiLeaks, the wider public is able to read the unvarnished and attributable views of a senior, expert official, speaking frankly. Occasional on-the-record assessments from senior security officials say much the same thing in more guarded language.[5] The really puzzling thing is why this does not resonate into the public debate. Faced with a gangster-run state on our doorstep, why do not our politicians take the necessary steps to quarantine it and counter its malign effects? One reason is clearly the 'war on terror', which has diverted attention and effort to deal with the threat from radical Islam. Even in the narrow world of counter-intelligence, Chinese spies seem to attract more attention than Russian ones. Admittedly, Beijing's agencies have formidable hackers and are good at stealing military and technological secrets. But they do not murder people, rig our decision-making, or disrupt our alliances. Russia's spies are part of a much wider picture: an effort to play divide and rule, to exploit the greed of Western politicians and officials by paying them to make Kremlin-friendly decisions, and to deal ruthlessly with dissent abroad. This last element leads to flagrant law-breaking by Russian spies, which brings surprisingly little comeback.

One example is the Litvinenko case, mentioned above. His killing, in the view of British officials, involved the FSB. I dealt with this at length in *The New Cold War*.[6] A second instance is portrayed in a book by two British investigative journalists, Mark Hollingsworth and Stewart Lansley, dealing with what looks like the assassination of Stephen Curtis, a 45-year-old lawyer for Mr Khodorkovsky.[7] Mr Curtis had helped mastermind the shift of Yukos from a shambolic collection of assets marked by rows with investors into a \$15bn oil and gas company. Some called that evolution merely cosmetic; others believed it signalled the end of robber-baron tactics and the adoption of good management and transparent corporate governance. Mr Curtis was also a legal adviser to Mr Berezovsky and to other senior Russian figures.

Mr Curtis dealt with frightening people. But he was not easily frightened. When a friend warned him, 'You are dealing with the Devil,' he replied: 'I will jump on their backs and ride all the way down to hell.' That proved unpleasantly prescient. After Mr Khodorkovsky was arrested in 2003, Mr Curtis was – all but literally – in the firing line, as the man who knew the intimate details of his finances. He feared prosecution in Russia on the same trumped-up charges – tax avoidance, money-laundering and embezzlement – and a contract killing at the behest of Mr Khodorkovsky's emboldened business rivals. In the weeks before his death he was under surveillance from investigators hired by minority shareholders in Yukos and by people apparently working for the Russian state. His security consultants found evidence of bugging at his castle in Dorset. He hired a bodyguard and in mid

February 2004, worried by escalating death threats, offered (friends say) the British authorities information in return for government protection. A week before his death he told a friend: 'If anything happens to me in the next few weeks, it will not be an accident.' On 3 March 2004 his helicopter was approaching an airfield in Dorset in poor but not dangerous weather when it suddenly lost power and crashed into a field. An official investigation said that the pilot, Max Radford, had become disorientated during the final stages of his approach to the airfield and found no evidence of an explosion (though tampering with the controls would have also brought the aircraft down).[8] Mr Curtis's former bodyguard Nigel Brown, a former Scotland Yard detective, believes his client was killed and is puzzled that the police did not launch a murder inquiry.

It is not just lawyers for fugitive oligarchs who have reason to be worried. A remarkable BBC radio programme in the summer of 2010 entitled 'Why Russia Spies'[9] gave a tantalising glimpse into the closely guarded world of British security and defence worries. It was perhaps a sign of private concern in Whitehall about Russian activities that the radio producers were allowed the access that made the programme possible. Its opening sequence sounded like a flash-back to the Battle of Britain: listeners heard fighter pilots scrambling to intercept potentially hostile aircraft. These Russian antics mostly involve the lumbering 'Bear' (Tupolev Tu-95) bomber, a propeller-driven hulk that first went into service in 1952. It is a useful plat-form for launching nuclear missiles, but it is easily spotted and no match for any NATO air force. Sometimes, however, the Russian sorties involve the 'Blackjack' (Tupolev Tu-160), a sleek supersonic machine with advanced radar-dodging technology that still creates headaches for NATO. In 2008 news leaked of an incident the previous year when a Blackjack approached northern England at a speed and height that mimicked a real nuclear attack. The target was somewhere between Leeds and Hull. Though the Russian plane turned back just before actually entering British airspace, for a few nerve-wracking seconds defence commanders wondered if World War Three might just possibly be imminent.[10]

The real damage was to British credibility, not nerves: the over-stretched RAF was short of planes to meet the potential intruder. (That was in 2007: its ability to defend British airspace was weaker at the time of writing and is set to be eroded still further by defence cuts.) The frequency of such probes is surprising – as often as one a week in some periods, and more than fifty since 2005. It is not just Britain that suffers these unwelcome attentions. In 2011, Russian bombers intruded on Dutch airspace on at least three occasions.[11] Though irked and sometimes alarmed, defence chiefs dislike discussing the subject. They say that in a real war few Russian planes would get airborne and all would be shot down long before they were near NATO air space. In peacetime, they do not want to give Russia the satisfaction of knowing that its sabre-rattling has an effect.

As well as showing off and tying up scarce defence resources with military stunts, Russian efforts also involve spying on Britain's nuclear deterrent. It is fashionable to deride this as a Cold War legacy. Those who want Britain to give it up should perhaps ask themselves why Russia spends so much energy trying to unpick its secrets. It is still quite possible to imagine a scenario in which America is unwilling to risk a nuclear confrontation with Russia over a security conflict in Europe. In the autumn of 2009, for example, Russia and Belarus conducted the Ladoga and Zapad-09 manoeuvres.[12] This was in fact one exercise, but divided into two in order to avoid having, to invite observers from NATO, as stipulated by arms-control treaties for drills involving more than 13,000 soldiers. The real exercise was not defensive, but aggressive. The combined forces, some 20,000 strong, were rehearsing how to isolate the Baltic states from the rest of Europe, invade and occupy them. In case of reinforcement by other NATO countries, the rehearsal showed that Russia would respond by using tactical nuclear weapons. This drill was followed by another exercise by Russia's Strategic Rocket Forces (the custodians of its main nuclear arsenal) in which the target was Warsaw,[13] showing how closely Russia's conventional defence planning is linked to the use of nuclear weapons – and how important the British nuclear deterrent remains. Imagine for example that America, facing a defence budget shrivelled by economic weakness, were preoccupied elsewhere, say in a confrontation with Iran that blocked oil supplies through the straits of Hormuz (which could easily be manufactured by Russia) or with China over Taiwan. A reminder from Britain that it has an independent nuclear deterrent and is prepared to use it in response to a Russian nuclear attack on any British forces in the Baltic could tip the balance between peace (meaning victory) and a conflict (which NATO, without America, would lose). Such a scenario is in current conditions extremely unlikely. But if that British response becomes impossible (for example because our deterrent is no longer credible) then the whole basis of Western defence weakens. If a future Russian leadership could assume it did not risk the ultimate penalty for military adventurism (and especially if NATO knew it too), then bullying neighbours, with the threat of armed force at least in the background, becomes more likely.

It is therefore interesting that Akula-class submarines, the pride of Russia's dwindling navy, have resumed a Cold War-era tactic, lurking off the Forth of Clyde in the hope of picking up the acoustic signature of Britain's Trident submarines as they enter and leave their base. This distinctive pattern of noise allows sophisticated detection equipment to track and potentially destroy the other side's submarines. Once you know what you are looking for, it is much easier to find it. The Royal Navy's Vanguard-class submarines now devote considerable time to fending off these attempts. Given the secrecy that traditionally surrounds anything to do with submarines, any public mention of such concerns is a sign of how seriously naval chiefs take the Russian activities. Whispers in the shadows of Whitehall suggest a still greater incidence of such activities, including the targeting of undersea anti-surveillance installations. Akula-class submarines are also patrolling far afield – even to the coasts of the United States, where one such vessel surfaced as if openly inviting attention.[14] Russia's aim is to intimidate and divide NATO, forcing the alliance to focus on hard questions that its members would rather avoid, and for which the various national publics have no appetite. If, after stirring up a divisive discussion in NATO, Russia concluded that Poland and the Baltic states were diplomatically and militarily isolated, it then would find it easier to bully them over other matters of concern such as energy supplies, trade or domestic politics. In assessing that scope for manoeuvre, intelligence plays a vital role.

Russia was most interested in the Western reaction to its exercises. What conclusions did military attachés draw? Could NATO tap Russian battlefield communications in real time? Most importantly, how did other countries respond to the quiet but sharply expressed concern from Tallinn, Riga, Vilnius and Warsaw? Was the West's reaction to tell these frontline countries to calm down and be quiet? Or was it to offer them reassurance? In fact, the reaction was not what Russia expected. Though some officials tried hard to play down the significance of the exercises (one called them 'a twitch of the dinosaur's tail'), America ordered a response that included in 2010 a major special-forces exercise, a marine amphibious landing in Estonia and a reinforcement drill in Latvia, with more to follow. NATO warplanes held a large air exercise involving mid-air refuelling. America's National Geospatial-Intelligence

Agency (formerly the Defense Mapping Agency) has compiled a detailed 3D electronic map of the Baltics. NATO contingency plans now for the first time include the Baltic states, involving the use of Swedish airspace and Polish troops. This was presumably not what the Russians wanted. So why did they do it? The chief reason for this self-defeating gambit was a flawed assumption: that the West does not really care about the Baltic states and brought them into NATO only for political reasons. In fact, America at least has shown that it does care about its new allies and is willing to make efforts to prove it.

Monitoring all this closely was the spy-infested Russian mission to NATO. This quasi-diplomatic outfit enjoys a remarkably privileged status at alliance headquarters in Brussels, with regular briefings, spacious offices and security badges that allow its members preferential access to meetings, documents and other facilities. This friendly treatment dates from the days when NATO tried to soft-soap Russia about the alliance's expansion to the former Soviet empire. By opening up to Russia, NATO hoped to dispel any fears about its intentions; belief persists among some member countries that differences with Russia are merely the result of misunderstandings, and that confrontation would be a sign of failure. This approach is heartfelt, particularly in Germany, where it is an article of faith among senior officials that Russia must be embraced and reassured, not deterred. The theoretical argument about whether relations would be even worse without this approach is unresolvable. What is clear is that attempts to build trust have proved unsuccessful in practical terms. On issues such as terrorism NATO puts cards on the table, and receives in return Russian offerings dressed up as serious intelligence, though in truth they are little more than could be found out on the internet. The Russian spies posted to the NATO mission are numerous, ubiquitous, unscrupulous and energetic. They bluntly and repeatedly

approach officials whom they regard as promising targets. They
are adept at keeping their distinctive ID badges concealed and
slipping into meetings to which they have not been invited. Their
chief targets are the alliance's future military thinking, especially its
contingency plans; new capabilities, for example in cyber-warfare
or missile defence; and NATO's codes and communications –
the alliance's central nervous system. They have a sharp eye on
counter-intelligence: trying to find out what NATO members
know about Russia, and where it comes from. They like to have
a clear idea of who is being trained for what, by whom, where,
and how well.

A paradox here, as so often in intelligence work, is that many of
these secrets are both closely guarded and yet not very interesting.
NATO's abilities and capabilities have shrivelled since the end of
the Cold War. Many of its members spend risibly little on defence.
Many of the member states' governments have little interest in
Russia, and find it hard to share the worries of countries such as the
Baltic states and Poland. In a crisis, NATO's effectiveness depends
almost wholly on the United States. Russian intelligence penetration of NATO probably peaked at a time when it revealed a lack
of secrets, rather than their existence. Russia's lavishly resourced
spies do not mind about that. For a start, NATO HQ is a good
place to recruit highfliers from the countries that matter – chiefly
America, Britain, France, the Netherlands, Norway or Turkey
– who will go on to careers in their national defence and security establishments. Secondly, Brussels is a great place for agent-
running. Belgian counter-intelligence is weak. Only a handful of
officers deal with Russia. They have no powers of arrest and face
grave difficulties in obtaining warrants. All this is a serious problem
for the hard-pressed NATO Office of Security.

A deeper reason for Russian behaviour is a paranoid mind-
set conditioned partly by the Cold War, partly by the alliance's

expansion, and partly by the NATO-led bombing of Serbia in 1999.* With the Soviet Union out of the way, Russians believe, America and its allies turned a neutral front yard into a *cordon sanitaire*, deliberately designed to humiliate and constrain the former superpower, and breaking a promise made to the Soviet Union in exchange for German reunification.[15] What if NATO decides next to help one of Russia's near neighbours, say Georgia, or Ukraine, or Moldova, in some military flare-up? When dealing with a powerful and unpredictable military alliance on your borders it is better to have too many sources than too few. Nobody is going to complain about having too much information about NATO's inner workings. The more the diligent spies report that NATO is ineffective and distracted, the more the instructions come back to dig deeper and find the real story.

Other international organisations are at even greater risk. The mental barriers to giving away secrets are lower (betraying your country or its military alliances is one thing, betraying an anonymous bureaucracy is another). Whereas NATO at least tries to keep spies at bay, the headquarters of the European Commission and European Council in Brussels are a security nightmare: a warren of badly policed offices and unvetted staff, where outsiders can walk in and out almost at will on the flimsiest of pretexts. The European Parliament, newly important since the Lisbon Treaty carve-up gave it and the EU's big countries the main role in the union's decision-making, is a particularly vulnerable target. Its members (and office staff, on their behalf) can demand almost any document they like from the European Commission. Staffers are

---

* Many worried that a supposedly defensive alliance was waging an aggressive war against a historic Russian ally. Yet NATO got involved only reluctantly and belatedly, after the multiple massacres in the preceding Bosnian war, and when Russian foot-dragging had stymied efforts to stop a Serbian attack on Kosovo.

lightly vetted (or not at all) and can ask for a briefing or an informal chat with any official.

The EU, it should be noted, is not in the position to treat Russia the same way. For a start, it has no intelligence-gathering service of its own. Weak leadership, squabbles and bureaucracy plague its misnamed 'External Action Service', which is supposed to spearhead a more decisive and better-informed EU diplomacy. An intelligence agency requires much greater grip and focus than a diplomatic service. If the EU cannot yet run a foreign ministry and embassies properly, it has no chance of developing a spy agency capable of dealing with a tough target such as Russia. The only advantage of this is that a bad intelligence agency is more damaging than none at all. If you don't spy, you can't bungle; you can't be fooled by bad sources or get good ones into trouble. The disadvantage is that politicians may lack full knowledge of the people and thinking that they are dealing with. The EU is also unable to get proper intelligence from its member states. For the handful of member countries (chiefly Britain and France) that do have real intelligence services, the job is mostly outwitting the EU on matters of national interest, not helping the Eurocrats to raise their game. Even when European and national interests do overlap, the EU is seen as too leaky to be trusted with more than the stalest crumbs of intelligence.

As with all intelligence agencies, it is one thing to gain a flow of information, and another to use it correctly. American decision-makers are overwhelmed by a 'fire-hose' of classified, secret, top-secret and urgent information produced by that country's sprawling intelligence 'community'.[16] Much of it is dross, either recycled or poorly sourced. Much less is known about Russia's use of intelligence, although it is clear that Mr Putin takes a close personal interest in the output of his country's agencies – people who know his daily routine say he habitually spends a couple of hours a day reading its reports and cables, while shunning more conventional (and perhaps more useful) sources of information.

For whatever reason, however, Russia does seem to have the knack of searching through floods of data to find the most usable bits. EU officials who deal with Russia, for example, have told me that they frequently have the impression that the other side already knows every part of their negotiating position. It is easy to scoff at this: why should anyone care if the Russians bamboozle the Eurocrats? The answer is simple. If Russia understands which countries are the die-hard supporters of a particular EU policy that it does or doesn't like, which are the wobblers, and what is the negotiating position, it knows where to apply diplomatic pressure (or when not to waste time and effort fighting a lost cause).

The EU talks to Russia about matters of vital interest to every member-state's citizens, but a prime example is energy. Here the picture has shifted sharply over the past decade. Ten years ago, Russia was seen as a bright prospect for Europe's future oil and gas supplies, and a source of nuclear expertise, fuel and technology. Since then corruption and incompetence at home, and bullying behaviour abroad have eroded Russia's clout, to the point that even Germany is now sceptical about its reliability. In the past, Germany was heavily dependent on Russian gas. Its biggest energy companies were closely tied to Gazprom, and the former German Chancellor, Gerhard Schröder, took on the chairmanship of a controversial Russian–German gas pipeline on the Baltic seabed soon after he left office in 2005. In his time Germany resisted any attempt to talk toughly to Moscow on energy and other issues: many outsiders saw that as sinister. They feared that the gas supplies had anaesthetised the country's prudence and scepticism when it came to policy towards Russia.[17]

That has changed. Russia's squabbles with transit countries such as Ukraine have interrupted gas supplies to Europe and rattled

German confidence. Angela Merkel, Mr Schröder's successor, is instinctively more hawkish about Russia. Corruption and incompetence in Gazprom and elsewhere have raised fears about Russia's ability to meet its long-term supply commitments. New gas supplies are available from elsewhere – chiefly Liquefied Natural Gas (LNG), which can be delivered by sea from distant suppliers. Only five years ago this was scarce and expensive. But technological change has made tankers and terminals cheaper, while new extraction techniques mean that more gas is on the market. The days when Russia's east-west pipeline monopoly created a lock on European energy supplies are over.

But Russia is now playing a hard defensive game. It no longer controls the bottleneck in supplies. Instead it wants long-term contracts, stakes in downstream distribution systems and market information. In Britain, those dealing with Gazprom's local subsidiary say that its behaviour is less that of a new entrant into the market, and more of an intelligence operation. The head of counter-intelligence for Germany's BfV security service, Burkhard Even, highlighted the role of Russian spies in

> supporting Russian companies . . . to gain a footing in the German energy sector. The interest is above all in alternative and regenerative energy, possibilities to increase energy efficiency, European energy interests and diversification strategies . . .[18]

Russia is in most respects a backward country – a source of humiliation to those who remember that the Soviet Union was the country that put the first satellite, living creature and human being into space. Closing that gap through the normal process of industrial development seems all but impossible. Despite remaining pockets of excellence in the education system, ambitious Russians head abroad, rather than building their businesses at home.[19] Though Mr Putin is personally determined that Russia become a world leader in nano-technology, building such hi-tech industry from scratch is hard: Russia does have plenty of brainpower, but it is starting ten years later than competitors in Germany, America and Britain. The only way Russia can hope to close the gap is by stealing secrets, either to take advantage of them in its own industry, or to trade elsewhere (principally to China). One way of doing that is snooping on other countries' communications.

Use Google Earth to search for 57°48'8.20"N 28°12'58.59"E and you will see a snapshot, taken from space, of a large collection of satellite dishes on the westernmost extremity of Russia, on the Estonian border, to the north-east of the main A-212 road from the provincial capital Pskov. Even viewed from on high, the gleaming metal and bright paintwork make it clear that this is a new installation; the long shadows cast by the guard fence and sentry posts around the antenna array indicate a high degree of security. Google now helpfully labels it 'Center FAPSI'[20] and an enterprising photographer has provided a fine picture of it.[21] Western intelligence officials were initially puzzled about the facility's purpose. Russia already has an archipelago of electronic listening stations: why build a new one exactly there?

The answer was that this particular corner of Russia overlapped, just, with the then footprint of the main Inmarsat 4-F2 satellite, which sits high over the Atlantic ocean in a geostationary orbit carrying a huge quantity of data between Europe and the United States.[22] Such data networks are of great interest to Russia. The ability to listen in to mobile phone calls, bug emails, observe web-browsing habits and obtain passwords are essential ingredients of other espionage operations, both in gathering politically sensitive information and in garnering compromising material that can be used for blackmail – and also in stealing other countries' commercial and industrial secrets.*

Industrial espionage was a big feature of Soviet-era intelligence too. But the economic planners who ran industry then were mostly incapable of putting into production the techniques and technology that the KGB's spies so painstakingly and brilliantly acquired during the Cold War. Many of those constraints have now gone. Russian state-backed high technology companies operate more effectively than their Soviet-era predecessors. One reason is that they are not shackled by the constraints of the planned economy. Another is that the paranoid culture of secrecy has faded. Their experts and executives can travel freely; Western controls on the export of sensitive equipment that frustrated Soviet engineers during the Cold War have lifted.[23] Not only can the stolen material be better used, but the threshold of treachery when obtaining it has sunk. In the days of ideological competition between East and West, even the most hard-up Western scientist might think twice about helping a totalitarian superpower whose very existence was based on lies and mass murder. Helping Russia sounds a lot less bad: after all, many Western businesses and politicians have deep interests in that country too. A German scientist or engineer who succumbs to a Russian approach to pass on secrets from his firm or university laboratory could be forgiven for thinking that if senior public figures can enrich themselves through connections with Russia, humble boffins can do the same.

Overall, America is the top target for Russian foreign intelligence. The partnership that has developed since the 'reset' is grudging and cautious, while the adversarial approach is deeply rooted and instinctive. As well as harassing and monitoring members of

* Of course Western intelligence collects information on Russia too. America's National Security Agency gathers electronic data from antennae in north-eastern Poland, close to the Russian border.

the Russian diaspora, a prime goal for the Russians is to assess and if possible influence policy-making. This includes scrutinising anyone who presents a direct or indirect challenge to the regime in Moscow through their activities in political life in Washington, DC, such as retired officials, commentators and policy-makers; and think-tank and academic experts who are involved in policy that affects Russia, its interests and its neighbours. Practical targets range from the symbolic, such as the repeal of the Jackson-Vanik amendment,[24] to the wonkish, such as understanding arguments in the Senate about arms-control treaties. A prime strategic interest is to weaken transatlantic security ties, thus strengthening Russia's position in Europe. This is behind the Russian demands (so far fruitless) for a new European 'security architecture' that would exclude America and give Russia a legally binding veto over the continent's decision-making. To that end, Russia stokes anti-Americanism in Europe and eagerly encourages American policymakers and thinkers to see the world in terms of bilateral deals between superpowers, rather than the sentimental old alliances of the last century. Russia is pushing on an open door in this: America's commitment to NATO is weakening, as is Atlanticist sentiment in Europe.

Another priority for Russian spymasters is to promote the interests of their country's business. The decision in 2010 to allow Rosoboronexport, the biggest Russian arms exporter, to renew operations in the USA is an example of a major breakthrough. Russia is interested in the listing requirements, disclosure rules and other hurdles that govern access to American capital markets (this is the ultimate goal for corrupt officials and businesses the world over: a listing not only brings in a cash windfall from foreign shareholders, but also gives an instant aura of respectability).

Russia also worries about the rapid growth of shale gas production in the United States. This means that America no longer imports LNG from other producers, creating a glut on world markets, which has allowed European countries to diversify their supply away from Russian pipeline gas. More generally, Russia seeks to limit America's influence in world energy markets as well as to promote the interests of companies such as Gazprom and Rosneft. Associated with this are politically exposed Russian citizens who find it difficult or impossible to gain an American visa. Russian officials lobby the executive branch to allow these individuals to enter the United States, and try to bring additional pressure to bear via Congress. A signal example here has been the case of Oleg Deripaska, a Russian tycoon whose efforts to visit America have been dogged by controversy.[25]

The final and most dangerous Russian aim is to penetrate NATO countries' security and intelligence agencies. Two notable successes in America in recent years are the cases of Aldrich Ames and Robert Hanssen. Ames was a senior CIA counter-intelligence officer dealing with the Soviet Union. Before his arrest in 1994 he betrayed more than a hundred operations and twenty-five agents in the KGB and other Soviet power structures who had entrusted their lives to America. Around ten were executed. Hanssen was a senior FBI officer whose job was supposedly catching Russian spies, until he was exposed as one himself in 2001.

Espionage pervades this story, but in its classic form is only part of it. In all, Russia uses multiple tactics in pursuit of its goals. One is lobbying and diplomatic pressure. This is traceable through a close examination of the trade press, which reveals the growth and scope of Russian lobbying efforts, as well as declarations made under the Foreign Agents Registration Act (which was used as a legal stop-gap to charge the spies caught in the summer of 2010). The second is the use of 'unorthodox' but legal tactics. These include threatening critics of the regime with legal action in English courts. The First Amendment protects freedom of speech in America, but it cuts no ice in London, where a defamatory statement risks a costly lawsuit, in which the author must justify the allegation with facts, or proof of fairmindedness or fact-checking. This has led a number of think tanks and analysts, even in America, to rephrase or withdraw their criticisms. Another carrot-and-stick tactic is to offer (or withdraw) access to meetings with Russian policy-makers such as Valdai, an annual shindig at which journalists, academics and think-tank experts are given a lengthy interview with Mr Putin.[26] More scandalously, Russian lobbyists may also offer to donate (or withhold) funds for research programmes at think tanks and universities. Such activities may involve agents working either at Russian diplomatic missions or undercover.

Russia also enjoys a direct presence in foreign media. The Russian taxpayer in 2010 regularly subsidised struggling foreign newspapers including the *Daily Telegraph* and the *Washington Post*, which printed special advertising 'supplements' called 'Russia Now',[27] highly flavoured to suit the official line and produced by *Rossiyskaya Gazeta*, a government newspaper with a disgraceful record of historical falsification and propaganda peddling.[28] The print editions try to make it clear that the inserts are not the work of their own journalists. But the paid-for material nestles on the newspapers' websites, with a layout very similar to that of the real journalism. A disclaimer in tiny print states: 'Russia Now is Paid Supplement [sic] to the *Washington Post.*' On the *Telegraph* website a more prominent one reads: 'This online supplement is produced and published by *Rossiyskaya Gazeta* (Russia), which takes sole responsibility for the content.' But it does not specifically say that money has changed hands. A casual browser could easily be confused.

Also in Britain, two prominent papers, The *Independent* and the London *Evening Standard*, are in the hands of Evgeny Lebedev, the son of a former KGB officer, Aleksandr Lebedev, who worked

in the Soviet-era *rezidentura* in London and is unfondly remembered by dissident émigrés of that era (he also became famous
in September 2011 for his unrepentant use of violence against a
fellow-discussant on a television programme).[29] The papers have
covered some otherwise boring Russian business stories with notable alacrity, and chronicled the social activities of their proprietor
(to be fair, hardly unusual in the British media). No consistent
signs have yet appeared of interference with the editorial line on
Russia itself. (The *Independent's* diplomatic editor, Mary Dejevsky,
is a well-known British specialist on Russia whose distinctively
optimistic line on the country's prospects and problems long
predates the paper's change in ownership.) None of the other
papers mentioned has adopted a pro-Russian stance, though the
general shrivelling of budgets for foreign coverage has certainly
weakened their ability to follow the intricacies of Russian politics
and business.

More worrying than the advertising largesse and changes in
ownership is the wider, subtler effect of Russian money on the
media. Russian agents are adept at cultivating their media contacts,
and in offering access in return for favourable coverage. Those
who write hostile stories may find that they are no longer invited
to Valdai. For professional Russia-watchers, an invitation to this
event, normally held in November, is tantamount to a job ticket.
Being barred can be a career-chiller, or killer. A tougher sanc-
tion, for journalists who are consistently critical of Russia, is a visa
blacklist compiled by the FSB.

Russian influence and subversion crops up across the entire
spectrum of public life in EU countries and America. Much of
what goes on cannot be discussed openly for fear of libel suits,
but occasional scandals give at least an outline picture. One is the
role of Russian agents in bribing, blackmailing or bamboozling
politicians. Sometimes the results are remarkably unsubtle, such as

when they slavishly follow Russian talking points and voting strategies in international bodies such as the Parliamentary Assembly of the Council of Europe and the Parliamentary Assembly of the Organisation for Security and Cooperation in Europe. Readers may be forgiven for never having heard of either outfit: they are well-funded talking shops that pass sententious resolutions of great prolixity and little weight. However, Russia finds them useful forums for its agenda, for example, highlighting issues that divide or embarrass its European critics.[30] More important than the bodies' activities, however, is their membership: they consist of lawmakers who also have important jobs back home.

Those who observe the meetings of these bodies notice how often attractive young Russian and East European women accompany some of the middle-aged male MPs who make up the bulk of their membership. In most cases these women have doubtless been hired solely for their research skills. But the suspicion remains that in at least some cases someone has assigned them to these elected officials, with the aim of influencing their decision-making or obtaining sensitive information. This does not necessarily involve treason. Some politicians are stupid and naive enough to hire and hobnob with questionable assistants without considering that anything might be amiss.

In 2010, for example, Britain's Security Service was alarmed to note that Katya Zatuliveter, a Russian citizen working in Parliament, had met a Russian intelligence officer based at the embassy in London. The spycatchers were convinced that they had spotted an active and dangerous spy. The use of attractive young women – lastochky (swallows) – to seduce Western targets was a mainstay of the KGB playbook. Ms Zatuliveter had a lengthy affair with her employer, Mike Hancock MP. He was a classic target: forty years older than her, portly, self-important, married – and also a member of the House of Commons Defence Committee and the Council of Europe Parliamentary Assembly. She later bedded a senior NATO official (also married) dealing with Russia and Ukraine. No young British woman could enjoy a comparable career in Russia.

The Home Secretary ordered Ms Zatuliveter's deportation. She appealed (odd behaviour if she were in fact a spy) – and MI5 suffered an unprecedented public embarrassment. The appeal tribunal included Sir Stephen Lander, the former director of MI5, as one of the three judges. The evidence MI5 presented in open court was unconvincing – and so too, apparently, was what it argued in the secret sessions. The tribunal concluded that it was unlikely Ms Zatuliveter was a spy: far more likely, she was just 'an immature, calculating, emotional and self-centred young woman'.[31] That she had met a Russian intelligence officer in London counted in her favour: were she really a spy, she would shun any such contact and meet her case officer only on her regular trips to Russia. It was astonishing that, even in secret, MI5 was unable to produce conclusive evidence of any wrongdoing. Nor was it clear why the service had risked publicly demanding its quarry's deportation. A quiet warning would have stopped any espionage in its tracks. And if Ms Zatuliveter was a real spy, why not watch her in action? One explanation may be that MI5's once-fearsome expertise in Russia has decayed severely since the end of the Cold War.

Whatever its practical failings, MI5 and sister services are right to believe that Russian citizens visiting the West under their own names are a far bigger part of the Kremlin's espionage effort than old-fashioned 'illegals'. A plausible example of the new echelon would be a comely young PhD student bearing a passport from an East European country (Commission officials responsible for counter-intelligence sometimes mention Bulgaria in this context). This 'student' of EU affairs is attractive, inquisitive and ruthless. She gets a job first as an intern, then as an assistant. That creates one line of attack. Simultaneously, she is researching her PhD (perhaps on EU energy policy, or trade relations with Russia, or some other topic of interest to the Kremlin). In one sense her behaviour is entirely legitimate. It is not a crime to ask questions flirtatiously, or to sleep with officials who answer them. Her identity may be forged, but is more often completely legitimate: perhaps acquired during a brief but perfectly convincing marriage to a Bulgarian. Only a detailed security vetting would uncover a family connection with Soviet-era intelligence structures and a stint learning spycraft in Russia. This 'student' (an amalgam of some real-life examples) will probably avoid any position where she comes under direct scrutiny: a job at NATO, for example, or in the commission's new External Action Service. But her flatmates, bedmates or officemates may work in just such roles, and she will be only one step behind. Indeed, secretaries in sensitive offices in the European Union's institutions turn out surprisingly often to have been born in the core countries of the former Soviet Union. They have EU passports now and it would be a suspicious soul who begrudged them a chance to make the best of the careers open to them. Nobody seems bothered by their presence or willing to check up on them; and if they did, it would be hard to know if a regular trip to see family in Russia was just that, or included a meeting with a spy agency. Such people are one arm of the Russian effort abroad and I will return to them later. But when they are not available, Russia's spymasters turn to another reservoir of potential agents: the diaspora.

4

Real Spies, Real Victims

The Russian diaspora's presence in the West reflects one of the great triumphs – and vulnerabilities – of the post-1991 era. The free movement of people from East to West was a defeat for the merchants of mind-control in Moscow, who feared that capitalist fleshpots would be an 'ideological distraction' for the hard-pressed proletariat of the 'world fortress'. But the new regime in Russia is more resilient. It flourishes on contacts with the rich world, which offers everything from financial services to luxury goods, and it places no obstacles in the way of those wanting to leave. The Soviet leadership created the largest prison camp in history, keeping hundreds of millions of people bottled up behind the Iron Curtain, with travel privileges tightly rationed and dependent on cooperation with the KGB. Now tens of millions of Russians have travelled abroad: they are free (visa regimes permitting) to work, holiday, study, marry and invest there. Whatever counter-intelligence worries the new era creates, nobody should wish for a moment that the clock be put back to the dark days before 1989. But for Russia's spymasters, targets and means of espionage overlap in this diaspora. These compatriots may know the secrets of the country they are living in. Or they may be able to help steal them. It is a sad truth that however far émigrés may flee oppression and corruption, their personal ties with their country of origin will always leave them vulnerable to bullying and blackmail.

The new problem is a greatly amplified version of an old one. As we will see in a later chapter, in the huge movements of refugees that followed the Second World War émigré communities from Soviet-block countries easily became pawns in spy wars. As the Cold War intensified, and the gulf between East and West deepened, personal ties across the Iron Curtain were increasingly scanty and easily scrutinised on both sides. Even so, they occasionally led to spectacular breaches in security. A successfully hushed-up scandal of the 1980s involved an émigré from one of the Baltic states (then still occupied by the Soviet Union) who worked as a dentist. That might seem an occupation of no interest to the KGB. But this particular dentist had a contract to provide treatment to the staff of a Western foreign ministry.* His files provided a perfect means of distinguishing between mainstream diplomats and intelligence officers working under diplomatic cover. When the spies were due for a dental check before or after an overseas posting, their agency's personnel office made the appointment, not the foreign ministry's. The intelligence officers' files had a distinctive coding – doubtless for budgetary reasons. The KGB, in a clever bit of spycraft, tracked him down and threatened his family members inside the Soviet Union with the many miserable fates awaiting those who displeased the authorities there. When news reached him of their troubles, he was distraught – and with no security training, an easy target.

The result was devastating. The intelligence service concerned went to great lengths to post its best and brightest young officers under carefully constructed diplomatic cover. They cheerfully did the worst jobs in the embassies they were assigned to,

---

* I am concealing the full details of this case out of consideration for his family.

toiling over visa applications and stationery invoices in the hope
of staying unnoticed. Had they worn neon lights flashing the word
'spy' they could hardly have been more conspicuous. The KGB
knew just whom to watch. Often it waited for years before taking
any action, allowing the targets to work diligently in the belief
that their efforts were unseen. In fact they left a toxic trail over a
web of contacts that the KGB could investigate at its leisure. To
this day, the damage done by the dentist is unknown. Unmasked
when some KGB records became available after 1991, he admitted everything and escaped prosecution. This KGB operation
was a brilliant piece of work, done with the greatest difficulty in
a well-protected NATO country at the height of the Cold War.
The task now is much easier. Russians who live abroad, working
in everything from finance to showbiz, are a force-multiplier for
the regime back home. Even if few have access to secrets themselves, their friends, relatives, colleagues and sporting partners may
do so.

Monitoring the activities of émigré and diaspora groups that
could pose a threat to the regime's interests has long been an intelligence target for the Kremlin. It pays particular attention to those
who previously occupied positions of power or influence inside
Russia. Even if they are not formally defectors, it views them
with great suspicion and monitors them aggressively. But ordinary
émigrés too may be eavesdropped and recruited, either willingly
or not. Some may end up serving just the narrow purposes of
Russia's intelligence services. Someone who works in the billing
department of a mobile phone company, in a tax office, in a bank
as Ms Chapman did in Britain, or in a credit-rating agency can
help expose a fake identity being used by a foreigner on a visit
to Russia, or assist in concocting one for Russian spies needing
to work abroad. During the Cold War, for example, the KGB
was able to recruit an agent in the London regional office of the

motor-licensing authority. This enabled them to find out which cars were used by the spycatchers of MI5.

The same insights are useful today. Does the Western business-man visiting Russia have a convincing credit history? Does his mobile phone number check out? What calls has he made? Does he have any frequent-flier cards? If so, what pattern of activity do they show? Does he pay taxes? If so, from which home address and on which sources of income? Someone with access to an immi-gration computer can check if records show any sign of previous globetrotting for the passport that this supposed international busi-nessman presented at his hotel.

Still more tempting targets are those in a position to obtain secrets or sensitive information. Even if they do not have the neces-sary access, they may know someone who has. In a lawless country such as Russia, it is easy to find ways of influencing them, either directly or through those that they care about. As a Canadian offi-cial put it after a spy scandal there: 'They're pretty good at apply-ing pressure, by appealing to their patriotism . . . or by remind-ing them that Mother is still back home.'[1] Such robust persuasion is easiest when émigrés actually visit Russia. The FSB can plant drugs or pornography, fake an allegation of rape, or concoct some other unpleasant difficulty, either against the victim directly, or against a relative or friend. The accused protests his innocence to grim-faced police who tell him to expect a lengthy stay in custody while the case is fully investigated. Without proper legal repre-sentation, facing scandal at home and possibly losing his job, the detainee is easy prey when an anonymous visitor in civilian clothes appears, explaining that the 'misunderstandings' will clear up in return for a little help. This cooperation can range from straight-forwardly betraying secrets to more subtle tasks such as reporting on colleagues' personal weaknesses, or simply providing anodyne information in order to test the source for later use.

In some cases, the victim hurries home and reports the entire affair to his own country's counter-intelligence service (one such agency is the source of the above outline of the FSB's modus operandi). If that happens, the Western side may try to use the person to feed disinformation to the FSB, or to obtain more information about Russia's wish list. Such instances are rare. Western spycatchers worry about how often such FSB approaches have been successful and unreported, and what may have happened as a result. The advantage of this kind of operation for the FSB is that its methods and officers are largely preserved: if the 'pitch' is unsuccessful and the source is never seen again, little is lost. If it works, the agent running can happen mainly or wholly inside Russia: after all, the target has completely convincing family reasons for visiting. Each time he visits, the screw can tighten a little. That is a lot easier than trying to recruit people in Berlin, London, New York or Paris under the noses of NATO counter-intelligence services.

A good example of what appears to be the use of the diaspora for intelligence purposes is the story of Axis Information and Analysis (AIA). This outfit described itself as an 'information agency that unites professionals having years of experience in collecting and analysing information about Asia and Eastern Europe'. It claimed to be focused upon 'states that constitute a threat to regional and international security, as well as upon areas of ethnic and religious conflict'. Its main mission was to produce rather good information about defence, security and intelligence issues. A typical day's headlines, on 25 February 2009, included items such as 'Former Czech chief-of-staff works in company with person suspected of ties with Soviet intelligence'; 'Estonian investigators pass opinion why did Herman Simm betray his native country'; 'Attempt of bombing of synagogue in Ukraine not considered act of terrorism' and 'Russia has at least 500 secret service agents in Vienna 20 years after Cold War'.

From 2005 I was a regular visitor to AIA's website, www.axis-globe.com.[2] The information was a clever mix of local media reports, seasoned with intelligent observations and occasional bits of first-hand reporting. It was topical, accurate, well presented and concise, if in slightly stilted English. So who was writing it? I had never met any of the people listed on the site as contributors, though after more than twenty-five years dealing with the region I would have expected to have heard of such evidently expert and well-informed colleagues. Nor had I met anyone else who had. Nor did Google show them as having any existence elsewhere. AIA said that some of its authors were still in government service and that they, and some other contributors, used pen names. It self-consciously added an air of mystery by claiming to use 'journalists, ex-diplomats, and *former officers of the special services of a number of Asian and East European countries*' [my italics].[3]

The site did not require payment and had no advertising. My initial assumption was therefore that it was part of an information-warfare effort, aimed at planting skewed stories or disinformation in a seemingly credible wider stream of news. But intense scrutiny of the AIA output, even on the subjects I knew best, revealed no consistent pattern that supported this theory. The tone was pleasantly astringent towards the Russian services and their rivals alike. I took discreet soundings from intelligence professionals in the region. They turned out to be fans of AIA, with the same curiosity about its origins and purpose. The site was registered via an American hosting company, with all further details privacy-protected. I tried writing to the supposed editor, Michel Elbaz, and got an evasive reply in return. Eventually I gave up worrying and simply used the site as a handy compendium of news and analysis, assuming that it must have some kind of business model that I was too stupid to grasp. Had I looked a bit harder, I might have found some clues suggesting the opposite.

The pace of contributions to the site slackened in late 2009 and it became inactive in 2010. It was still a useful repository for historical information – particularly as I was beginning to research this book. In mid-2010, the whole site went behind a pay wall, demanding a log-in and password but giving no indication of how to acquire one. Frustrated, I emailed Mr Elbaz again, simply asking him to invoice me for access to the archived material on the site. Any normal company would have responded to that – at least to ask how much I was prepared to pay. AIA did not respond. This fired my interest again. If AIA was not trying to make a profit, someone had sponsored it. But who? And why? It had no visible do-gooding or academic affiliation. I started investigating more vigorously.[4]

A bit more digging brought a real breakthrough: the identity of one of the AIA contributors. He turned out to be a colleague: Āris Jansons, a well-known Latvian journalist and an acquaintance of mine for nearly twenty years. He had worked at Radio Free Europe in Prague after the collapse of the Soviet Union. When its Latvian service closed in 2004, he returned to Riga to look for a job. In January 2006 he was browsing the web and noticed a mistakenly identified picture in an AIA story. He emailed the site to point out the error, and after receiving an initially dismissive reply from Mr Elbaz then received a rather friendlier letter offering him a job as the Baltics correspondent. Mr Jansons was intrigued. The money was good and, more importantly, the editorial quality was impressive. I have reviewed numerous emails between the two men, provided by Mr Jansons. Mr Elbaz's brief to his new writer was a model of editorial professionalism. He gave a step-by-step guide to AIA's needs. One priority was to avoid duplication with any other English-language source. Another was to use a snappy, and preferably intriguing, headline. Concision, relevance and topicality were vital. The only slightly puzzling aspect was an instruction to avoid any direct criticism of the regime in Uzbekistan. But that was hardly going to be a big deal for a correspondent in the Baltics. The first year went well, with generous pay and plenty of demand. Mr Jansons wrote excellent articles, under a pseudonym. After that, AIA began to plead poverty. Payments slowed and stopped. Eventually Mr Elbaz offered Mr Jansons shares in the company in lieu of pay, which he turned down. Mr Jansons found another job and apart from grumbling about his unpaid fees, thought no more of it: freelance life is like that.

So what was AIA really? It was run by a Russian: Mikhail Falkov. He had emigrated to Israel – as it happens from Soviet-occupied Latvia – in the 1970s. He is the longstanding owner-editor of IzRus, a prominent Russian-language website there. He is also a former PR adviser to the controversial Israeli politician, currently foreign minister, Avigdor Lieberman, a Soviet-born immigrant whose hard-line approach (towards both Arabs and dovish Israeli officials) and fondness for the regime in Russia arouse considerable controversy.[5] Mr Lieberman once worked as a nightclub bouncer. In April 2011 he was charged by the State Prosecutor's Office with fraud, breach of trust, money laundering, and witness tampering; he denies all wrongdoing, and the case was pending as this book went to press. In the eyes of his critics, he has imported thuggish Soviet-style attitudes and habits into Israeli politics. Mr Falkov's IzRus website in 2009 carried an article denouncing Israeli embassies abroad which could be seen to echo Mr Lieberman's dislike of his own diplomats. It said they were 'fertile ground for orgies, sex with minors, sexual harassment and bribery' which was 'hidden from the public'.[6] There would be those who might see Mr Lieberman, and his sidekick Mr Falkov, as prime examples of how Russia exerts its influence in other countries.

Mr Falkov declines to answer any questions about AIA's finances, genesis and aims. It may well be that from his point of view it was indeed a purely business venture, which simply failed to gain the advertising that he hoped for. I am not accusing him of anything improper. But a few lines of text on the website give a tantalising hint of another explanation for its existence: suggesting a connection with the world of espionage, not of mere news. On the 'about us' section of the site, visitors were told:

AIA is open to cooperation on a commercial basis with those who possess exclusive and current information on policy and security issues in the countries of Asia and Eastern Europe . . . AIA accepts orders for collecting and analysing information on any issue that concerns policy and security . . . [it] can be either supplied confidentially to the client, or appear on our website.

That would be an unusual offer for anyone wanting to quash suspicion of involvement in espionage. It is possible that someone at AIA was hoping to act as a private intelligence broker. I have discussed the issue with people who think it likely that the outfit was operating on behalf of a government, wanting to flush out either sources of information, or demand for it. The 'freelance news agency' willing to pay generously for research material commissioned by anonymous clients was a staple of Cold War espionage: readers may recall George Smiley using it. The sort of people who read the published material on AIA's website would have included those with an appetite – and a budget – for more sensitive information along similar lines. One explanation is that its website was designed, not necessarily with Mr Falkov's consent or knowledge, to note the people visiting it, and perhaps to log details of their computers or even to plant viruses on them. Another is that its backers were interested to see what kind of orders came in: that could cast an interesting light on the behaviour and needs of government agencies. I do not find this completely convincing: no serious intelligence service would go shopping like this without thorough scrutiny of AIA, which would reveal its suspiciously flimsy structure. Another option is that it was an attempt by a government agency to spot potential sources of information. Any new contributors making themselves known to AIA would represent an interesting pool of potential sources. Those with access to real secrets could then be put on first consulting contracts and then developed, either directly or indirectly, as real agents if they proved useful. But the danger of a trap – a 'dangle' in espionage parlance – would be great.

More likely in my view is that AIA was (not necessarily with Mr Falkov's consent or knowledge) a counter-intelligence operation. Defence, security and intelligence officials in the ex-Soviet region are often demoralised, disgruntled and outright discontented by the corruption and futility of their jobs. It would be most interesting for the FSB, say, to know which of them would be willing to nibble at the carrot of discreet extra income from a foreign information agency. People vulnerable to a phoney temptation could also be open to an approach by a real espionage service. Such potential weakness is best known about in advance. Widely read by just the right people, Axisglobe's site would have been a neat way of flushing out such potential sources. But its putative role as part of an active intelligence operation was probably quite brief. It established its credibility, reaped its harvest, and then drifted into decay. Its significance may have been chiefly the way that it combined, certainly not for the last time, the anonymity of the internet with the human resources that the Russian diaspora represents for the intelligence and security services in Moscow. On 7 June 2011 the site was bought by a Japanese blogger for $940. That at least was a commercial transaction.

So far I have outlined much of the profile of Russian espionage: in cahoots with gangsters at one moment, bullying émigrés to

cooperate at another, stealing industrial secrets the next, and turning to lobbyists and lawyers when that becomes necessary. This is
bad enough for countries inside the EU and NATO. It is far worse
for those on its fringes. I conclude this section with a detailed
look at the frontline of Russia's military-intelligence effort – the
subversion, special operations and dirty tricks being practised in
Georgia, a country that has challenged Russia's claim to a *droit
de regard* in the former Soviet Union. This idea is a central part
of Russia's foreign-policy thinking about its neighbours; nothing should happen that Russia does not know about, and nothing
should happen that Russia does not consent to.

Under the Tsarist empire from 1813 to 1917, briefly independent until 1921 and then part of the Soviet Union until its collapse in
1991, Georgia has a special place in the hearts and minds of Russian
officials. They see it rather as Americans do Florida, a prized spot for
recreation and the source of countless sentimental holiday memories. It is also a bastion of Russian influence on the Black Sea, and
a bulwark against historic rivals for influence in the region such as
Iran and Turkey. The idea that Georgia – an Orthodox Christian
country – might want to head westwards, joining the European
Union and even NATO, strikes most such Russians as preposterous effrontery, even if it is exactly what the overwhelming majority of Georgians want. Russia kept a military presence in Georgia,
against the will of the republic's authorities, until 2006, occasionally
displaying military muscle in a show of force. But the real threat was
not the demoralised and largely barracks-bound regular soldiers.

So far I have mainly dealt with the direct heirs to the KGB, the
FSB domestic security agency and the SVR foreign-intelligence
service. But in Georgia's case, another organisation is at work:
the GRU military-intelligence service.* Georgian officials term

---

* *Glavnoye Razvedyvatelnoye Upravleniye* (Main Intelligence Directorate).

it the 'most aggressive and destructive' of Russia's three spy services. With around 12,000 employees,[7] the GRU has maintained unbroken institutional continuity since Leon Trotsky created it in 1918 (and it draws on a long tradition of Russian military espionage going back to Peter the Great). Even in Soviet times, the GRU's motivation was more patriotism than communist ideology. Its officers tend to come from the provinces rather than Russia's metropolises, from humbler backgrounds than the elite spies of the SVR, and nowadays from more honest ones than the cronies and thugs of the FSB. Partly as a result, the GRU tends to stay clear of the dodgy money-laundering schemes and commercial shenanigans beloved of its sister agencies: it will take part when operationally necessary, but not out of simple greed. It is hard, for example, to imagine a GRU officer being involved in the swindles that led to the death of Sergei Magnitsky. The agency is also less subject to political interference than the SVR: it is directly responsible only to the defence ministry, which shields it somewhat from the feuds and machinations at the top of Russian officialdom. But its senior officers and people close to it run into trouble if they stray into national politics.[8]

The GRU's chief mission is to collect military information affecting Russian national security, especially plans, hardware and personnel moves. Those who watch it sometimes feel the agency is stuck in something of a time warp, with targets and tasking almost unchanged since Soviet times. GRU officers seem to assume that foreign countries have secret plans to attack Russia that must be uncovered. If they cannot be found, then the search must be intensified. GRU doctrine and methods have in the past been different too. It tends to go for the 'quick hit': overcoming a source's reluctance, squeezing out his secrets and then dumping him, shutting him up with money, threats or worse. GRU officers are trained in the use of force and are quite capable of using it. In this sense, the GRU is quite different from counterpart organisations such as America's Defense Intelligence Agency (part of the Pentagon) or Britain's Defence Intelligence (which works out of the Ministry of Defence in Whitehall). These are chiefly focused on analysing information; when their staff members venture into the field, it is mainly as embassy-based attachés.

The GRU's officers do work as military attachés too. But its role is much wider. Until the military reforms of 2009 it used to have responsibility for most of Russia's elite *Spetsnaz* special forces – the equivalent of Britain's SAS and SBS, or America's Delta Force. It continues to have a special-operations capability. A small cadre of illegals are posted abroad, mainly to act as saboteurs in time of war. The agency also runs an extensive military counter-intelligence effort inside Russia; it is responsible for satellite reconnaissance (a comparable function to America's National Geospatial-Intelligence Agency) and also for military electronic information collection, such as snooping on NATO communications. The GRU's officers are trained at the 'Aquarium' spy school and headquarters building in Moscow. In a sign of the agency's prestige, in November 2006 Mr Putin formally opened the agency's glitzy new building, on Narodnogo Opolchenia (People's Militia Street) in the heart of Moscow. A sycophantic news report[9] showed the indoor swimming pool (for training frogmen) a firing range, special windows incorporating anti-bugging technology and a hi-tech situation room.

The GRU has played a big role in Chechen counter-insurgency operations. A GRU operation killed the first president of the breakaway republic (a terrorist leader in Russian eyes), Jokar Dudayev. A missile blew him up when he unwisely emerged from hiding to make a call on his satellite telephone. Another high-profile killing was the car-bomb assassination of the exiled Chechen president Zelimkhan Yandarbiyev in the Qatari capital Doha in February 2004. This killed the Chechen leader and two bodyguards, as well as seriously injuring his 12-year-old son Daud.

Shortly afterwards the infuriated Qatari authorities arrested three Russians (possibly because Russia's foreign-intelligence agency, the SVR, which often has poor relations with the GRU, botched part of the follow-up). One of the arrested men, a first secretary at the Russian embassy named Aleksandr Fetisov, was released shortly afterwards either because of his diplomatic immunity, or possibly in exchange for two Qatari wrestlers arrested on trumped-up charges while in transit at Moscow airport. The other two men were identified as GRU agents, Anatoly Yablochkov and Vasily Pugachev. Both men received emphatic public support from Russian officials; their defence attorney was Nikolai Yegorov, a friend and former university classmate of Vladimir Putin. Both were sentenced to life imprisonment, but were extradited to Russia in December to serve their sentence there. On arrival, they received a hero's welcome and disappeared from public view. The Russian authorities said that the Qatari sentence was 'not relevant'.

Many Russians see the Chechen fighters as mere bandits and welcomed these operations. For Western countries worried about global jihadist violence, the nuances of Chechen insurrectionist politics paled against the need to maintain solidarity between big countries in counter-terrorism. But the GRU's operations in Georgia are quite different. They are directed against a country that has not attacked Russia. Its only crime is to see its history and future differently. The GRU armed and trained Abkhaz and South Ossetian forces that resisted Georgian independence in the early 1990s. The reluctance was understandable: Georgia's ethnonationalist leadership at the time made little effort to accommodate the views of the country's minorities. But the Abkhaz and Ossetian separatist militias also perpetrated ethnic cleansing against people in their territories, mainly Georgians, who disagreed.

After those civil wars ended in uneasy truces, many in Moscow assumed that Georgia could be maintained as a weak and pliant

neighbour. History proved otherwise. Georgia stabilised under
the rule of Eduard Shevardnadze, a former Soviet foreign minister, and then accelerated its reforms under the leadership of the
American-educated lawyer Mikheil Saakashvili. Seen (perhaps
rather romantically) as a lone outpost of Atlanticist sentiments in
the region, and (hard-headedly) as a vital part of plans to bring
oil and gas from the Caspian and Central Asian regions to world
markets, Georgia benefited from a huge CIA and Pentagon aid
programme. Georgian intelligence and security officers received
fast-track training in the United States and in other NATO allied
countries. The Georgian military received subsidised or donated
equipment, ranging from sophisticated battlefield radios to portable anti-aircraft missiles (provided secretly by Poland in 2007).[10]
The hope was to make Georgia a bastion of Western influence on
Russia's southern flank. But in the rivalry between the GRU and
its adversaries, the Russian side has so far been the winner.

The biggest disaster for the West was the war of August 2008.
The aim of foreign assistance to Georgia had been to make a conflict
less likely, by calming and reassuring the Georgian leadership in
the face of escalating military provocations from Russia. Instead,
it produced the opposite result. Georgian politicians wildly over-
estimated both their own military strength and Western support.
This was a colossal intelligence failure. NATO countries failed to
read Russia's intentions, and the way that their Georgian protégés
would behave under pressure. Intelligence officers in the region
reported the increasingly dangerous situation regularly and accu-
rately to their controllers. But analysts blurred or misinterpreted
those reports, controllers failed to pass them on with sufficient
urgency, and the services' political masters failed to appreciate
the implications of what they were being told. That the whole
affair happened when many top decision makers were on holiday
did not help. A particularly striking and systemic failure was in

America's CIA. The small analysis division dealing with Russia has attracted particular criticism (belatedly) from its 'customers' else-where in the US government for interpreting raw intelligence in a framework that took great account of Russian sensitivities, fears and interests, but discounted other interpretations.

The American, British and Estonian training of Georgian human and electronic intelligence resources created structures that still lacked the clout and insight to interpret or influence events adequately. Decision-making circles were thoroughly penetrated, certainly by electronic means and possibly through the use of witting traitors or unwitting intelligence assets, recruited and run under the noses of the agencies responsible for security. Russia knew what Georgia knew, and how Georgia would react. It was therefore able to provoke the Georgian leadership successfully into attacking the breakaway province of South Ossetia, in the belief that a short victorious war would topple the separatist regime there and forestall a Russian troop build-up that the Tbilisi authorities believed was a prelude to a full-scale and potentially devastating military offensive.

That proved a disastrous miscalculation. Russia counterattacked, and the expensively equipped Georgian forces performed, for the most part, poorly (though to be fair the best part of the armed forces were in Iraq, or on leave having just returned from duty there). Command and control broke down. Expensive battlefield radios didn't work (leaving officers to communicate by insecure personal mobile phones). The reserve forces fared particularly poorly.[11] Russia's victory owed more to weight of numbers than to military prowess. But it was a triumph for the Russian intel-ligence agencies, which had a startlingly clear picture of events on the Western side. In one revealing cameo, telephones at a major NATO military facility in Europe became unusable: the NATO Office of Security (NOS) was aware that they were penetrated, but

was unable to take immediate countermeasures. Officials instead
had to use their personal mobile phones (which may have been
even less secure than the landlines). Russia knew to a high degree
of certainty that America would not go to war to defend a friendly
country that was under attack; it also knew that the European
Union was in no state to act as a decisive, well-informed mediator.
It was able to follow in detail the zigzag diplomacy of the French
president, Nicolas Sarkozy, and the evolution of the amateur-
ishly imprecise ceasefire document that he finally produced with a
triumphant flourish on 13 August.

Since the war, many in the West have come to see Georgia as a
faraway country of which they never knew much and would now
like to know less. Certainly Mr Saakashvili's erratic behaviour in
the run-up to the war in 2008 did little to boost his country's credibility. It will be a long time before any NATO country's spymas-
ter sticks his neck out on behalf of a Georgian leadership that has
gained a reputation for chaos and unreliability. Politicians in the
EU and America still maintain rhetorical support for Georgia's
territorial integrity, but have produced scant support in practical
terms. Foreign assistance efforts in Georgia have wound down, as
have Georgian efforts to meet Western concerns about the rule of
law and political pluralism.

These trends are indeed cause for concern. But whole-scale
pessimism is unfounded. Following the lost war, Georgia has
picked itself up and resumed reforms and economic growth. For
all its faults it remains the only post-Soviet success story outside
the Baltic states. Outsiders flock to observe its tax system and
administrative reforms. The Georgian leadership has also, belatedly, begun taking security more seriously, and paying heed to
the long-standing suggestions and complaints of their Estonian
and other advisers. Tighter scrutiny and better counter-intelligence tradecraft have begun to pay off, most recently in July

2011 with the arrest of a presidential photographer, who confessed that he had been recruited by Russia to spy on Mr Saakashvili. The round-up started in November 2010 when nine Georgians and four Russian citizens were arrested on suspicion of spying for Russia. The Georgian Interior Ministry described the group as consisting of military pilots and a sailor and a number of business-men who had passed on data about flight schedules and military equipment and procurement, as well as the personal details of top Georgian officials.

A documentary broadcast on 5 November, the GRU's 'birth-day', on the Georgian Rustavi-2 television channel featured a double agent, code-named 'Enveri', shown only with his face hidden, who said he had worked for the GRU at the Georgian port of Poti in the late 1980s. On the instructions of Georgian intelligence, he made contact with his old employers and met three GRU officers who gave him instruction in how to embed secret material in innocent-seeming email attachments. Enveri allowed the Georgians to spot dozens of other locals and a GRU liaison officer, Yuri Skrilnikov. When this officer attempted to meet his source in May 2010 Georgian counter-intelligence officials arrested him, along with another Russian citizen and a Georgian. Both had previously worked at a Russian military base in Georgia until its closure in November 2007.

Enveri reported that his Russian case officers were interested in NATO warships' visits to Georgian ports and Western training of Georgian military forces. But the true aims of the GRU are wider and more alarming. An analysis by Georgian officials lists them as: discrediting the country's foreign and domestic political course; preventing accession to NATO and European integration; denting foreign investors' confidence; creating 'spots of instability' to high-light the state's weakness; creating a pro-Russian 'fifth column'; consolidating Russian control over South Ossetia and Abkhazia;

supporting secessionist tendencies in other parts of Georgia; and creating an intelligence network inside the government.

In other countries, such tasks would be mainly the job of the SVR – the foreign intelligence service. But in Russian eyes, Georgia is not 'foreign' enough for that. Instead, the military intelligence agency, the GRU, has the main role. The FSB, once a big presence, now plays a second fiddle, chiefly in targeting the Georgian diaspora inside Russia; in previous years it was involved in scams such as protecting a counterfeiting operation in South Ossetia that produced large amounts of forged American currency.[12] The GRU's prime targets are Georgia's defence capabilities, links with NATO, energy security, the transport infrastructure (especially ports), the structure and composition of the border police and all electronic communications. But it also mounts special operations, including bombings and other stunts. These, Georgian officials say, are run from the southern regional headquarters in Krasnodar, with a sub-station in the coastal resort of Sochi. At least according to the Georgian authorities, the GRU is also actively involved in stoking violent political protest by marginal parts of the country's opposition. On 26 May 2011 the Interior Ministry in Tbilisi released an audio recording of a bugged meeting in which an opposition leader, Nino Burjanadze, and her son appeared to be expecting the intervention of GRU special forces if a planned violent demonstration turned into an insurrection.

Georgia also believes that Russian intelligence officers, mostly from the FSB but also from the GRU, are recruiting ethnic Georgians in the occupied district of Gali in Abkhazia, either with bribes or blackmail, in order to carry out acts of terrorism and sabotage.[13] This has involved at least twelve incidents since 2009. The targets have included railway installations, bridges, public buildings, public squares, offices of political parties, ministries, the American embassy and the NATO liaison office in Tbilisi. Two people have been killed so far, but many more would have been at risk had the bombings succeeded as planned. In one house search, for example, Georgian police found nine canisters of hexogen explosive, five of which had been modified with homemade shrapnel. The ringleader of one of the groups arrested, Gogita Arkania, said in a witness statement that he had been recruited, trained and directed by Major Evgeny Borisov, who is part of the Russian military contingent in Abkhazia and used to be based there as a 'peace-keeper' before the war. Though he is formally part of the FSB border guards, Georgian counter-intelligence officers believe Borisov is an active operative of the GRU; however, this cannot be independently verified and Mr Borisov has made no public statement. Telephone intercepts obtained by Georgian intelligence show intensive traffic between mobile phones registered in Arkania's and Borisov's names with a mobile number belonging to the Russian Defence Ministry, at exactly the times that bomb attacks took place in Georgia, for example against the American embassy on the morning of 22 September 2010.

In at least one case, a GRU operation against Georgia was let down by an elementary blunder. On 2 October a bomb placed near an important railway bridge at Chaladidi in the western Khobi district failed to go off. But the next morning the European Union's Monitoring Mission received a phone call from a Russian military officer, asking for more information about the bomb blast that he claimed passengers had reported on the railway. Georgian officials were baffled – until local residents found the device a few days later. The only possible source for this mistaken enquiry by the Russian officer could have been the GRU unit that instigated the botched attack.

Russia can afford to make mistakes. Georgia cannot afford Russia's successes. The international media and Western countries have shamefully neglected this bullying campaign by a hostile big state against a friendly small one. The effect is to create a climate of impunity in which the Kremlin and its spymasters feel that the risk of these attacks is minor and the rewards are substantial. Georgian complaints to Russia are either ignored or met with dismissals that range from the airy to the vituperative. Sometimes Georgia is accused of spinning fairy tales; sometimes the charge is Russophobia. Western officials accept privately that Georgia has reason to complain. But they see no political or professional benefit in taking up the issue. It is hard to grab foreign official and public attention about allegations of foreign involvement in a largely non-lethal bombing campaign in a country that is seen as marginal and difficult. Raising the complaints risks making Georgians look paranoid. And if they do gain attention, the result may be to underline the country's reputation as a trouble spot, not a reliable partner and prospective EU and NATO member.

The operations described in the preceding pages are unpleasant but for the most part clumsy: assassinations, bombings, military sabre-rattling, the blackmail of émigrés, the bedding of politicians. It is now time to turn to the more subtle methods used by Russia's spymasters, chiefly in Europe and North America: the use of fake (and increasingly of real) identities to place career intelligence officers undercover on long-term foreign assignments. This is a world of closely guarded secrets in training and doctrine, of meticulous planning, deep paradoxes and tangled psychology. It could hardly differ more from its portrayal in spy fiction and in Hollywood films, as I show in the following chapter, which introduces the reader to the real world of spies and spycraft.

5

Spycraft: Fact and Fiction

Spies break rules for governments that try to enforce them. In this contradiction lies the fascination of the espionage world and also its greatest weakness.* Espionage involves breaking laws, perhaps of your own country, more often of its allies and certainly in the country being spied upon. The reason is simple. Secret information may come through deduction and inference, or from exploiting the other side's carelessness by bluff and subterfuge. But the blunt fact is that for the most part secrets must be stolen. This means instigating treachery, using bribery, burglary, blackmail or outright violence as necessary. That is a long way from the normal tasks expected of a public servant. It attracts a certain kind of person, often flawed or troubled, and shapes them to its needs, to the point that deceit arouses not repugnance, but professional curiosity and admiration. Before looking at the battlefield of the East–West spy wars, it is necessary to understand the mentality, training and selection of the soldiers.

The first quality of a good spy is to shun and shed the social mores that hamper deceiving, cheating and manipulating people.

* I focus in this chapter on solely HUMINT (the recruitment and running of human sources) not SIGINT (electronic intercepts) or geospatial reconnaissance (via satellite). I am also leaving out, among other intelligence professionals, the analysts and reporting officers who make sense of the spies' work.

An early exercise during IONEC (the six-month 'Intelligence Officers New Entry Course') at Britain's Fort Monckton spy school on England's south coast is to gain as much personal information as possible from people in a pub: a prize goes to anyone who obtains passport details. A second is to borrow money from strangers. Some well brought-up trainees find this so demeaning that they quit. Other agencies use similar training games. Israel's Mossad sets recruits the task of inveigling entry into a stranger's apartment and appearing on the balcony drinking a glass of water; watchers in a car park below will see who succeeds. Spying is a job for the nosy and devious, not the shy and the scrupulous.

If moral ambiguity is part of the lure, another element is the glamour of secrecy. Nobody cares how and where the government trains its tax inspectors; but the location and topography of Fort Monckton, the names of the courses and their content are secrets.* Outsiders catch only fleeting glimpses of life in the shadows, usually in carefully sanitised form. Secrecy and flawed fictional depictions fuel misperceptions. These would not matter were spying a branch of government service with limited relevance to the outside world, such as drafting fire regulations. But espionage is connected directly into nations' most vital interests and their most ruthless pursuit. Those wanting insights into complicated geopolitical competition in finance, law or diplomacy are more likely to read the *Economist* than a novel. But concerning the no less intricate world of espionage, every cinemagoer and novel-reader has a (usually mistaken) impression of life in the shadows. This is one reason that the arrest of the ten Russian spies in America in June 2010 attracted such ill-informed commentary.

---

* This former Napoleonic fort, once used by Britain's wartime Special Operations Executive, is not as secret as perhaps it should be. Its postcode is PO12 2AT; other details including a telephone number are available on the internet.

Drama and suspense require that fictional spies swing into action at a second's notice, rather than wasting time writing operational plans and worrying about overspending their budgets. They are untroubled by the nagging concerns of counter-intelligence: the weaknesses – human, financial, bureaucratic, operational and technical – that an enemy could exploit. Routine and discipline are the tiresome exception, not the mundane rule. Equipment appears as if by magic and always works. These exciting exploits bear as little relation to real espionage as *Star Wars* does to astrophysics. Though spies such as le Carré's cerebral George Smiley do exist, in real-life espionage brain-boxes are as rare as sex-gods. Real intelligence officers – as the professional employees of state spy agencies are called – generally do not know how to pick locks, steal cars, create explosive devices from household chemicals or disable an assailant with a single punch.[1] They hate standing out in a crowd, don't wear flashy clothes and certainly don't flirt. Their job is to get unnoticed from A to B, to perform task C and return. Scriptwriters would find that rather dry.

Moreover few intelligence officers steal secrets directly: it is too hard to get the right access, and too risky to exploit it when gained. Their main role is recruiting others to do the dirty work. Here the real talent kicks in: successful spies tend to be good at dealing with people – unobtrusively, imaginatively and persuasively. They could easily be executive coaches, psychotherapists, salesmen, confidence tricksters or (scraping the barrel) journalists. Their job is to extract information and consent by concocting and administering the right cocktail of pressure, ideology, flattery and money.

Each ingredient has its drawbacks. Blackmail can be a jolt that offers an opening for other, more durable means of persuasion; but the resentment it creates limits its usefulness. The victim twists and turns in his mind, desperately seeking a way out – which may be suicide, flight or confession, not treason. Blackmail works best when it comes from a third party, with the intelligence officer appearing as a friend, brokering a deal that involves betraying (initially minor) secrets. Ideology plays a diminished role but can also be useful. A Russian intelligence officer may play on anti-Americanism (most often in allied countries, but sometimes even in the United States). Western recruiters have used Russians' dislike of the regime's authoritarian crony capitalism. Flattery is the most potent technique. A friendly voice passing favourable judgement on work overlooked by an unappreciative boss is one of the most formidable weapons in the intelligence officer's arsenal, particularly when dealing with a 'developmental' agent: one who is on the road to treachery, but not yet arrived. When and if the real nature of the clandestine relationship becomes clear, flattery can be crystallised in the form of a rank or a medal.

A final complementing ingredient is money. This can be paid as 'expenses' or 'salary', whichever seems less demeaning. (Many of the biggest traitors, from Britain's Kim Philby to Estonia's Herman Simm, have insisted that they were not mere turncoats but the other side's employees.) Money on its own has its limits though: it buys information, but not loyalty. The sneaking suspicion in any intelligence relationship based chiefly on cash is that if a higher bidder comes along, the first customer can easily come last. A taste for treachery is often accompanied by a fast-growing appetite.* Praise a source for what he does and he demands more. Criticise

---

* A related problem is that a single money-grubbing source may sell the same, slightly tweaked, information to several agencies: to America's CIA and Germany's BND for example. A dubious piece of information checks out from several seemingly different sources, and counts as solid. Yet behind it is just one agent, single-mindedly maximising his income. It is this that lay behind the colossal blunder that Western intelligence made over Iraq's supposed weapons of mass destruction.

him and he will say that he needs to take still greater risks – and demands more. Recruiting an agent from an impenetrable country such as North Korea is even harder; he may demand a huge sum of money for making any contact at all, and then disappear. Has he been caught? Has he simply disappeared to Brazil to enjoy life at your expense? Was the whole thing a dangle designed to boost the other side's operational funds? You will never know.

The rules that hamper terrorists and money-launderers have also hit espionage. Opening an anonymous bank account in Vienna, accessed perhaps with a password, or by presenting half a torn postcard (the bank had the other half and would simply check that they fitted), was easy thirty years ago. Now banks are supposed to 'know their customers'. In clandestine work, even a passport or home electricity bill requires forgery; creating a credit history that will stand up to checking is a serious nuisance. These hassles are potentially lethal. Imagine that you are a North Korean official in Vienna, who is considering selling some secrets. Your home is subject to regular searches by your fearsome State Security Department. If they get suspicious, you go home to eat grass in one labour camp while your wife gnaws tree bark in another. If you are paid in wads of €500 notes and keep them in a bank safety deposit box, you not only miss out on the interest: if you survive long enough to get the money out, you will find that large quantities of cash, gained from an undisclosable source, are more of a problem than a delight.

Some spy agencies therefore run a notional bank account for a source, letting interest build up on the 'salary'. Assuming the agent reaches retirement, the money is a nest egg for his new life. This also avoids the danger of conspicuous consumption, which can easily attract unwelcome interest. Another trick is to pay agents in rare stamps. These are easily portable, highly concealable, readily exchanged into cash – and leave no trace. Other means include gambling chips from casinos, especially from chains that allow them to be exchanged for cash in any one of several countries. Keeping intelligence officers themselves supplied with money is tricky too. Those working under alias need credit cards that will withstand a credit check. But they may also need to make or receive payments that leave no electronic trace. Here the kind of dodgy money-transfer company that Ms Chapman seems to have been associated with during her time in London (which I describe in the next chapter) can come in useful. Also handy are prepaid debit cards that can be topped up with cash. These featured in the contents of the Boston home of two other spies, 'Donald Heathfield' and his wife, listed in the search warrant obtained by the FBI.[2]

Good spies are not only manipulative and ingenious; they also need good memory skills: when writing things down is dangerous, the easy and accurate recall of number plates, phone numbers, map references and passwords is vital. Spies are naturally inquisitive, and pedantic when it comes to facts, figures, times and dates. They have good Thespian skills, being able to think themselves deeply and convincingly, like a Stanislavski-trained actor, into someone else's character. All these qualities, however, do not eliminate the paradoxes of spying: first, that using secretly obtained information necessarily endangers its source; second, that systematic attempts to be inconspicuous risk being noticed; and third, that the sort of people who deal in broken promises are unlikely to be good at keeping them.

For those running spy agencies the last of these is the worst. The people most drawn to the shadows are often those people most unsuited to working there. Though some spy for noble or intellectual reasons, for others their motivation is part of the problem, not its solution. The lucrative opportunities that the private sector offers ex-spies can erode loyalties, especially in later years as the job market looms. Those with a philosophical or mystical bent sometimes feel themselves to be part of a lay priesthood, armed with the powers of the curse and the confessional. This can shade into weirdness. Espionage also attracts those obsessed by secrecy for its own sake, and, most lethally, those for whom betrayal is a tantalising extra thrill. Breaking the other side's rules brings a buzz; sidestepping your own team's a bigger one. The more adept you are in the dark arts, the more tempting it is to use them widely. At a harmless level, that can involve simply fiddling expense accounts, charging meals and taxis to operational funds. It can mean bending the rules to do a pal a favour. It also invites sexual shenanigans. Spies only rarely use bedroom arts in pursuit of official business: their bosses usually veto such plans, wisely fearing that emotions may impinge on the operation. Outside work, intelligence officers are often formidable adulterers and fornicators – they know all too well how to cover tracks and avoid suspicion. In a life constrained by rules and routines, the temptation to throw over the traces can be huge. Betraying spouses can be a step to betraying secrets.

Regular counter-intelligence screening can uncover suspicious patterns of behaviour, or anomalies in the subject's private life. But the more senior and experienced the subject of scrutiny, the harder it is to trip him up – and the more damage he can do. Aleksandr Poteyev, the American agent at the heart of Russian intelligence who betrayed Ms Chapman and her colleagues, had apparently escaped routine lie-detector tests by virtue of seniority and good connections. Spies are necessarily practised and skilful in fending off unwelcome questions and concealing their real intentions and feelings. The endemic duplicity of the profession makes it hard to deliver sincere praise or to appreciate it.

The mutual dislike that often exists between spies and spy-catchers poses a further problem. Counter-intelligence officers tend to be suspicious, methodical types who like every fact to be nailed down and distrust flair, initiative or anything irregular.

It would be only a slight exaggeration to say that they see their field-officer colleagues as a self-indulgent menace to security. For their part, the active spies are at heart intuitive rule-breakers with a strong sense of the rightness of their own judgement. They think the spycatchers' silly rules hamper the chance of doing any real work. (This is one reason why his former colleagues from the elite foreign-espionage division of the KGB detest Mr Putin, who was a lowly counter-intelligence officer during his time in Germany.) The rivalry can be debilitating. When agencies such as the FBI or Britain's Security Service scent a spy on their turf, their priority is to arrest him to protect the nation's secrets. When the CIA or SIS (the official title of MI6) finds one, their instinct is to watch, not pounce. The longer the game, the more they learn about the other side's methods and sources, and the greater the chance of a successful ruse – recruiting the traitor as a double agent, feeding disinformation to the other side, or trying to flush out his case officer or controller.

The constant aim of intelligence work is to provide otherwise unobtainable information to policymakers. But spy agencies vary in size, techniques, susceptibility to political interference and most of all effectiveness. A good index of excellence is discretion: crudely, the lower the profile, the greater the success. Sweden's *Kontoret för särskild inhämtning* (Office of Special Collection) is a clear winner. It has no published street address, let alone a website.[3] Another variable is necessity. Countries facing an existential threat tend to take their security seriously. Those that don't (Belgium springs to mind) see it as a low priority. Poor countries find it hard to keep their spy services honest, as the rewards for misbehaviour are proportionately greater for those on low salaries. Spookish meddling in public life is a big problem in many ex-communist countries, where compromising information is political currency. An agency's ability to bug politicians' telephones can easily divert its attention from threats to the national interest.

The essential elements of espionage everywhere – boredom, deceit, secrecy and ambition – are an inherently toxic compound. The success or failure of a spy service depends on its ability to mitigate the negative effects of this compound, through selection, training, morale, discipline, scrutiny, and procedure. For all the high stakes and sharp wits, the biggest part of espionage is therefore meticulous, careful work; it can even be rather dull. The focus on routine also reflects the paradox that the most successful breaches of a rule are unmarked. A truly successful operation goes unnoticed by everyone but those who ran it. Every trace left restricts future options and increases the risk of the other side limiting the damage, taking countermeasures and tracking down sources. The hallmarks of successful spying are pedantic planning, plentiful patience, prudent precautions, and most of all invisibility.

The risks sharpen the focus. Officialdom often wastes public money. Errors in espionage mean not just unwanted buildings or ill-conceived regulations but deep damage and ruined lives. Treason bears heavy criminal penalties. In most operations, therefore, the human costs of failure outweigh the benefits of success. The resulting caution is in constant tension with the central means of espionage – rule breaking – yet it is vital that it does not overwhelm it. An intelligence officer who flinches at this might as well be a diplomat.

Imagine, for example, that you are a spymaster considering a potential source – someone, perhaps, like Sergei Skripal, a Russian intelligence officer who for many years passed his country's secrets to Britain. If your service successfully recruits and runs him, your country gains invaluable information about Russia's military capabilities and intentions, about its decision-making processes, about the weaknesses and strengths of its security procedures, about its intelligence-gathering efforts abroad, and much more besides. Your country is better informed and safer. Your taxpayers have got value for money. Your political masters will be pleased. Your career will flourish. But your source, if caught, is likely to end his days in a hard labour regime camp somewhere near the Arctic Circle (Mr Skripal was sentenced to thirteen years in 2006; he was one of the four prisoners that Russia swapped for Ms Chapman and her colleagues).[4]

The danger can be even greater. If your operation in China, Iran or Syria is blown, your source faces not just prison, but death, perhaps by torture. For their induction into the Soviet GRU military intelligence service, recruits were shown a film of the fate awaiting those who betrayed its secrets (the account comes from a defector who was undeterred). It showed a man, gagged and wired to a steel stretcher, being trundled to the door of a furnace prior to being burned alive:

He strains to the point of breaking his own bones, and tearing his own tendons and muscles. It is a superhuman effort. But the wire does not give. And the stretcher slides smoothly along the rails. The furnace doors move aside again and the fire casts a white light on the soles of the man's dirty patent leather shoes. He tries to bend his knees in an effort to increase the distance between his feet and the roaring fire. But he can't.[5]

To save a source from such a fate means a lot of dull errands. Go to the Hotel Sheraton in Kiev and leave this envelope at reception to be collected by Mr Brown. Go to the DHL office in Riga and pay cash for the delivery of this envelope to a Mr Smith in Dublin. Go to a bank in Helsinki, leave one package in a safe-deposit box and collect another. Buy a coffee and read a newspaper in the glass-walled metro station at Moscow's Sparrow Hills between eleven and twelve every Saturday, wearing a red scarf. That is a

signal to Mr Skripal (en route to his regular sports club) that everything is all right. If he is wearing a hat, he's OK too.

The precautions are necessary because of the time-consuming
yet vital assumption that the other side may be watching. Most
messages can be exchanged via brush contacts or dead-letter
boxes. A memory card the size of a fingernail can carry gigabytes
of data, though any non-specialist examining it will find only some
anodyne tourist snaps. Mr Skripal can wrap it in chewing gum and
stick it to a park bench, or to the side of his seat during his regular Sunday night cinema trip – having first made sure he is sitting
next to a woman with a white shirt and red scarf. Meetings are
rare and preferably in third countries. Spycatchers suspicious of Mr
Skripal see only normal life in Moscow, and harmless recreation
elsewhere: an overnight trip to a football match in, say, Kiev. Even
detailed scrutiny of the CCTV recordings in his hotel there will
not reveal the meeting that took place in its penthouse suite, with
a case officer who rented it in the guise of a foreign businessman.

Another Russian source might take his holidays in Vienna, and
have a long-standing interest in the Central Cemetery. Its 250
hectares* feature interesting graves from Freud to Mozart. It has
another advantage from an espionage point of view: the long paths
and clear sightlines give plenty of opportunity to see if anyone is
watching. Assuming all is clear, he can be picked up by a scruffy
van parked in some remote corner of the grounds. Inside are
comfortable chairs, a bottle of vodka, and a case officer eager
to debrief him. Half an hour later, he is wandering round the
cemetery again. Spycatchers' resources are finite: if scrutiny reveals
nothing, then they turn to something more promising.

Such elaborate precautions are costly and make sense only for
the most highly placed source. Yet if anything goes wrong, he ends

---

* 650 acres.

up rotting in a labour camp. Every stage needs to be hammered out in advance. Can that hotel penthouse in Kiev be dependably booked in advance? Can the source plausibly stay there on his official salary? Where exactly are the CCTV blind spots? Who will make the reservation? How will the bill be paid? Will the credit card be traceable? What passport will be used? Who will sweep the room for bugs? Each new precaution creates a new difficulty and something else to go wrong. The ideal operation has as few moving parts as possible. It is better to rely on split-second timing, which practice and professionalism can perfect, than on elaborate schemes that are vulnerable to the unexpected.

Take the Vienna trip: what happens if it is pouring with rain? A dedicated grave-spotter may take a short damp walk to see a famous tomb, but not a long one. So what is the back-up plan? A nearby church? Is it always open? What if a service is happening? And how to communicate if the plans go awry? Sussing that out requires lots of legwork. The officers working on this team will know Vienna's tourist attractions backwards by the time they have finished. Organising brush contacts, dead-letter boxes and signals in Moscow is even more difficult, and involves a stream of innocent-seeming bag men (and bag ladies), scarf-wearers and scouts who will turn up and run errands, dependably, punctually, and inconspicuously, right under the noses of the Russian FSB. Compounding the cost of all this is the need to avoid any recognisable pattern of behaviour. Too many visits to Vienna, or to Kiev, arouse attention. A dead-letter box is most secure when it is used sparingly, ideally only once. So the attrition rate is high. No sooner has an impressively guileful idea been worked out than it starts wearing out.

Such difficulties and precautions beset every stage of agent-running: identifying a potential source, softening him up ('cultivation' in spy-speak), presenting bluntly the offer of cooperation ('pitching'); keeping him safe, motivated and productive ('agent-running'), debriefing him ('elicitation') and when he is no more use standing him down ('terminating him'). A promising source may be a 'dangle' – someone presented by the other side in the hope of flushing out some clues about the way you work. If a source is willing to betray his own country, his loyalty to the person who brokers the betrayal must also be questionable. Even if he starts off genuine, suppose he comes under pressure from the other side, and betrays you and your methods? Maybe he will prove a time-waster, just in search of easy money for old news? The adversary's 'wish-list' is one of the most sought-after pieces of intelligence in the whole spy world. If you know what the other side does not know, you are in a good position to mislead them and to conceal your real secrets.

At a more trivial level, methods and tradecraft are vulnerable too. If a double agent reveals dead-letter boxes, his side can put them under observation in case another, unknown, agent is using them too. Who empties them? Maybe an embassy-based archivist or visa clerk not previously under suspicion as an intelligence officer. Then you have a new target. Giving a clever communications gadget to a newly recruited source can backfire. If he is caught or switches sides, anyone else using a similar device is at greater risk. A 'walk-in' who turns up at an embassy in a sensitive country demanding to speak to an intelligence officer can hardly be ignored. But even the initial vetting of such an approach is risky. Whoever meets the visitor may be being set up for embarrassment or expulsion. For someone based at an embassy in Moscow, this will mean a career-blighting departure to London, perhaps after first being humiliated in surreptitiously filmed clips broadcast on the evening television news.[6]

The spotlight also endangers all a case officer's previous contacts and operations. Marc Doe, a British official based at the embassy in Moscow who was exposed in the Russian media after a bungled operation, turned out to have a diplomatic cover job that involved channelling embassy funds to human-rights organisations long denounced as fronts for Western interests by the Russian authorities.[7] That was an excruciating blunder. For these hard-pressed and vulnerable outfits, the furore weakened their defence.

But the greatest risk remains recruiting the wrong person. Sign up the wrong source and you will give away far more than you gain. Hire someone with a fragile ego and a short temper and you risk a major security breach. The case of Richard Tomlinson, a renegade British spy who published a book in Russia about his recruitment, training and quarrels with his bosses, has been costly and damaging for Britain's intelligence agencies and their foreign partner services.[8]

In past decades the most formidable spies on both sides were 'illegals' – sent on long-term clandestine assignments, using stolen or fake identities, and without the benefit of diplomatic cover. One of them was Sir Paul Dukes, described in chapter 8, whose work under the noses of the Bolsheviks in the years following the Russian revolution makes him probably the most brilliant spy in the history of MI6. But after the debacles of the 1940s (of which more later) Western countries stopped trying to send agents to live undercover behind the Iron Curtain: the difficulty of creating sufficiently credible false identities for people to function inside a closed totalitarian society was just too great. The KGB and other services, however, made great efforts to send their agents to the West, sometimes for lifetime assignments. Some of the agents unearthed in June 2010 were just this kind of classic 'illegal'. Such spies are formidably expensive. By Russian estimates, creating an illegal identity costs around $1m per head. Still, even if they do nothing for decades, they may, in the right place at the right time, justify their mission. An extreme case is for a military-intelligence agency wishing to acquire a special-operations capability in the event of war. Simply establishing the illegals deep behind enemy lines will be well worth it when it comes to the outbreak of war ('Day X' in Soviet parlance) when invisible sabotage capability is priceless. In peacetime they can be vitally useful too, even when they do little or no actual spying themselves.

To understand why, imagine that you are a Russian intelligence officer working under diplomatic cover, tasked with gaining information about the British Parliament, or America's Congress. You have hundreds of potential targets: lawmakers, their staffers, even cleaners and technicians. But you are an obvious subject for surveillance. Your every meeting and every move carry a risk. You simply cannot afford to hang around in the bars of Westminster or Capitol Hill, chatting people up. Eventually even the most over-worked or demoralised counter-intelligence officers will notice you. So you need eyes and ears in the circles you wish to infil-trate, someone to spot people with access to the information you need, to identify their weaknesses (financial, sexual, psychological or political) and to cultivate them. A journalist, lobbyist or think-tank researcher would be ideal. You cannot play that role, but an illegal can.

If a potential source has strong convictions, an illegal can help turn loyalty to treachery with a 'false flag' operation. A stand-ard KGB task in the past, for example, was to find out how East European émigrés were supporting dissident movements in the homeland. A good approach was to pose as an ardent anti-commu-nist, representing a bunch of wealthy donors (preferably based in a faraway country) wanting to target their support effectively. Such a person, eager to gain 'analysis' of the real situation, could cred-ibly pay expenses and stipends to those who kept him informed. This still works today. If you are targeting left-wingers, pretend to be from Cuba; if you want to recruit Muslims, a claimed link with the Palestinian cause will do the trick. If the target is Jewish, or a conservative Christian sympathetic to Israel, say that you are working for Mossad. For an embassy-based intelligence officer to assume such an identity is complicated and risky. An illegal can adopt it more convincingly. For the target, checking the authenticity of such an approach is tricky to impossible: how can, say, a Polish expatriate working in an energy company know if the friendly compatriot enquiring about the workings of the gas market is really an undercover officer of his country's *Agencja Wywiadu* (foreign intelligence service) as he claims? He may be a Russian illegal, or working for the Saudis or Chinese. How to check?

Illegals can also help funnel funds from the buyer to the seller of secrets. But they cannot help with, and indeed are part of, a bigger problem: getting value for the money paid. A hint of this comes from the published fragments of intercepted communications between 'Moscow centre' – the headquarters of Russian espionage – and two of its illegals in America. The bosses are tut-tutting about the house lived in by 'Cynthia and Richard Murphy': does it belong to them (which would fit their cover story)? Or is it really the property of the Russian state? It is easy for each end to feel cheated by the other: the illegals regard everything they spend as a claimable expense. They are in effect doing two jobs: their cover profession and real spying. It is quite fair that the motherland should subsidise their property, cars or children's education. For their part, spymasters worry that operational funds are dribbling away into peripheral expenses, padding further a lifestyle that for most Russians would already seem unimaginably pampered and pleasant.

Illegals are also useful in the humblest parts of spying. Joe Navarro, a twenty-five-year veteran of FBI counter-intelligence, points out that one of their functions is simply to acquire legal documents such as a passport, driver's licence, university ID card or utility bills that can then be used as the basis for future forgeries. He describes illegals as like cancer: they have usually done their worst by the time they are detected. No electronic intercept or embassy-based spy can gain access to things that an illegal living as an average American can manage:

a car, a home, a library, neighbourhood events, air shows on military bases, location of fibre cables, access to gasoline storage facilities, a basement to hide an accomplice, a neighbour's son serving in the military, and so on. A mere walk . . . can give you access to vehicles parked at a garage sale that have stickers from government installations or high tech companies doing research. These individuals can be tracked or befriended . . . [Illegals] get invited to parties, meet people and gain access to individuals with knowledge, influence or information.[9]

For a service with the money and patience to run them, illegals clearly have many uses. They present one of the trickiest problems in the counter-intelligence universe. Whatever they do or don't do, they are certainly no laughing matter. The real question is whether they justify their costs. From a Western perspective now, the answer is 'usually not'. It makes more sense to use lots of disposable junior intelligence officers working under light cover than to concentrate resources on a small number of costly assets with elaborate cover stories. The classic work on this is a declassified CIA study called *Principles of Deep Cover* by a long-dead intelligence officer who used the pseudonym C.D. Edbrook.[10] He writes:

Because the deep-cover agent must usually devote a large share of his time to carrying on his ostensible legitimate occupation, his intelligence production is quantitatively small. He is therefore an expensive agent, justified only by the uniqueness of information he produces, or can be expected in the long term to produce. The establishment of a deep-cover operation should consequently derive without exception from the object to be achieved, not from the availability of the agent or the opportunity for cover.

The danger of distraction is clear: Edbrook's paper cites a CIA agent who spent four years building a cover story by attending a university in order to gain a job as a salesman in a particular target area. He then lost interest and resigned. This certainly seems to have been the case with some of the Soviet-era illegals sent to America on long-term deep-cover missions during the Cold War. Eventually unearthed thanks to the Mitrokhin archive, they proved to have done very little or no spying, and in some cases had lost contact largely or wholly with their controllers. Edbrook continues:

> The rational preparation and conduct of an operation can there-fore have no other guide than its purpose, and this purpose must therefore be defined at the outset . . . A deep-cover mission is not justified if it can do no better than wander along the fringes of an intelligence target, eliciting scraps of information and misin-formation, or 'collect information available in the normal course of cover work and spot potential agent material.'* It is wasteful to have a deep-cover agent doing the routine jobs that can be done just as well by an official-cover man or his ordinary local agents and informants. The targets that call for deep cover are those to which official government representatives lack access or in which they must conceal their interest or from which only an

---

* Mr Edbrook is presumably quoting from another CIA document not yet declassified.

independent channel will elicit information not meant for official consumption.

Thinking in the spy world has moved on a bit since this, exploiting the increasingly blurred boundaries between government service and life outside. Thomas Patrick Carroll, a former American intelligence officer turned academic and security consultant, has coined the term 'natural capacity' for a kind of spying which is self-financing, ubiquitous and effective. He posits the following scenario: America wishes to know about the people, materials, finances and political associations of an international airport in the Middle East. The traditional approach would be to post intelligence officers, probably under official cover as diplomats, to recruit the necessary sources. Under 'natural capacity' the CIA would have at the airport an authentic, profitable private firm, backed by real investors. It could survive any amount of scrutiny, and would provide anything that policymakers needed to know about the airport. 'Natural capacity' could also include a mining company searching for mineral deposits in Afghanistan, or an NGO* providing mobile hospital services with access to remote parts of the Philippines where extremists lurk.[11]

Mr Carroll's speculative account of a desirable future for American intelligence sounds uncannily like the way that Russia behaves already. Its energy companies, banks and other commercial, journalistic and academic outfits give it 'natural capacity' of a kind that British or American spymasters for now can only dream of. Ms Chapman's hybrid identity in the West – genuine in every respect but her intentions – fits into that well. But Russia's spymasters have also shown they can use human and financial resources the old-fashioned way, by running deep-cover illegals. It is hard

---

* I think this creates horrific problems for real NGOs and should be off-limits.

to see how Western services can match that, even if they wanted
to. For a couple plucked from Tomsk in the 1980s Soviet Union,
a move to the West under an illegal identity probably seemed like
a good career move – and so it must have appeared to the illegal
'Donald Heathfield' and his wife Ann Foley, who were originally
from Tomsk but who spent twenty years living undercover in the
West. The other way round looks less attractive. It is hard to imagine the CIA recruiting two able graduate students in Wisconsin or
Kansas for a twenty-year mission living undercover in Siberia. Yet
the fact that something is illogical or undesirable from a Western
point of view does not mean that a Russian decision-maker would
see the issue in the same way. Blessed by natural abundance, and
with Soviet-style thinking still lurking in the background, Russia
tends towards extravagant use of resources of all kinds.

The illegals' controllers in Moscow may well have been wasteful in using their assets' costly and carefully designed cover. One
of the illegals in America, 'Cynthia Murphy', was asked to collect
information about the world gold market. Any competent trader
or banker in Moscow could have done that without needing any
clandestine cover. Decision-makers in all countries tend to overes-
timate the value of secret information, Russians more than most. It
may well be that these illegals wasted time satisfying their masters'
fetish for material marked 'secret', which in fact contained little
that was not available from open sources.

Amused complacency, however, is not the media's usual
response to, say, the leak of toxic industrial waste. Even if the
discharge does not prove damaging, it focuses attention on the
physical or procedural flaws that caused it. The arrest of the illegals
showed that American public life was wide open to penetration
and that Russia has put substantial resources over many years into
trying to exploit that weakness. Why was nobody worried? A big
reason was the FBI's clever news management. It is often said that

spies like the shadows. But like any outfit dependent on taxpay-ers' money and politicians' willingness to spend it, intelligence and security services pay careful attention to their image: in their case as mysterious, austere and self-sacrificing guardians of the ultimate national interest. Though they do not hold press conferences or run advertising campaigns, they use nudges and winks, discreet briefings of selected journalists deemed 'sound'; and the occasional release of carefully honed material to the wider public.

This clashes with an operational need: to mislead the other side. Crowing about successes risks endangering sources and methods. Keeping silent about them risks giving an impression of idleness and incompetence. Britain's Secret Intelligence Service (the offi-cial label for MI6) was thrilled to have smuggled Mr Gordievsky to Finland. The temptation to show off a brilliant piece of tradecraft was great. But once you explain how a diplomatic car picked up your fugitive from a remote rural bus stop and took him across the border in a heat-insulated baggage compartment, you will be less likely to pull the trick off again. The same principles apply to disasters. If you are penetrated or betrayed, then owning up to the damage risks giving the other side some clues about what they achieved – and failed to achieve. Some spy services never pros-ecute traitors for just this reason. Those who are caught are quietly retired or shifted to other jobs, leaving the other side guessing whether their asset was blown, or was just the victim of a random bureaucratic shuffle.

It is against this background that all the public information relat-ing to the detained illegals such as Ms Chapman must be judged. The American authorities weighed every line of the criminal complaints they issued against the arrested spies. Clearly, it was necessary to provide enough information to crack the defence of those arrested, leading to an immediate admission of guilt. The American authorities did not want to risk a trial in which FBI agents could have been subject to embarrassing and potentially damaging cross-examination about sources and methods. Another priority was to cause maximum annoyance and confusion to the Russian side, chiefly by making the 'damage control' effort as painful, costly and disruptive as possible. That meant overstating what the American side didn't know, and understating what it did. In the world of mirrors and mind-games, planting doubts is a powerful offensive weapon. Exaggerating the time during which the spies were under surveillance, for example, discredits everything they did in their bosses' eyes. A cardinal principle of intelligence work is that anything provided by a compromised source must itself be considered as compromised. The farther back in history that the taint goes, the bigger is the area of contamination. Similarly, the Americans may not have succeeded in intercepting and decoding everything sent from Ms Chapman's laptop.* But the Russians cannot be sure. If burst transmissions over ad-hoc networks between nearby laptops are hard to monitor then it would be a neat counter-measure to mention them frequently in the criminal complaint. It will be a bold Russian spy who includes them in his operational planning in future. A correctly concocted mixture of overstatement and ambiguity will cast a corrosive cloud over Russian intelligence operations for years.

It is also necessary to understate some bits of a successful operation. If the key to cracking the spy ring was a flaw in Russian tradecraft, it would be a mistake to highlight it: after all, the other side may make the same mistake again. If the vulnerability came from code cracking, that too must be concealed. If the clues came from a penetration agent in Moscow, his welfare must be weighed

---

* Ms Chapman and another junior illegal ferried laptop computers between Russia and America, rather more often than planned because of repeated technical glitches. When they worked, the laptops were used to send clandestine radio transmissions to intelligence officers based at Russian diplomatic missions.

against the need to curb or catch the spies he has betrayed. Is he so valuable, and will he be at such great risk, that he must be exfiltrated before the spycatchers pounce on their quarry or limit his activities? Protecting him may set off alarm bells and send the hostile agents scurrying into hiding. The spycatchers' nightmare is a failure on all fronts: damage done, the horse bolted, and nothing gained.

America's criminal complaints against the illegals were nicely balanced. They trumpeted the Bureau's success, humiliated the Russian side, but gave away rather little about sources and methods. It is not clear, for example, how the FBI obtained the 'was it in Beijing?' code word that one of its agents used to gain the confidence of Mikhail Semenko, a Russian working under his own name in Washington DC. They put heavy emphasis on traditional surveillance: bugging phones, entering premises with a search warrant, looking at safety-deposit boxes. That the FBI can do that will surprise nobody. They highlight what look like some bad mistakes in the Russians' tradecraft. Donald Heathfield's wife had a photographic negative in a safety deposit box that bore a Russian brand name, Tasma (TACMA in Cyrillic). For someone purporting, as she did, to be a Canadian real estate agent, that was a huge breach in a cover story. Another of the illegals is said to have written a vital email password on a bit of paper next to a computer, which was noted by FBI agents during a clandestine visit to the apartment. If these blunders indeed happened, those in the Russian intelligence headquarters in Yasenevo responsible for training illegals will be unpleasantly surprised.* But the FBI may have exaggerated or misleadingly portrayed the slip-ups. During their debriefing sessions the agents may deny having made these

---

* Known as the 'Forest' or the 'Sanatorium', the SVR headquarters is a Finnish-built skyscraper complex in the district of Yasenevo, just south of the Moscow ring-road.

errors. Ideally, both their competence and their loyalty will be questioned.

The complaints published by the American authorities are also interesting for what they do not say. They do not give any detailed account of the illegals' tasking: what were they really trying to do, and how? The overall instruction is to create convincing cover stories: but for what purpose? Heathfield is said to have tried to find out about America's bunker-busting bombs. The complaint alludes indirectly to his attempts to befriend Leon Fuerth, a former senior administration official, and to contacts between 'Cynthia Murphy' and a Democratic Party bigwig (which I cover in more detail in the next chapter). The reader learns a lot – perhaps a surprising amount for those unused to the spy world – about the mechanics of spying: the cover stories, the foreign travel, the code words and the use of laptops. He learns very little about the substance.

The official explanation is that the Russian illegals indeed failed to make any real headway in America. They consumed much of Moscow's money and time, but succeeded only in infiltrating suburbia. A neat twist in this portrayal is that even this bit of the Russians' mission looks unsuccessful. They may have deceived their neighbours, but from the very beginning they were under the eagle-eyed scrutiny of the FBI. Nobody in America needs to feel embarrassed, because no secrets were stolen. That is comforting but not wholly plausible. For a start, the idea that the FBI and its overseas partner agencies would manage (or want) to keep ten people, some of them seasoned intelligence officers, under constant surveillance in multiple countries for a period of many years is fanciful. Even for a well-funded US government agency, the cost in time and money would be colossal. More to the point, it would be risky: a small slip-up would set alarm bells ringing in Moscow and quite possibly lead to the quarry vanishing. It is more likely that only some were under long-term surveillance and that even this was not constant. It is probable that all ten came under complete observation only at the end.

Establishing assets able to move easily in a hostile environment is in itself a major achievement for an intelligence service. Whether they were spotting potential recruitment targets, collecting information, or servicing other agents, the illegals' activities cannot be regarded as harmless or benign. As I show later, even the junior Ms Chapman had previously helped out with a questionable money-transfer operation, involving apparent identity theft and other shenanigans. It is hard to believe that all her counterparts in America were less active. She and Mikhail Semenko were regularly conducting secret communications with Russian intelligence officers. It is unlikely that they were merely exchanging test transmissions or remarks about the weather.

Another factor that may have sanitised the FBI's account of the illegals' activities is the political climate. Anybody who had fallen seriously into the clutches of one of these illegals would be unhappy to have the fact broadcast. Humiliating influential people by highlighting their cooperation with Russian espionage would be a mistake on almost any count. It would make unnecessary enemies – something that an agency with acute political antennae knows to avoid. It would raise the question of whether these individuals should be prosecuted, with all the embarrassment and unwelcome publicity involved. Nor would the FBI see any great need to make an example, assuming such people are dupes, not traitors. The Bureau could just identify the people acting as sources for the illegals and deliver a quiet but sorrowful warning, explaining that they were on a slippery slope that could have all too easily ended up in disgrace or jail. Such a conversation would almost certainly end with an admonition to discuss its content with nobody – a course of action strongly in the interests of both sides. In short: absence of evidence that the illegals were effective is not the same as evidence that they were not.

A second political dimension is US–Russian relations. As noted earlier, for all its shortcomings, the 'reset' is one of the few bits of Mr Obama's foreign policy to have shown any sign of success. Although the White House could not ignore the FBI's evidence of extensive and potentially damaging Russian espionage, it would be quite natural for the country's political leaders to try to limit the wider diplomatic fallout by presenting the illegals as more comic than sinister. Were the public to believe that the spies had done serious harm to the nation's interests, it would be a lot harder to explain why senior figures in the administration saw fit to hobnob so cordially with their Russian counterparts.

For all these reasons, the illegals' arrest was presented to avoid any great sense of alarm or urgency. The message from background briefings was of patronising sorrow rather than anger: it was a pity that Russia still felt the need to play these strange old-fashioned games, both because of what it said about the thinking in Moscow and also because these fossilised spies – sad relics of the old days of superpower rivalry – had achieved so little. Yet as I show in the next chapter, the illegals' activity in America and elsewhere gives no grounds for such complacency.

6

Spies Like Us

Gathered in the same room, Richard and Cynthia Murphy, Donald Heathfield and Anne Foley, Juan Lazaro, Vicky Peláez, Michael Zottoli and Patricia Mills, Mikhail Semenko and Anna Chapman would have seemed like a bunch of unremarkable Americans. They spoke English fluently, with varying accents; they had jobs ranging from the humdrum to the glamorous. Their neighbours and work colleagues noticed nothing extraordinary about them. But when they did meet for the first time, it was in a courtroom, shortly before their deportation to Russia. The ten were at the centre of the FBI's most spectacular and successful counter-intelligence operation for decades: Operation Ghost Stories. According to the American authorities' criminal complaints, they and persons unknown

unlawfully, wilfully and knowingly, did combine, conspire, confederate, and agree together and with each other to commit an offense against the United States.

It stated that the FBI's investigation has revealed that

a network of illegals is now living and operating in the United States in the service of one primary, long-term goal: to become sufficiently

Americanized, such that they can gather information about the
United States for Russia, and can successfully recruit sources who
are in, or are able to infiltrate, United States policy-making circles.[1]

Richard and Cynthia Murphy lived in the New York suburb of
Montclair.[2] She had two undergraduate degrees from New York
University and an MBA from Columbia Business School, and she
worked in a financial services firm in New York. Her stocky, bearded
husband had studied economics at the New School in New York,
where his heavy accent and gloomy manner aroused only mild curiosity. Nina Khrushcheva, his Soviet-born supervisor, was puzzled by
his claim to be of Irish extraction; to her well-tuned ear he sounded
'instantly Russian'.[3] But America is built on the idea that people
can reinvent themselves, shedding identities from the old world and
adopting new ones. Murphy was no different. Nothing else he did
seemed to arouse any interest at all. As far as any outsider could
see his main job was caring for the couple's young daughters Katie
and Lisa, aged eleven and seven in June 2010. That was when their
parents – real names Vladimir and Lidiya Guryev – were arrested.

Murphy's mission in America was unexciting, ferrying cash
to other illegals. His wife had a more glamorous life at Morea
Financial Services, a specialist tax firm dealing with the rich and
famous. That was a perfect cover for her clandestine mission, to
befriend wealthy Americans with political connections – including Alan Patricof, a close friend of Hillary Clinton. According to
the criminal complaint issued by the Department of Justice, Mrs
Murphy's bosses in Moscow described Mr Patricof as:

a very interesting 'target'. Try to build up little by little relations with him moving beyond just [work]* framework. Maybe

---

* Square brackets signify material redacted by the FBI before the complaint was
made public.

he can provide [MURPHY] with remarks re US foreign policy, 'roumors' [sic] about White House internal 'kitchen', invite her to venues (to [major political party HQ in NYC], for instance) etc. In short, consider carefully all options in regard to [financier].[4]

Two more of the illegals were equally unremarkable. Michael Zottoli and Patricia Mills (real names Mikhail Kutsik and Natalya Pereverzeva) studied and worked in Seattle before moving to Arlington, Virginia. Their task, as reported by the FBI, was also little more than to ferry sums of money around between other agents. The supposedly Uruguayan-born Juan Lazaro (Mikhail Vasenkov) was a 'bag man' too, bringing money from an unnamed South American country to America, apparently in collaboration with his wife, a radical Peruvian journalist called Vicky Peláez. His illegal mission had started in 1976.[5] It clearly included some spying, as this bugged exchange from 2003, involving his wife's trip to an unnamed South American country, indicates.

Lazaro: When you go . . . I am going to write in invisible [ink] and you're going to pass them all of that in a book.
Peláez: Oh, OK.
Lazaro: I'm going to give you some blank pieces of paper and it will be there . . . about every thing I've done . . .[6]

It is easy to mock the pointlessness of these people, apparently the least serious of the illegals, sent at vast trouble and expense to a foreign country in order to carry out tasks that most people manage with a mouse click. But it is not a laughing matter.[7]

By far the most serious of the spies in terms of intellectual fire-power and access to decision-makers in America and elsewhere was Andrei Bezrukov, who lived in Cambridge, Massachusetts under the alias of Donald Howard Heathfield, with his wife Yelena

Vavilova (Tracey Lee Ann Foley). The elder of their two sons, Tim, was a student at Georgetown University in Washington, DC. Ms Foley was a real-estate broker. Her website carried convincing if fictional pabulum, describing her as:

> a native of Montreal [who] lived and was educated in Switzerland, Canada and France. Prior to her career in real estate she worked as a Human Resources officer in Toronto and ran her own travel agency in Cambridge, Massachusetts that specialised in organising trips to French wine regions for small groups of enthusiasts. Ann's cultural awareness and international experience make her sensitive to the needs of other people. She strives for excellence in everything she does. Ann succeeds through her ability to ensure quality service, honesty and integrity. You will appreciate Ann's enthusiasm and commitment to make sure that your real estate goal becomes a reality.
>
> Ann resides in Cambridge with her husband and two teenage sons. She and her family are fond of travel. They have enjoyed visiting much of Europe but are particularly in love with Asia. Ann also appreciates gourmet food, ballet and spending time with her children.[8]

Her husband's cover story was similar: bland and at least superficially convincing. Months after his deportation, his website www.futuremap.com was still promoting his consultancy firm's expertise:

> Future Map Institute is [sic] global think-tank focusing on creating practical policy proposals (strategies) for dealing with most pressing problems. It collectively maps anticipated developments in a number of domains and tracks their evolution. The institute relies on the network of on-line collaborators and organises virtual conferences on critical issues.[9]

Behind this waffle was a serious mission. Heathfield, in the view of American officials close to the case, was by far the most important of the spies they had under surveillance. His cover story gave him an entry into the highest levels of American business, academia and government, and a convincing reason for seeking the inner-most thoughts of the people at the top of any organisation. For Heathfield's career was only partly phoney. Although he used the stolen birth certificate of a Canadian baby who died in 1963, his qualifications were genuine. He had indeed studied international economics at York University in Toronto,[10] earned a master's degree in public administration from Harvard's John F. Kennedy School and worked as a management consultant.

His striking quality was blandness: not one of the dozen or so associates I have quizzed can remember a distinctive quirk, foible or habit that made him stand out. He was bilingual in French and English (although with a faint accent in both). He joined professional bodies on his own merits, and networked assidu-ously with alumni, colleagues and other business associates. For Heathfield did not just pretend to be a management expert: he actually became one. He is probably the only spy in history to write an academic paper as part of his cover story. It appears as a chapter in *Scenarios for Success*,[11] a collection of papers originally presented at a 'Future Studies' meeting in Oxford in 2005. One of the editors of the volume, Bill Sharpe, recalls a colleague 'deeply involved in the subject' and a friendly and collaborative editing process[12] that mainly involved the 'debranding' of Heathfield's work – in other words removing the frequent references to his trademarked 'FutureMap' decision-mapping software. Piquantly, Heathfield seems to have become rather fond of his assumed iden-tity. 'I know it was his cover but it bled through the surface and got into his soul,' says a former associate.[13] Since his return to Russia, he has tried to reknit the shreds of his reputation. His profile on LinkedIn, a business-networking site, has been updated with his new job, as an adviser to the chief executive of Rosneft, an oil company with close ties to the Kremlin.[14] But it also gives a fragment of his real life: five years studying history at the Tomsk State University, from 1978 to 1983 (though what he did between graduating and appearing in Canada in 1992 remains a mystery).*

Aficionados of 'Future Studies' believe that it offers organisations useful tools for analysing the future. Critics dismiss it as 'bullshitology' – a caricature of management expertise, laden with buzzwords, clichés and impenetrable jargon, both sententious and unfalsifiable. But in a country like America where management expertise is a kind of lay priesthood, its practice gave Heathfield access to the secrets of the confessional. When Bill Sharpe heard of Heathfield's arrest, he realised what 'jolly good cover' his contributor's role would have been:

> Once you're in an organisation doing that kind of work they give you absolutely everything . . . they put you in touch with other people in the area, take you to meetings. They share all their thinking.

Another business associate says Heathfield's sales pitch, always to people at the top, was, in effect, 'I have created a black box that helps you mitigate risk and plan for the future.' They merely had to tell him their secrets and fears. Heathfield's software product was professionally designed by a reputable company at substantial cost. But was it any good? Like much other expensive material bought by business executives, the data produced by Heathfield's software may have been less a real tool for decision-making than

---

* I contacted Heathfield via LinkedIn, offering him a chance to review this chapter and give his comments. He replied by giving an email address, but never downloaded the file I sent him.

ammunition for boardroom battles. Among the experts he showed it to was Yaneer Bar-Yam, a physicist and the founding president of the New England Complex Systems Institute, who politely describes it as a 'working prototype' rather than a breakthrough:

> The specifics of the model he showed me were more of a conceptual sketch than an implementation of fundamental mathematics . . . a mock-up – on the lines of 'this is what it would look like if it works'. It's another thing to have something that really works.[15]

Stripped of its jargon, the software pictured priorities and approaches inside an organisation, with the aim of getting people with different viewpoints to work together. Heathfield's intern, who used the software for a university project, remembers it less than fondly:

> It had very few capabilities – it was essentially a long-range calendar with a few bells and whistles. We were students and wanted to appease our professor, so we used it in a study on the hydrogen economy[16] . . . it didn't have much utility. The interface was impossible: buggy, jerky, hard to zoom in and out.[17]

Despite its flaws, the software may have been designed to provide its promoter, not its users, with insights. Jerome Glenn of the Millennium Project, a UN-linked outfit that ponders the future with help from forty 'nodes' around the world, recalls meeting Heathfield exhibiting his software at a conference in 2007. Keen to see his product used at the prestigious project, Heathfield offered it free of charge. Mr Glenn also found it unsatisfactory and did not want to spend time learning to use it. Heathfield was indefatigable, returning every two or three weeks to press his case and ultimately offering to provide an intern, whom he paid $500 a month in order to promote the software inside the project. Even that was not enough to clinch the deal.

But his consulting work provided a good vantage point. 'It's a smart strategy to monitor the think tanks that monitor global change,' says Mr Glenn. Had he known that Heathfield was a Russian he would have taken immediate steps to have the software checked, he says.[18] The advantages for a spy of having a proprietory programme installed on important people's computers in places ranging from Iran (where the Millennium Project has a 'node') to Beijing barely need stating. Even if the software is initially innocuous, an 'update' can deliver a piece of malware (malign code) that could copy emails, search a computer or a network for key-words, upload files to a remote server, or steal passwords. Leaving electronic espionage aside, Heathfield's work also provided a laissez-passer to business, academia and government. A case study cited in his published chapter involved:

a group of graduate students at the Elliott School of International Affairs at George Washington University working under the guidance of Leon Fuerth, a research professor and former National Security Advisor to Vice President Gore. The concept of 'Forward Engagement' put forth by Professor Fuerth focuses on identifying major future contingencies that are likely to affect the long-term future of the United States. Those contingencies, from the aging of the US population to catastrophic terrorist acts, have important implications across multiple domains, from environment and energy to international relations. Dealing with those contingencies will require a proactive forward engagement by the US government. In order to make legislators aware of the implications of these major societal developments and to build the momentum for appropriate decisions among the public, a 'big picture' of future challenges must be constructed first.[19]

It is easy to see how useful such access would be. Students involved in such a project would be prime recruitment targets: the sort of people likely to move onwards and upwards in America's defence, security and foreign policy establishment. Faculty members at Georgetown would also be well worth getting to know, in order to tap their past government experience – or their future roles. Mr Fuerth is a well-connected figure in Washington, DC. His version of events is as follows:

Heathfield introduced himself to me at the conclusion of a speech that I gave at a public meeting in Washington. He expressed his interest in the subject of Forward Engagement, presented himself as an entrepreneur vending his own software for long-range assessment in corporations, and requested an opportunity to see me to continue the discussion. We met from time to time, whenever – as he claimed – he was in Washington on business. He volunteered to let my students work with his software to see if it helped their assignment for my class. His description of the work that my students were doing looks accurate. However, as I recall, their judgment was that, while the concept of Heathfield's software was interesting, the software itself had very limited capabilities insofar as their end-of-semester project was concerned.

Heathfield's personality was low-key and friendly, and he appeared to be seriously interested in the subject of foresight and how to develop and use it. Eventually, however, I learned that he was presenting himself as someone who had played an important role in developing Forward Engagement. At that point, I made it clear that this should stop, and he dropped out of touch. Heathfield is not and never was a 'partner.' He was one of many persons with parallel interests, whom I have gotten to know as the result of my work in this field . . . Heathfield played no part in the development of these ideas.[20]

Mr Fuerth may well have had little time for Heathfield. But the Russian spy's bosses were clearly interested in Mr Fuerth. He appears to be the person named as 'Cat' in encrypted communications to Heathfield from the Moscow headquarters of Russia's Foreign Intelligence Service. They encouraged him to continue cultivating the source.[21] However in this case the main role played by Mr Fuerth and the George Washington University may have been in bolstering Heathfield's credentials, rather than in active intelligence gathering. His long-term mission may have been to move closer to the national-security world – always the prime target in Russian eyes. Professor William Halal of Techcast, a forecasting outfit, used to see Heathfield regularly during his frequent trips to Washington, DC. 'He tried to meet anyone who was doing anything of consequence,' he recalls.[22] Heathfield also discussed with him a planned move to the American capital, with every sign of seriousness. That would have given him better access to companies that sell defence- and intelligence-related products and services. But the most tempting target could have been the think-tank world: the soft under-belly of the American security and intelligence community, where retired officials, those hoping for jobs, and those taking a break from government mix and mingle with outsiders.

Heathfield's efforts were not just in America. His intern recalls, 'He was always travelling – I had no idea how he was funded – back and forth between Singapore, Boston and Canada.' His website also suggests partners in China, including with the Chinese Academy of Social Sciences, an influential government think tank, with the Beijing Academy of Soft Technologies[23] and an outfit called Chinagreenfuture.[24] Emails to these organisations asking for details of Heathfield's involvement in their activities went unanswered but the connection was strong: his elder son interned in China in 2008.

Clearly part of Mr Heathfield's image was simple invention. He cites in the 'resources' section of his myfuturemap.com website a reputable firm of business coaches called Coachinc.com. Asked to confirm Mr Heathfield's claimed connection, the CEO, Sandy Vilas, replied immediately: 'Never heard of him.'[25] But chasing down other leads presents a more complex picture. In a lengthy presentation about Futuremap's virtues at an event in Singapore sponsored by the local French Chamber of Commerce, Heathfield's local partner Fabrizio Battaglia used a slide giving the logo of nine well-known international companies, including ABB, Alstom, AT&T and T-Mobile.[26] Heathfield's own website says that he has worked with big companies such as 'General Electric, AREVA, Boston Scientific, Ericsson, Motorola, Microsoft, Michelin, Philips, STMicroelectronics, SAP, T-Mobile, and United Technologies.'[27]

Most of these companies replied that they could not trace any connection with Mr Heathfield. (Mr Battaglia did not respond to repeated requests for comment.) Among the exceptions was ST Microelectronics, which confirmed that its 'internal educational organisation', ST University, 'occasionally collaborated' with Global Partners (a reputable Boston-based firm where Heathfield used to work) for sales and marketing courses involving him as an 'external consultant'. It insists that it never bought his software or hired him directly, 'nor was the relationship . . . of any signifi-cance in duration or value'.[28] The France-based international utilities firm Veolia was the only firm to acknowledge a serious connection. It hired Heathfield to design strategy and speak at management training events. Benoit Bardon, who worked with him closely for six years, recalls a 'smart guy' with 'brilliant meth-odology' who showed no interest in intelligence-related matters. Gerard Bridi, an American-based consultant who worked closely with Heathfield (and endorsed him on his LinkedIn profile) says that he typically charged his clients $3,000 a day.

A bit of puffery is not unusual in the self-promoting world of consultancy. It is also understandable that huge companies, with operations in dozens of countries, find it hard to say whether a particular consultant has or has not been hired at any point over the past fifteen years. But two points stand out. One is how easy it is for a plausible and well-educated person to disguise phoney origins and appear to be a genuine expert. The other is how much damage can be done by allowing such a person access to the inner workings of companies that are involved in defence contracting, energy security, communications and the like. The most likely modus operandi for someone like Heathfield is to recruit sources as unwitting collaborators with Russian intelligence. His consultancy job allowed him to ask well-placed sources to write occasional background reports for anonymous consulting 'clients', in exchange for a lucrative fee or well-padded per diem payments. He needed to make no mention that the result was going to a foreign government, let alone to Russia.

It may help the reader to picture three possible examples of such an approach. Imagine yourself to be an influential American – perhaps a senior partner in a professional-services firm with a client list that includes government agencies and big companies. How suspicious would you be of an intelligent and attractive woman assigned to help with your taxes, who shows a flattering interest in your political connections? Or of a brainy, jargon-spouting consultant wanting to future-proof your business? Or of a plausible-seeming fellow-alumnus who networks assiduously at events that you attend? Most likely, they are all just what they seem. But any of those three could be an illegal, working for Russia, China or some other country, trying to make you a witting or unwitting ally in their attempt to steal secrets and exert influence.

For specific targets of direct national-security importance, someone claiming to be an American citizen (or British, or from another

NATO member) may find it marginally easier to gain trust speedily. But in other respects Heathfield's elaborately acquired illegal
identity – a Canadian citizen with a stellar professional career – was
unnecessary, and even a hindrance. One of the appealing aspects
of Western society is that employers and business associates tend
to take the people they deal with on trust. If someone is charm-
ing, brainy and effective, those characteristics will matter far more
than whether they hail from Tomsk or Toronto. Had Heathfield
started his mission twenty years later, his bosses could have sent
him to Canada quite legally on a student visa. From there he would
have gone to the Kennedy School, and finally moved into consulting, without breaking any law or needing any clandestine connection, other than perhaps a wealthy 'relative' in Russia to pay the
bills. He could even have changed his name, as many immigrants
to North America do, from the hard-to-pronounce Bezrukov to
something easier: Heathfield, perhaps. Much if not all of his assiduous networking and self-promotion would have followed an all but
identical path. He might still be living in Cambridge, Massachusetts
today, rather than working in Russia as a consultant to an oil
company. Indeed in some respects his cover story may even have
been positively harmful. Some of his former associates say that they
would have been more forthcoming had they known he worked
for the Russian government: they found his relentless commercial-
ism rather off-putting. Professor Bar-Yam, for example, who had
previously found Heathfield's software commendable if flawed,
says his reaction to the spy scandal was 'very neutral':

So Russia was sending people to learn about local culture? You
might see it as a cultural exchange. I am not sure that's a bad thing.
If there's conflict between countries it is very important that there
is an exchange of information to bring broader understanding.[29]

An illegal identity also has the great weakness of all complex plots: just one loose end can unravel the whole deception. A former student of Tomsk University, now living in America, remembers the couple clearly from the early 1980s: 'Lena' (who later became Heathfield's wife 'Ann Foley') was a ballet-loving young woman, who had studied at the city's prestigious German-language high school and toured Japan with a Soviet tourist group. That was a striking privilege at a time when travel to capitalist countries was restricted to the best-connected, and was especially rare for those living in strategically important 'closed cities' such as Tomsk – these were places quarantined by the KGB, where visits by foreigners where banned, and whose inhabitants were generally prohibited from visiting countries in the 'capitalist camp'.

Bezrukov transferred to a university in Moscow – an unusual move up the Soviet academic ladder that indicated powerful sponsorship. When the communist world was almost hermetically sealed from the capitalist one, it was highly unlikely that any tendril of an illegal's old life would appear to trip up the new one. The chance of Tomsk alumni meeting in Cambridge, Massachusetts was about as likely as an encounter on the moon. Yet the erstwhile fellow-student[30] could easily have bumped into Heathfield and his wife on the street. Denial would be risky, explanations even more so. It might force the controllers in Moscow to abort the whole mission, ending a decade or more of meticulous and costly work.

Technology and the internet create problems for old-style illegals too. Spycatchers in Britain used to wonder why Soviet block embassy staff showed such interest in cemeteries and country churchyards. Eventually the penny dropped: they were looking for the gravestones of dead children, in order to obtain their birth certificates and then apply for passports, driving licences etc. But the scope for this is shrinking. Biometric data are unique to each individual. Birth and death registries are increasingly computerised.

Google makes tracing connections easier. In Heathfield's case, a news announcement in the Canadian press in 2005 of the death of his 'father', Howard William Heathfield, also mentioned that the real infant Donald had predeceased him. Had the phoney 'Donald' already been under suspicion, the death notice could have given a dangerous clue to an alert spycatcher.

Fashioning a fake identity that fools a layman is one thing. Creating one that generates a real passport and other documents is harder. But providing an alias that will withstand determined scrutiny – for example of the kind carried out on an applicant for a security clearance – is now formidably difficult. The slightest anomaly or flaw becomes fatal. For this reason, the best penetration agents are not illegals but traitors: people like Kim Philby, a blue-blooded trueborn Englishman who decided at university to devote his life to the communist cause, and simply waited until SIS hired him.[31] Herman Simm was at least in his own eyes in the same category. But traitors cannot be ordered up at will. Instead, Russia's spymasters are turning to a new and more potent category of illegal. Unlike Heathfield and his colleagues, they do not rely on stolen identities. They use their own.

7

The New Illegals

The clearest traces of this new echelon of Russian spies (one might call them the 'legal illegals') were left by Ms Chapman and the rather less glamorous (but more impressive) Mikhail Semenko, a fluent Mandarin speaker who worked at a travel agency but hung around Washington think tanks. Like Heathfield, Semenko maintained a profile on the business networking site LinkedIn.[1] This gives his genuine Russian academic credentials, from Amur State University and the Harbin Institute of Technology in China, as well as his American alma mater, Seton Hall. It describes him, in convincing resumé-speak, as a:

> highly creative and analytical professional with recent education and diverse experience involving development assistance, meeting and event planning, partnership building, and high-level client relations. Natural leader and communicator with in-depth knowledge of government policy research, program management, international negotiations, and delivery of formal public speaking presentations.
>
> Solid history of success creating new public policy events, expanding program participation and membership, and establishing connections between diverse cultures. Multilingual with native

expertise in Russian, fluency in English, Mandarin Chinese, and Spanish, and intermediate skills in German and Portuguese.

It lists his interests in 'non-profits, think tanks, public policy, advocacy and educational institutions' and his specialities as: 'International Relations, Foreign Policy Analysis; Program and Project Management; Policy Research and Writing; Senior Executive Council Coordination; Marketing and Sales Management; Membership Recruitment Initiatives; Client and Public Relations.' Like Heathfield, Semenko constructed a suitable web presence, marketing his expertise with an enjoyable and interesting blog on the Chinese economy. In mid 2011 it was still available at china-economytoday.wordpress.com. It describes him as 'an expert in Chinese economic policy' with fluent Mandarin and 'Rusian' [sic], available for translation and consulting. The last blog entry, on 24 June 2010 (just before the spy scandal broke) was a thoughtful piece about the undervaluation of the Chinese currency. Two days earlier, an interesting posting dealt with Chinese business manners; before that came a witty piece about the mangled 'Chinglish' of confident but inexpert Chinese English-speakers. Semenko matched Heathfield in audacity, but lagged behind him in other respects. Whereas Heathfield, two decades his senior, hobnobbed with the big beasts of American business and government, Semenko moved in a lower orbit, impressing people with his youthful eagerness rather than his expertise. But even in the wonkish world of Washington, people who speak both Russian and Mandarin fluently are thin on the ground. Semenko's mission, according to a decrypted message from his bosses in Moscow, was to 'search and develop ties in policymaking circles'.[2] That would have presumably meant gaining a job in a think tank and then perhaps in government, where he could have worked as a passive or even an active asset. At some point he, like many other foreigners working in

America, would have swapped his H1B visa (issued to highly quali-
fied foreign workers) for a Green Card and then American citizenship. That creates an important line of defence for a spymaster. A
detailed background check would have exposed Heathfield as a
fraud. He had stolen a dead baby's birth certificate. But a similar
check on Semenko, whether or not he eventually became a US
citizen, would have produced nothing incriminating. His account
of himself was not untrue. It was just not the whole truth.

Semenko was recruited at university and trained during gaps
in his academic career. Had he grown up in a country where
co-workers and fellow-students could be quizzed, and foreign
travel records scrutinised, he would have been left dangerously
open to discovery. A Finnish, Indian or Brazilian student would
find it hard to explain or conceal frequent trips to Russia. But it
is all but impossible to check out the credentials of someone like
Semenko, who divided his time between his native Russia and
China. If such a Russian says he spent a summer at a relative's
dacha when in fact he was at spy school, how will the bureaucrat
ticking the boxes on his American security clearance spot it? Had
Semenko become an American citizen, discriminating against him
on grounds of origin would have been offensive and possibly illegal. Only a Western penetration agent inside Russia's own security
and intelligence apparatus would have been able to uncover him.
As we will see, that seems to have been the case – on this occasion.

But even Semenko's entry-level spying activities are worth
analysing. Among the think tanks he targeted was the American
Foreign Policy Council.[3] This is a small, hawkish outfit, which
has a long (and in my view admirable) record of contradicting the
consensus among Washington-based Russia-watchers. One of its
Russia experts until recently was J. Michael Waller, a proponent
of the theory that the former KGB retained influence in Russia
after the Soviet collapse, and returned to power with Mr Putin in

1999.[4] Another is Ilan Berman, an expert on Russian links with Iran and the Muslim world, and a consultant to both the CIA and the Pentagon. Keeping an eye on those in America who truly understand Russia may be more valuable than more overt Kremlin activities (discussed in previous chapters) such as peddling propaganda that all is well, and soft-soaping those who believe it.

On 26 June an undercover FBI agent made contact with Semenko, pretending to be a Russian intelligence officer. The exchange (initially in Russian) went: 'Could we have met in Beijing in 2004' to which Semenko replied: 'Yes we might have but I believe it was in Harbin'. This was no casual chat: the FBI agent was using a code-word to establish his credentials. Semenko's response showed that he had accepted the American's bona fides. The FBI agent then asserted that the most recent data swap on 5 June between Semenko's laptop and that of a Russian official had failed. He admonished Semenko to take more care of the 'sensitive' equipment. Semenko then accepted a package containing $5,000, which the FBI agent told him to take to a dead drop at a park in Arlington the next day. He did so and was arrested shortly afterwards.

A far snazzier version of Semenko was, of course, Ms Chapman.* Her career took her via an unwitting English husband, Alexander, to the glitziest nightclubs in London and New York, and a social life that has attracted prurient attention[5] from the tabloid newspapers, not least when he sold topless pictures taken during their marriage. But the revelation that a young Russian woman has not

---

* I made repeated attempts to gain Ms Chapman's side of the story for this book. I received two messages in return from her Facebook account. One read: 'How can you possibly write a book without 1 decent article in press that is based on some what [sic] true facts? No interview, no nothing . . .' The other noted: 'I was the one who suffered and you will be the one to gain? :)' I responded: 'I hope my book will sell well but even if I win a Pulitzer prize (which I won't) you will always be more famous than me!' I received no answer to this, or to an extensive list of questions.

only breasts but a sex life is news only by the standards of the popular press. Her cover story was utterly convincing: a young Russian
who marries a British man, working first in banking, then in an
executive jet company, and then in real estate. These are all jobs
that can be useful for an intelligence service. But nothing about
her personal or professional life distinguished her from hundreds of
thousands of other young women from the ex-communist world
who head abroad in search of fame, fortune, marriage and travel.

Later on I plot her meteoric career on her return to Russia. A
convenient first point of analysis of her career before that is her entry
on LinkedIn.[6] Like those of her colleagues it is an artful mixture of
truth, exaggeration and outright falsehood. She was born in Russia
and speaks English fluently, with a mild accent that disguises her indif-
ferent grammar.[7] She also claims conversational German and basic
French. After that, it gets more complicated. Illegals commonly set up
an identity in one country and then use it as a springboard for a more
effective and espionage-focused life in another one. Ms Chapman
built up an English CV and gained a real passport by marrying a
British citizen, before moving on. It is unclear who paid for her jet-
setting lifestyle: certainly not her work as a personal assistant or as a
humble banking adviser. Southern Union, a company with which
she was associated, may have provided some. She says she received a
grant from a Russian government fund that supports start-ups. This
may have been a disguised payment from Russian intelligence.

She returned to Moscow in 2006 to try to set up a Western-
style real-estate company called domdot.ru. She describes it as a
'search engine in real estate for [sic] Russian speaking audience'
and her own role as 'running all aspects of business, setting strategy
for development, international expansion, people management,
investors reporting.' Business contacts who had email dealings
with her say she made an unremarkable but professional impression.[8] But it seems to have got nowhere. She then moved to New

York, where it is unclear if her business idea, a property search engine called NYCRentals.com, was part of a cover story or a real business. The business plan on its website was written in careless, Russian-inflected English that would have inspired little confidence among potential investors:

By specialising on narrow region it will allow for a system to gather not only information about letting but also create rich with information database with building, city infrastructure, other useful and relevant for choosing real estate to live area specifics.[9]

A video interview she gave about it for an entrepreneurship event in New York was notably light on content and heavy on flirting with the camera.[10] Plans were not far advanced: she bought the NYCRentals.com website only on 22 June 2010, for $25,350.[11] Her private life, however, was another matter. Former friends in New York describe her as a hard-partying and insatiable networker. Among her conquests was a multi-millionaire businessman from New Jersey, more than twice her age. The *New York Post* called her a

flame-haired 007-worthy beauty who flitted from high-profile parties to top secret meetings around Manhattan [with] a fancy Financial District apartment and a Victoria's Secret body.[12]

She seems to have come on to the spycatchers' radar quite late in the story. The FBI says that on 'approximately ten Wednesdays' in the first half of 2010, Ms Chapman used a laptop to exchange clandestine messages with a Russian government official.* On one

---

* In fact an intelligence officer based at the Russian mission to the United Nations in New York, under the diplomatic cover of 'second secretary'. It appears that most if not all the illegals were run from the Russian mission in New York, not from the embassy in Washington, DC.

occasion the official drove a minivan past the coffee shop, long enough for Ms Chapman to send a burst transmission from her laptop to a computer in his car. On another, she was inside a bookshop while the official was passing near by. On a third occasion, the official appears to have noticed that he was under surveillance and aborted the mission. The same official had already been spotted carrying out a brush-pass with one of the other illegals in 2004: it is likely that he led the FBI to Ms Chapman, not vice versa.

In the curious sting operation that followed, an FBI undercover agent posing as an intelligence officer based at the Russian consolate made contact with Ms Chapman, saying that he urgently needed to meet her. As with Semenko, he used a series of pass-phrases to establish his credentials, claiming to be called 'Ilya Fabrichnikov' – a code name that she had previously been given from her controllers in Moscow. She was willing to discuss the technical problems she was having with her computer and hand it over to be repaired; she also agreed to a second meeting at which she would be given a passport in a false name which she was to pass on to another female illegal. On 26 June, a Saturday, the FBI man called Ms Chapman again, saying that he needed to meet with her that day. She phoned back and asked if the meeting could be postponed until the next morning but then changed her mind and agreed to meet that afternoon. She seems to have made little attempt to check his bona fides, and discussed both her technical problems and her Wednesday electronic hook-ups. Mr 'Fabrichnikov' (evidently a native Russian-speaker, although the pair spoke English later in the conversation) then asked her if she would be willing to pass on the document, saying: 'There is a person here who is just like you . . . but unlike you she is not here under her real name . . . we have to give her new documents . . . are you ready for this next step?' Ms Chapman replied:

'Shit, of course.' She received the false passport, a description of its intended recipient and instructions about how to recognise her. Ms Chapman was to ask: 'Excuse me, but haven't we met in California last summer?' The other party would reply: 'No, I think it was the Hamptons.' Ms Chapman handed over her faulty computer.[13]

This was all oddly hurried behaviour by the FBI. It strongly suggests that the American officials had to force the pace, probably because their source in Moscow had bolted, and would soon be missed. Ms Chapman belatedly had second thoughts about the meeting. She hurried to a pharmacy and then to a mobile phone shop where she bought a cell-phone and two international calling cards. She took only limited anti-surveillance measures, the thorough ones that would be expected from a well-trained intelligence officer who realises that the hunt is on. She phoned her father in Moscow, to be told that a senior SVR officer dealing with the illegals had disappeared. That was oddly sloppy tradecraft. So was giving palpably fake identity details on the customer agreement, where she described herself as 'Irine Kutsov' of '99 Fake St'. A cardinal principle of undercover work is to tell no unnecessary falsehoods and shun any indulgence in humour. A simple 'Jane Smith' and an unremarkable but illegible scribble for the address would have been more consistent with the professionalism normally expected of one of the oldest and savviest spy services in the world. Evidently alarmed, the next day she went to a police station in Manhattan and handed in the passport – apparently claiming that she had been given it in error. When FBI officials arrived they arrested her.

But whom had they caught? Anna Vasilyevna Kushchenko was born on 'Defender of the Fatherland Day', 23 February 1982. Her grandfather was a Cossack, her father in the KGB and her favourite children's story was a bombastic Soviet fable called 'The Tale of the Military Secret'.[14] She enjoyed acting it out, making her grandmother play the role of the hateful 'bourgeois', who tortures a little boy to make him confess the 'hidden secret' of the Red Army (which is, of course, the inspirational power of communism). By the time she was ten that world had collapsed, and with it the prison-like constraints it imposed on its inmates. Ms Chapman's generation had the world in front of them. One childhood friend, Elena Slesarenko, went on to win an Olympic gold medal in 2004. Another classmate is said to have ended up in Japan as a successful model. Ms Chapman's interests turned abroad too. At the age of sixteen, as the film *Titanic* came out in Russia, she penned a drawing of its star Leonardo DiCaprio so popular with her classmates that she and her sister earned pocket money selling photocopies.

When Ms Chapman was thirteen her father Vasily was posted back to Africa, while she stayed behind in Volgograd with her grandparents. Her grandfather was ill and the young teenager learned a toughness and self-reliance that would later stand her in good stead. In a chaotic and poverty-stricken country, she yearned for the comfort and glamour of life in the West. A song that epitomises those years – enough for Mr Medvedev to be caught on video clumsily dancing to it over two decades later – is the 1990 'American Boy' by the girl-band *Kombinatsiya*.[15] When Ms Chapman told a school friend, Valeriya Apanasenko, 'I'll find myself a husband in England, I'll go there and live there,' she was at least unconsciously reflecting its stilted and saccharine English lyrics, which bemoan the lot of a 'simple Russian girl', who has never been abroad and is waiting for her 'foreign prince' to whisk her away to a world of luxury.

Her first stop was Ramneki, a smart Moscow suburb, where she lived before a stint with her family in Zimbabwe. She was not a star pupil: her mother Irina, a former teacher, describes her as having 'solid Bs'. None the less, perhaps thanks to her father's professional connections, she was able to study at the University of People's Friendship in Moscow, a shabby but trendy establishment known since Soviet days for its lively social scene and large numbers of students from developing countries. But this was just a staging post. Aged 19, she met the 21-year-old Alex Chapman at a rave in London's Docklands in the summer of 2001. The English boy came to Moscow while she finished her studies. In March 2002 they married in a civil ceremony. Ms Chapman told a friend that she had married her husband in order to obtain a British passport (it was later cancelled by the authorities). That is in itself not a sign of an intelligence connection: Ms Chapman would not be the first Russian woman to marry a gullible foreigner in the hope of acquiring his nationality and name. The couple lived in the unglamorous inner-London district of Stoke Newington.[16] According to her own account of her life, Ms Chapman worked at a hedge fund, Navigator Asset Management. People recall that she partied hard, often in the company of rich nightclubbers. Her boss, Nicholas Camilleri, described her later as a 'green, wet behind the ears' type of girl.[17] She then moved briefly to a junior job at NetJets, a company that provides executive jet services to wealthy customers. Ms Chapman claims that she was:

- Primarily involved in selling private jets to companies and individuals in Russia
- Conducting research on East European markets, keeping updated on territory social events and business news, participated and helped organise NetJets European marketing events
- High-end client interaction, targeting Senior Executives and key decision makers within multi-national global organisations and wealthy individuals
- Cold-calling prospects based on research obtained from industry sources

- Developing proposals and formulating documentation in line with client requirements
- Working to timescales as set by the client, with a sales cycle of between one week and one year, depending on the complexity of sale
- Post-sales relations to ensure smooth running of processes, involving customer service problem-solving

For a three-month stint in a junior position, some might think that was on the effusive side. If Ms Chapman was even on the books of the SVR at this point, her main role was probably acquiring cover, with a view to some serious spying later on. But the people who use executive jets are often of interest to intelligence services; bugging their conversations, for example, would require placing and removing a recording device on an aircraft. It might also be useful simply to know who was travelling with whom, and where. The same applies to her next job, as an adviser in the small business division of a branch of Barclays Bank in Ealing, west London. Ms Chapman's LinkedIn profile refers caustically to her post as 'slave' – and also places it in the more glamorous-sounding investment banking division of Barclays Capital.

But slaves can be good spies. Understanding how the rules work inside an organisation helps those wanting to bend or break them. Even a junior bank employee may be able, for example, to make credit checks. That would be handy for the SVR's N-line department (which establishes identities for illegals). It needs to see if its work is accumulating the right degree of solidity. It could also help evade or manipulate 'know your customer' requirements: useful for anyone needing to establish a bank account in a hurry. A lowly employee may also have access to customers' account details, meaning that such a person could see if potential targets for recruitment had money worries. (If Barclays has kept logs of

Ms Chapman's activities, spycatchers may find them rewarding subjects of enquiry.) A glaring instance of resume padding came in a Russian television interview where Ms Chapman claimed to have worked for the billionaire Warren Buffett (who indeed owns Netjets but was hardly her boss).[18] In fact, her experience of the overlap between spycraft and finance was of a different, less prestigious and more troubling kind.

Despite her unremarkable professional career, Ms Chapman was fast ascending the London social ladder. Her marriage came under increasing strain and the couple parted in 2005. Mr Chapman says that following the split his ex-wife slept with a series of wealthy older men. Another Russian woman, Lena Savitskaya, who claims to have shared a flat with Ms Chapman for two years, says that her friend moved in the same circles as, among others, the fugitive Russian oligarch Boris Berezovsky. A picture from those days shows the young women partying with two junior members of the European aristocracy: the heir to the Grand Duchy of Luxembourg and a minor member of the former Russian imperial house of Romanov.[19] She also hung out in London nightclubs patronised by members of the British royal family, befriended the managers and seemed to show eagerness to get to know their best-known clients personally, leading some British tabloids to wonder if her real mission had been to bed a prince. That seems unlikely: intimate friends of the royal family are subject to intense if discreet background checks to exclude any security risk. Any such scrutiny would have exposed not only Ms Chapman's family connections with Russian officialdom but also some curious business activities that she was already involved with at this time.

Her presumed acquaintance with Mr Berezovsky is a more plausible sign of real intelligence activity. In the eyes of the Russian authorities, the tycoon is the epitome of the influence-peddling and sleaze that characterised the presidency of Boris Yeltsin. Mr

Berezovsky was a friend of the former Russian president's daughter, and at one point had an office in the anteroom of the then-prime minister, Viktor Chernomyrdin. Mr Berezovsky was closely associated with Mr Putin in the early years of his rule, brokering deals and easing the transition between the old and new regimes. Some even wondered if the tongue-tied ex-spook from St Petersburg, who initially seemed so ill at ease in the limelight, would end up the puppet of the wily master manipulator. Mr Berezovsky lost out, fleeing the country in 2001.* He maintains a caustic commentary on the corruption and incompetence of the Putin regime, and conducts bewildering political and business manoeuvres in the countries of the former Soviet Union. In June 2007 British police arrested and deported a contract killer only minutes away from Mr Berezovsky's office. 'I was informed by Scotland Yard that my life was in danger and they recommended that I leave the country,' the tycoon told a journalist at the time.[20] Friendship with Mr Berezovsky would provide insights into his movements, routines and security procedures – just the sort of information that an assassin would need. Mr Berezovsky declined to comment. But the most startling aspect of Ms Chapman's life in London has nothing to do with her glitzy friends; the clues to it lie in the dry documents of London's Companies House.

At first sight, the now defunct company Southern Union appears to have done little of consequence. Founded in 2002, its declared activities were wholesale trade in food 'including fish, crustaceans and molluscs' and 'other monetary intermediation'. It bears the same name as a former large money-transfer firm based in Zimbabwe, run by a bank close to that country's ruling authorities, which transferred millions of pounds a month, often using

---

* He gained political asylum in Britain in 2003, taking up a promise made when he brokered the release of two British hostages in Chechnya in 1998.

ingenious financial mechanisms to avoid currency-control rules and local hyperinflation. The British Southern Union published its last accounts in 2009 and was wound up on 1 February 2011. A Steven Sugden, born on 20 May 1974, became a director in 2002, also registered at the Chapmans' address in Stoke Newington. An outsider might wonder if having a lodger in the couple's one-bedroom flat was rather a tight fit. In 2006, Mr 'Sugden', according to company documents, moved to Dublin.

Had Ms Chapman not been unmasked as a spy, Southern Union and its directors would have escaped scrutiny. Yet the documents I have obtained and the evidence of witnesses suggest a tangled story reeking of identity theft, money laundering and secret-service dirty tricks. The story starts with a prominent Zimbabwean businessman called Ken Sharpe, who is a friend of Ms Chapman's father. Mr Kushchenko introduced Mr Sharpe to his Russian wife, Joanna, a former dancer.* In 2002 the Chapmans honeymooned in Zimbabwe, staying with the Sharpes. Most whites in Zimbabwe fare poorly. But those close to the regime can flourish mightily. American diplomats say Mr Sharpe is friendly with the regime of the Zimbabwean dictator, Robert Mugabe, and active in controversial construction schemes and also the gemstones trade. 'In a country filled with corrupt schemes, the diamond business is one of the dirtiest,' said a cable published on WikiLeaks, snappily entitled 'Regime elites looting deadly diamond field'.[21] It would be easy to see why someone involved in such business might feel at home in Russia, and be disinclined to open his business affairs to scrutiny. At any rate, Mr Sharpe declined to respond to questions. The Sharpe family is clearly connected with the London company bearing the Southern Union name. Ken

---

* She is sometimes described as a 'belly' dancer and sometimes as a 'ballet' dancer. This may be a confusion caused by pronunciation.

Sharpe's sister-in-law Lindi Sharpe is listed on a document from September 2002 authorising the appointment of a director. This is puzzling. A search of Companies House shows no Lindi Sharpe connected with Southern Union.[22] It is not clear therefore how she was in a position to make such an appointment. In 2006 she and a Kenneth Sharpe were listed on the UK electoral roll at an address in London.[23] Nobody there responded to questions.

By Mr Chapman's admission, Southern Union was the couple's principal means of support in the early years of their marriage. It paid him £40,000 a year plus a £10,000 payment in return for becoming a director.[24] That is not necessarily sinister: it could just have been a generous father-in-law asking an old friend to make sure that the newly-weds had an income. Mr Sharpe strenuously denies any wrongdoing, or indeed any connection with the UK end of Southern Union. He has said he was a client of the Zimbabwean end of the operation, but did not found it, operate it, or benefit financially from it. But according to Mr Chapman, his Southern Union, as well as handling large numbers of transactions with southern Africa, chiefly Zimbabwe, also made payments on the direct instructions of Ken Sharpe. A foreign intelligence service needing to send money to pay sources and fund operations would have found the company's capabilities interesting.

The links in this chain are individually just curiosities. Why are Russians and Ukrainians involved in what looks like a large money-smuggling operation in Zimbabwe? That could just be people from one corrupt country turning a profit in a place with a similar business culture. But the story is about more than that. One of this operation's patrons appears to have been a Harare-based Russian intelligence officer – Ms Chapman's father. That links the world of Russian espionage (itself often overlapping with organised crime, as we have seen in previous chapters) with the questionable money-transfer business in Harare. The nature of that business is odd too. As noted, spy agencies love the ability to make untraceable payments for clandestine purposes. Finally, the British dimension adds extra spice. In short, an enterprise able to make large numbers of effectively untraceable transactions all over the world, based in one of the most lawless countries imaginable, and with personal ties to Russian intelligence, was operating under the noses of the British authorities. It also had a phantom owner.

Within a month of his marriage breaking up Ms Chapman's husband Alex ceased to be a director. The only remaining director then was Mr 'Sugden'. The name, date of birth and signature fit a man of that name, a married father of two who works in the telecoms business in Tunbridge Wells – but the Kentish Mr Sugden has never met the Chapmans or heard of Southern Union.[25]

An obvious place to find answers to these questions would be Southern Union's accountants, Manningtons of Heathfield, East Sussex. But its senior partner Alan Staples, whose signature appears on the company documents, says he has no instructions that permit him to answer my repeated questions about the circumstances in which his reputable firm registered the company; or whether he or colleagues met in person with anyone purporting to be 'Steven Sugden'; or took any steps to verify his identity. The main bank involved was HSBC. It declines to comment on whether it has ever had a banking relationship with Southern Union or any company trading under that name. Mr Chapman declines to comment on the circumstances in which 'Mr Sugden' became a co-director, or indeed on anything relating to Southern Union. It is unclear why the signature used by the director 'Steven P. Sugden' varies between documents but on some occasions is the same as the signature of the real Mr Sugden of Tunbridge Wells.

All this is odd enough. But the mystery deepens when we follow Mr 'Sugden' on his purported move to Ireland. The trail

leads to Rossmore Grove, a cul-de-sac in the plush Templeogue
south-western suburb of Dublin, coincidentally not far from the
Russian embassy. According to documents at Companies House
in London, Mr Sugden moved there in 2006, first ostensibly
to number 10, then to number 12. This is odd. Templeogue is
misspelled on more than half a dozen documents. One thing that
people tend to get right is their own address. Much odder is that
James Farrell, the owner of 10 Rossmore Grove for the past thirty
years, has never heard of either a Steven Sugden or of Southern
Union. The neighbouring house, 12 Rossmore Grove, was until
recently rented out to a number of East European (mainly Polish
or Lithuanian) migrant workers. Nobody there recalls a Steve
Sugden either. (Nor, incidentally, have the British or Irish authorities approached the occupants.) Only on 1 September 2010, more
than a month after the spy scandal broke, did someone purporting
to be Steven Sugden apply to have Southern Union struck from the
register. It was dissolved on 1 Feburary 2011.

A strange clue to this mystery comes from Zimbabwe, where
a Steven Sugden works for Mr Sharpe, at his company Augur
Investments, a Ukrainian company registered in Estonia. A profile
for a 'Steven Sugden' on an obscure social-networking site called
Hi5 claims the same 20/05/74 birth date as that cited in the
company documents (and belonging to the real Mr Sugden of
Tunbridge Wells). The Hi5 profile also had two other notable
features: it said that the Zimbabwean Steven Sugden was based
in Dublin and listed his languages as English and Russian.[26] What
happened next could be seen as a panicky attempt to cover tracks.
I identified and contacted (by Twitter, Facebook and email) the
ten or so friends listed on the site. Within twenty-four hours, the
mysterious Zimbabwean Mr Sugden cancelled his membership of

Hi5, deleting the profile.* After a few initial responses, none of
the friends was prepared to give any details of Mr Sugden's background or to confirm his identity. Also within twenty-four hours
of my enquiries starting, someone deleted an entry for a Steve
Sugden based in Dublin on another social networking site, names-
database.com,[27] claiming him to be part of the 'Class of 1992' from
Blackrock College, a leading Dublin secondary school. (Blackrock
College School says that nobody called Steven Sugden ever studied there.) A request for contact to a Skype address for a Stephen
P. Sugden in Zimbabwe went unanswered. A Twitter feed in
the name of stephenpsugden has been protected so that outsiders
cannot read it. An email then arrived, in lamentable English, reading as follows:

> My name is Samantha Procter, i am an assistant to Mr Sugden;
> It is my understanding that you are trying to contact mr Sugden
> in order to discuss matters related to the book you are currently
> working on; Mr Sugden is currently away from the office. Please
> may you forward all relative information to me, which i will bring
> to the attention of Mr Sugden upon his return;

Repeated requests for clear answers to my questions brought
belated and inconclusive replies and then a threat of legal action.

An innocent explanation for this could go as follows. By an
unlikely coincidence, two people, both called Steven P. Sugden,
share the same date and year of birth and remarkably similar signa-
tures. One of them is from Tunbridge Wells, the other genuinely
from Zimbabwe. The latter, who just happens to speak Russian,
becomes a director of a London-based company established

---

* Luckily my web-savvy son Johnny suggested that I make a screenshot of the
Google cache version of the site.

through questionable means by a relative of his boss. He initially uses the address of a one-bedroom flat rented by his friends the Chapmans, protégés of his boss, and thereafter gives a forwarding address in Dublin. He does so carelessly, misspelling the suburb and even getting the house number wrong until he later corrects it. For prankish reasons he establishes some phoney credentials on the internet purporting to show that he was at school in Dublin. When outsiders start asking questions, he takes fright and clumsily covers his tracks.

Another more sinister version could be that Ms Chapman, in cahoots with her father, was involved in a front company in London that moves money around either on SVR business or as part of some private scheme involving Russian officials and their foreign funds. One director is an employee of her father's friend, a Russian masquerading as a Zimbabwean who has bolstered his flimsy invented identity with genuine personal data from a real person of the same name in the UK. He has created phoney inter-net clues to add authenticity. When Ms Chapman moves on, so does Mr 'Sugden', giving a misspelled – and misnumbered – Dublin address. My enquiries arouse first alarm and then attempts to escape scrutiny. Without answers from the Zimbabwean Mr Sugden it is hard to rule out either version.

Precisely what bits of Russia's foreign espionage effort may have been involved, or for that matter how much of Zimbabwe's natural wealth was plundered, can only be a matter of specula-tion. The operation seems a bit sloppy by the traditionally high standards of Soviet and Russian tradecraft. Why use a living person's identity? Why give two successive next-door addresses (in each case misspelled) in Dublin (another address for a Southern Union company, in Northampton, was also misspelled).[28] Britain's Security Service started an investigation but soon dropped it. It hunts spies, not criminals. Although its officials punctiliously

refuse to discuss operational matters, on or off the record, I infer
that it believes Mr 'Sugden' to have used a rather sloppy mixture
of SVR techniques for commercial, not espionage purposes. If so,
that exemplifies the blurred boundaries between Russian officialdom and wider business interests.

What is clear, however, is the damage done to entirely innocent bystanders. Steven Sugden's name is still listed at Companies
House as a director of three defunct companies (Southern Union,
Intercon Trading and Africa Connection). The real, Kentish
Steven Sugden is not directly out of pocket, though investigating
the issue has cost him and his family considerable time and worry.
Anyone doing a credit check on him might note, for example,
that the companies had on occasion been less than punctilious in
submitting their annual reports and accounts; an outstanding loan
of £12,000 might also affect his creditworthiness in some eyes.
Companies House is unwilling to delete him from their records;
the police are unwilling to accept that a crime was committed;
Britain's Security Service (MI5) has asked him to cease his own
investigations into the matter in order not to jeopardise its own,
which has fizzled out. The blameless Mr Farrell, and the Crowe
family that own 12 Rossmore Grove, have had the addresses of
their properties used in a way that is certainly fraudulent and looks
sinister. In short, law-abiding people can have their identity and
address stolen by the Russian secret service or (at a minimum) its
officers' family cronies, and used for clandestine, or even nefarious,
purposes, and when this is uncovered, nobody will do anything
to help. I return to this subject in the conclusion. None of these
awkward questions has clouded Ms Chapman's return to Russia.

For a profession that prides itself on obscurity, publicity is a
sign of shameful failure. Most spies retire quietly to the shadows
after they are exposed. Not so Ms Chapman. Her metamorphosis
from a provincial teenager to life as a go-getting émigré, then as

a failed spy and finally to being her country's leading political sex symbol says only a little about her, but a lot about Russia's attitude to spies, the West, women and its own rulers. The spy scandal in which Ms Chapman featured came at a bad time for Russia's rulers. The country had suffered the harshest recession in the G-20 in the previous year, and in the summer of 2010 an outbreak of wildfires had shamed the authorities. A thick, stinking smog enveloped Moscow, making one side of Red Square invisible from the other. Blame fell on the poorly privatised state forestry services, which had all but abolished the vital function of fire prevention. Contempt for the regime was growing elsewhere too. Promises of modernisation had proved empty. Trust in the security services and the police had plunged since Mr Putin took power.

The spy scandal thus cast an unwelcome light on two of the regime's weakest points: corruption and incompetence. The illegals appeared to be an expensive throwback to old Soviet tactics. They had – at least according to the published version of events – failed to gain any secrets and had been under American observation from the start of their mission. Despite the failure of their mission, some of them deserved praise for their personal talents and dedication: Heathfield's brains, Semenko's language skills, or even Lazaro's decades of service all stand out; among the women, the professional career of 'Cynthia Murphy', a financial adviser to rich Americans, was a solid achievement. Yet from the beginning it was the most junior and incompetent of the spies who became the celebrity.* She has posed semi-naked for glossy magazines; she hosts *Mysteries*, a lightweight television programme; she has an iPhone app allowing people to play poker with her electronic avatar and has even registered her surname (in fact her

---

* Her website (annachapman.ru) gives details of her exploits. Curiously, it was registered in April 2010, before the spy scandal broke.

ex-husband's) as a trademark. Chapman-branded products from cosmetics to consumables are on sale or in development. In an article headlined 'Anna Inc',[29] *Newsweek* magazine even termed her 'Russia's hottest cultural icon'. As well as her showbiz, media and marketing efforts, Ms Chapman has a job at a financial entity called FondServiceBank. This is mainly notable for its close links with the defence industry and for its initials FSB. Grigory Belkin, a spokesman, says it jumped at the chance to have her. 'It's very prestigious for any bank to have an employee with a specific background . . . linked with doing helpful things for the state.'

Ms Chapman has also moved into politics: with a prominent but nominal role at *Molodaya Gvardiya* (Young Guard). Founded in 2005, this is the youth wing of the ruling United Russia Party. Though it portrays itself as an apolitical do-gooding organisation, keen on ecology, education and cleaning up government, it is in fact part of a wider Kremlin attempt to forestall any mass protests that might threaten the regime. A nightmare for the 'political technologists' who advise Russia's rulers is a movement on the lines of Ukraine's 2005 Orange Revolution – a spontaneous youth revolt against a corrupt and incompetent regime, prompted by blatant election rigging. Russia may seem unpromising ground for this, but this does not mean that the authorities are complacent. Like the parallel organisation *Nashi* (Ours), the Young Guard offers its members excitement, glamour, perks such as holidays and a professional and educational leg-up. It also has a thuggish streak, harassing opposition figures and interfering foreigners.

She appears less useful to her real-life business employers. Yulia Shamal, head producer at the 'Mysteries' show, says the new presenter doesn't have time to do research but does come to editorial meetings. 'Anya remembered she knew this clever successful person, an artist actually, who not only saw a UFO but managed to take a picture of it,' says Ms Shamal, struggling to find an example of her star presenter's editorial talents.

Ms Chapman's biography does not suggestion that she was a class act. But she was an effective one. Her glib but accented English, imperfectly tinted hair, garish clothes and unremarkable professional career were not a clever bluff, but the real thing. Neither ferociously clever nor blessed with steel nerves or hypnotic people skills, she never sought to match, like Heathfield, the talents of the global elite; her forte was to dance with them, to date them and to work alongside them. As a spy, her tradecraft was startlingly sloppy. In London, her company Southern Union was unable even to spell its phoney address properly on official documentation. Her written English was embarrassingly bad. Under pressure from the FBI she failed even to buy a mobile phone without mistakes that would shame a trainee in the first week of a course at Fort Monckton. In a panic, she called her father on an easily intercepted telephone line.

If that signalled the decline in professionalism of what was once the most efficient bit of Soviet bureaucracy, the way Ms Chapman got her job highlighted something else: nepotism. It is easy to infer that she had gained her plum job, complete with generous taxpayer backing for her business, thanks to birth not brains. Andrei Soldatov, the spy-watcher and author of *The New Nobility*, says: 'All she did was to try and exploit her father's connections in the SVR for money.' Yulia Latynina, a leading opposition journalist, refers to Ms Chapman as 'a very high-class prostitute in the West, with the state paying for all of her beautiful underwear and all her expenses'.

If it is hard to see what service Ms Chapman has rendered to Russia abroad, it is easy to see what she has done on her return. The failed spy has been a blank canvas on which the regime's propagandists have painted their own image of Russia: unstoppable abroad, electrically exciting at home, youthful, daring and sexy. But the first priority was damage control. Aleksei Navalny, an opposition activist who has made his name with an online campaign against corruption in big business, notes that a bad image for Russia's spies also damages Mr Putin, who has played heavily on his own background in the KGB. Mr Putin's former senior speech-writer Simon Kordonsky, now a professor at the liberal Higher School of Economics, sees the regime's eagerness to get its spies out of American custody as a manifestation of 'corporate solidarity' among Chekists, who felt compelled to show that 'one of their own cannot be taken'. But as her celebrity status grew, Ms Chapman's allure, not failure, quickly became a dominant theme. Some seasoned KGB veterans seem genuinely awestruck by her nerveless approach. Viktor Cherkashin, a former counter-intelligence officer in Washington and West Germany who retired in 1991, says she has the right mix of qualities for the modern age.

A person who can behave so naturally, be such a well-known figure in Russia, be part of high society, present a TV show – anyone who can behave like that is an ideal member of an illegals programme.

The growing hype was laced with another potent ingredient: anger over the spies' betrayal. A Russian official told the *Kommersant* newspaper that an assassin had already been dispatched to deal with the defector who betrayed the illegals, though this seems to have been bravado.[30] Mr Putin, after an evening singing patriotic ditties with the returned spies, said grimly that traitors end up 'in the gutter' and blamed 'treason' for the spies' exposure. This approach fits broader propaganda themes favoured by the regime: cynical Western penetration and manipulation of Russian society, the ruthless use of foreign money, and the Soviet-style heroism of the state's servants in difficult conditions.

In Russia's glitzy, sex-obsessed media culture, Ms Chapman's mysterious past and curvy figure were an easy sell. Joanna Seddon, an expert on branding, sees the ex-spy as a classic example of a celebrity who has 'leveraged her misfortunes into not only media popularity but also tangible wealth'. She likens Ms Chapman to Martha Stewart, the billionaire American businesswoman who launched a triumphant commercial comeback after her five months in jail for insider trading. Each woman, she notes, 'maintained the rightness of her actions throughout her troubles, providing a reason for her public to believe in her'. Having averted disaster and created a commercial triumph, the culmination of the propaganda response was to turn Ms Chapman into a political asset for a tired-looking regime that presides over a drab and increasingly backward country. Ms Chapman's symbolic role in Young Guard provided the perfect platform. Yana Lantarova, the organisation's Federal Charity Director, gushes about her new colleague:

> She's a very profound person – she loves her homeland sincerely. In the short time that she's joined us she's learnt how to speak sincerely and convincingly about it.

Ms Lantarova adds helpfully that Ms Chapman 'fires up' the movement's male members. The enthusiasm is not universal. Kirill Schito, a member of the movement's governing council and of the Moscow municipal assembly, is slightly less flattering, insisting that the benefit is 'mutual' and that Ms Chapman is 'quite smart'. But however artificially staged Ms Chapman's initial foray into politics may have been, it has struck a genuine chord among at least some ordinary Russians. Support is most enthusiastic in her native Volgograd. Referring to the legendary Second World War Soviet spy, local journalist Stanislav Anishchenko explains:

Our national hero is Stirlitz, a spy that fought against fascism. Anna Chapman is Stirlitz as a girl. So our media made her a hero and we organised the song contest. People always need heroes – that's why Anna Chapman was born.

The star-struck Mr Anishchenko even organised a song contest in honour of his city's most famous daughter. The winner was 'Anna Chapman is not Mata Hari' – a reference to a Dutch dancer and courtesan shot for spying in the First World War. It captures the nationalistic pride that Russians hold in their spies, though the doggerel lyrics are equally dire in the original Russian as in this loose translation.[31]

> America's symbols of freedom,
> The model of democrats' wisdom,
> It's a home, not prison for nations,
> The immigrants' high expectation,
> You get comfortable life as a present,
> The White House guys are so pleasant,
> They can't sleep without your well-being,
> Without helping earning your living,
> It's not so easy as it sounds,
> Sometimes all dreams fall to the ground,
> One day that a girl is simple and shy,
> Can wake up and find she is a spy,
> If only poor Anna could know,
> That this road is not safe to go,
> Then you'd give up business for sure,
> And go to the place where's secure,
> To Mars or better to Venus,
> To meet no misters, no peers,
> To look at the earth from a distance,

But suffer from lonely existence,
The world is full of secrets, believe me,
You cannot get it, just leave it!
You don't want surprises? – keep an eye open!

Be Glorious, all spies of Russia!
Be famous from Europe to Asia!
Your work and efforts are priceless,
Your fame and your records are doubtless,
You went through fire and water,
Kept busy the police headquarters,
Said nothing in chambers of torture,
Kept heads up in all misfortunes,
Anna Chapman is not Mata Hari! (repeated four times)

This knee-jerk nationalism is a perfect antidote to public apathy and disgruntlement. Ms Chapman also contrasts sharply with the ranks of United Russia, mostly filled with balding middle-aged men. Sergei Markov, a Duma deputy with close Kremlin ties, says:

People are bored with the talking heads on the TV; they are interested in adventure and in action. Spies like these are really popular in the country. She fits the bill perfectly and she is really attractive.

He also sees Putinesque qualities in Ms Chapman's curves:

Vladimir Putin is regarded as a sexual champion as he is very cool and very sexy. Both [Ms Chapman and Putin] are spies – both of them young, healthy, energetic, sexually attractive – and they met publicly. This is about making United Russia sexier and cooler . . . a successful political message needs to be combined with a successful non-political message.

This linking of Putin and Chapman has already started to sink into the popular consciousness. In May 2011 a shoot-em-up game called *Voinushka* (Punch-up) was launched on popular Russian social networking websites. A youthful-looking khaki-clad Mr Putin features as the commander, setting tasks for the person playing the undemanding game. He has a redheaded assistant, showing voluptuous décolleté, wearing a Soviet-style military hat and toting a rifle. The game's designers say they did not consciously choose Ms Chapman as a model.

It would be easy to dismiss this as harmless fun and games – a kind of circus in which an exotic bout of public service turns into an equally exotic private-sector phenomenon. If Ms Chapman and her colleagues seem to have done no real harm in the West, except perhaps to our image of invulnerability, then maybe it is time for bygones to be bygones. Outsiders may ogle her lightly clad figure, but must be resigned to the fact that her most interesting feature – her career in intelligence – is forever cloaked in shadow. Moreover, that someone who embodies superficiality rather than achievement has become a female role model speaks volumes about Russian femininity. Ms Chapman also embodies the contradiction between the regime's xenophobic attitude to the West in general, and its senior members' personal enjoyment of foreign fleshpots. As the journalist Ms Latynina notes caustically: 'This great heroine of the Putin youth was crying, crying buckets when she was told she was going to be banned from Great Britain.'

Sleazy and sex-crazed, crass yet sinister, xenophobic yet obsessed with the West, an artificial creation of an ailing regime: Ms Chapman is emblematic of the country that recruited, ran and promoted her. She exemplifies too the threats and the failings of Russian intelligence: nepotistic in recruitment, with an increasingly blurred line between the professional and private duties of its officers, but still able to plant undetectable and effective agents in our midst.

I have explained Russia's motivation for spying, how it spies, and why we should mind. The next section of the book looks at the history of Western espionage efforts against Russia. Despite some occasional successes, these have in many respects been feebly focused and disastrously executed, something of which British and other Western taxpayers are largely unaware. The biggest losers in this saga of fiascos have been not the Western spymasters and their staff, but the locals who trusted them. This section also sets the scene for the final part of the book, looking at one of the most serious and damaging episodes in recent years: the case of the Estonian Hermann Simm. In both the Western bungles and Russian triumphs, the Baltic states of Estonia, Latvia and Lithuania play a central role. Too small to be able to determine their own destiny,* they are also too important for outsiders to ignore. That has been a fateful combination: both Russia and the West have tussled for influence in the Baltic region and states, and used them as springboards for espionage efforts elsewhere.

---

* Compared to Russia, the Baltic states are tiny. But so are most countries. Their combined land area is around the size of California; the total population of the three countries is just under 7m, rather less than Greater London (7.8m). Lithuania, with 3.2m, is the largest, Latvia has 2.2m people and Estonia has 1.3m.

8

The Cockpit of Europe

A Hollywood blockbuster would hardly do justice to the stories. A masterspy disguised as a ragged pianist plays in his foes' canteen – and receives a knighthood for his efforts. A blundering colleague believes his enemies' tale of a vast underground army just waiting for his visit, and pays for his credulity with his life. Bungling spymasters dismiss espionage scoops that could change history. Souped-up torpedo boats, once the pride of Hitler's navy, rocket across the sea on moonless nights, their heavily armed passengers bearing ciphers, radios, treasure – and cyanide pills. Hidden in forest bunkers, desperate men risk death by torture in a forgotten and futile war. A star military commander in the Waffen-SS becomes a top man in British intelligence. Among his superiors is an undercover KGB colonel. Neglected and misunderstood, these events from past decades are the background to the spy wars of the present day.

Big countries' interests collide in the Baltic, often secretly and mostly tragically. In the past hundred years the region has been the front line of two big wars and several small ones, with coups, uprisings, pogroms and guerrilla struggles as footnotes.[1] The tides of history have swept the Estonians, Latvians and Lithuanians along, just as they have drowned their now-forgotten ethnic

cousins.* The region was one of the central killing grounds of
the Holocaust: Germans and local collaborators murdered around
228,000 Jews, around 90 per cent of the pre-war population.² It
is also a spies' playground. Trade, tourism, culture and family ties
make foreign visitors plentiful and inconspicuous, whether they
have really come to admire the architecture, do a business deal,
see relatives – or empty a dead-letter box. Targets are plentiful and
loyalties fluid: locals know from bitter experience that fortunes
shift and that many irons in the fire are better than one.

The stories include colourful characters such as Arthur Ransome,
better known as a best-selling author of children's stories in which
the plentiful clues to his previous espionage career have long
remained unnoticed.³ Among others are Sidney Reilly, Britain's
'ace of spies'; Paul Dukes, the only MI6 officer to be knighted for
his work in the field, and traitors such as Kim Philby. Shadows still
cloak the region's intelligence history.⁴ Details in an official British
account are skimpy and stop in 1947.⁵ American records are mostly
still classified. Swedish records were allegedly destroyed, though
they later turned up in the basement of a retired general.⁶ But the
outlines are clear. The Baltic was the hub of Western spymasters'
botched efforts to topple the Bolshevik leadership in Russia in the
five years following the revolution. After the Second World War
they backed a bogus underground partisan movement there. In
the 1990s they barged back into the region, believing it to be an
ideal springboard for intelligence operations against Russia.

The story starts with the Bolshevik revolution. In Britain,
France and America politicians wanted Russia's secretive and

---

* The Kreevians died out in the nineteenth century in Latvia. Probably the
last mother-tongue speaker of Livonian died in 2009. The Prussian language
became extinct in the eighteenth century, though German colonisers adopted
the placename. Around ten thousand Vepsians survive, mostly in Russia. The
Vends ceased to be a distinct ethnic group in the sixteenth century.

fanatical new rulers explained. Could they be enticed back into the war with Germany, or at least prevent the Kaiser's high command switching forces from the East to frustrate the allied advance in the West? Were the Bolsheviks really hell-bent on fomenting revolution elsewhere, or just prone to verbal flourishes about it? As spies sought answers, Mansfield Cumming, founder of MI6 (and in spy jargon the Chief of the Secret Intelligence Service) proposed on 18 January 1918 the creation of a new 'Baltic area' division dealing with Russia.[7] By 1923 the British espionage effort centred on the Estonian capital, Tallinn, with networks of agents run from substations in the Latvian capital Riga, and Kaunas (Lithuania's 'provisional capital' since the loss of the historic capital, Vilnius, to Poland).[8] The governments of the three newborn states, foreshadowing a similar reaction in 1991, were glad to see the British presence grow.* Too weak to manage their own security, they welcomed an outsider with similar geopolitical interests but no direct desire to meddle in their affairs. America, in those days, was an untried newcomer in European security. Sweden was too close and too self-interested, Germany too familiar and too weak. France, though a great power, had no historical ties to the region. The simultaneous weakness of both Russia and Germany gave a unique chance to start, or re-start, a history harshly interrupted by centuries of colonial rule.[9] But for Russian leaders both then and now the loss of the Baltic provinces seemed an unfair, costly and temporary sacrifice.[10]

As initial British, French and American efforts to bribe or browbeat the Bolsheviks into rejoining the war against Germany

---

* Britain had longstanding commercial and cultural ties with the region. An Anglican church in Riga opened in 1859, built on English soil specially imported by the wealthy merchants who traded furs and timber. A Scot, George Armitstead (known as Džordžs Armitsteds in Latvian), was even the city's mayor in 1901–1912.

faltered, attention turned to toppling the regime. Countries that cherished order were turning to subversion.[11] (Prevention would have been easier: a British military official posted to Russia in 1917 to monitor political radicals stopped Karl Radek and Fritz Platten, two well-known revolutionaries, from entering Russia; unfortunately he failed to notice that the third member of the party was Lenin.)[12] Officials took an apocalyptic tone. Admiral Sir William Hall, director of British Naval Intelligence, speaking on his retirement in November 1918 at the end of the First World War, said: 'Hard and bitter as the battle has been, we have now to face a far, far more ruthless foe, a foe that is hydra-headed and whose evil power will spread over the whole world, and that foe is Russia.'[13] Cumming took a similar view, telling his Stockholm station in late 1918: 'The only enemy now to be considered are the Bolsheviks.'[14]

The communist grip on power in August 1918 was precarious. The Bolshevik-controlled territory – barely bigger than the old sixteenth-century Muscovy – was short of food and chaotically run. Rows blazed about politics, economics and strategy. Anti-Bolshevik forces still presented a lively if fragmented opposition: an uprising the previous month by the ultra-leftist Social Revolutionaries had narrowly failed. A big British expeditionary force under General Frederick Poole had landed at Archangel on Russia's northern coast, aiming to provide muscle and leadership to the White Russian forces. The Red Army was in disarray. Allied leaders expected a swift victory.

This aspect of the struggle was purely military. Britain played a leading role in the Russian Civil War, intervening to help the White (monarchist) armies on four fronts.[15] A British poster of the time gives a flavour. It shows a British soldier, laden with arms, hastening to help three soldiers in the uniform of the White Army, fighting a hideous gap-toothed Bolshevik monster. It reads:

My Russian Friends! I am an Englishman. In the name of our common cause I ask you just to hang on a bit longer, like the good chaps that you have always been. I have delivered, and will deliver in unlimited amounts, all that you need; and most importantly I will deliver you new weapons with which to destroy those disgusting, bloodthirsty red monsters.[16]

But that British soldier was representing his bosses, not the masses. Strikes and mutinies showed that many in Britain's big industrial towns, either war-weary or radicalised, regarded the Russian revolution of 1917 with sympathy and admiration, as did many idealistic intellectuals. Communism seemed merely an advanced and vigorous version of socialism. The murderous and dictatorial side of the Soviet regime, apparent to first-hand observers in the 'Red Terror' of August 1918, was yet to become fully visible. Outsiders' desire to eradicate Bolshevism was both stoked and constrained by fear of its attractiveness. Western rulers worried that efforts to crush the communist experiment might backfire, leading to the radicalisation of their workers – and, worse, their soldiers and sailors. But letting the Bolsheviks stay in power was dangerous too: Lenin, Trotsky and the others had made it clear that world revolution was their goal. If they succeeded in Russia then other countries would soon be facing a communist threat too.

The other front, seemingly less risky, was domestic subversion, which was to fail just as badly as the military intervention. Amidst the pressure and panic of their early months in power, the Bolshevik leadership found the time to manage an elaborate deception operation that would leave British and French spy chiefs humiliated. According to Aleksandr Orlov, later a top Soviet defector, Lenin in the summer of 1918 decided that as the foreign powers were trying to overthrow him, it would be a good idea to catch the plotters red-handed and expose them.[17] The Bolshevik leader gave the task to the fearsome head of the Cheka secret police, Felix Dzerzhinsky, who decided to centre the deception operation on the regime's most effective fighting force, the Latvian Riflemen. Conscripted into the Tsarist army, the Latvians had become radicalised by their careless ill-treatment and high casualty rate, but were not fanatical Bolsheviks. Given the choice, many of them might have preferred a socialist Latvia to a communist Russia.

The first thread in Dzerzhinsky's web involved a short sallow-faced former naval ensign with a complicated name who offered a neat way into the British spies' plans and thinking.[18] An informer for the Cheka, he had already been approached twice by Commander Leslie Cromie, the British naval attaché in Petrograd.* On 7 August he opened the trap by responding to Cromie's overtures, with the claim that his friend, Colonel Eduard Bērziņš, a senior Latvian officer, wished to cooperate with the allies. This was exactly what British intelligence officers were hoping for, and they were all too willing to believe it. A week later the two men appeared at the Moscow apartment of the British envoy Robert Bruce Lockhart. An intriguing character in every sense, libidinous, extravagant, brainy and moody, Lockhart was a forerunner of Graham Greene's 'Quiet American' – just the sort of person that secret service work most disastrously attracts. Bērziņš explained to Lockhart, who was accompanied by two French colleagues, that the Latvians did not intend to fight the Bolsheviks' battles indefinitely and wished to go home. If they were sent north to fight General Poole's forces, they would like to surrender: could Lockhart arrange it? He also requested four million roubles to get to work on his fellow-Latvians' sympathies. Lockhart countered that it would be better if two Latvian regiments would switch sides

---

* Previously St Petersburg, soon to be Leningrad.

at the provincial town of Vologda, opening a second front against
the Bolshevik forces there, while those remaining in Moscow
would assassinate Lenin and the Bolshevik leadership. But he
wrote a *laissez-passer* to help the Latvians reach General Poole and
provided 900,000 roubles as a down payment.

By this the naive and impulsive Lockhart incriminated himself,
further endangered Cromie, and confirmed Bolshevik suspicions
of British meddling. He added to the disaster by putting the two
visitors in touch with Sidney Reilly, a spy based at the British
consulate in Moscow. Born Sigmund Rosenblum near Odessa in
Imperial Russia sometime in the 1870s, Reilly – later nicknamed
the 'Ace of Spies' – was a 'complex, unpredictable and undoubt-
edly self-serving individual mired in deception and conspiracy'.[19]
Like Lockhart he was wildly overconfident. He wrote in his
notes:

> I was confident that the terror [Bolshevism] could be wiped
> out in an hour and that I myself could do it. And why not? A
> Corsican lieutenant of artillery trod out the embers of the French
> Revolution. Surely, a British espionage agent with so many factors
> on his side, could make himself master of Moscow?[20]

Reilly was also a womaniser and remarkably careless. He
arranged a meeting with Bērziņš at the apartment of one of
his mistresses, but turned up late. While waiting, the Latvian
noticed an envelope in Reilly's writing that gave an address that
turned out to be the home of an actress, Elizabeth Otten, who
had allowed her apartment to be used as a meeting place for
Reilly and his spies. The Cheka began arresting all those who
visited it. One of them was Maria Friede, sister of a colonel in
the Red Army General Staff who was carrying secret documents from him, destined for Reilly. Her brother, duly arrested,

confessed his cooperation with an American intelligence officer who was later imprisoned.*

In another blunder, Lockhart's French colleagues confided in René Marchand, the Moscow correspondent of *Le Figaro*, in the bizarre belief that he was a spy for their government – which like the British and American ones was deeply alarmed by, and hostile to, the revolutionaries. Marchand, being in fact rather sympathetic to the Bolsheviks, immediately informed Dzerzhinsky. This added more details to those provided by the bogus Latvian 'mutineers'. Dzerzhinsky learned that the coup was planned for 28 August at a Party meeting in the Bolshoi Theatre. The Latvian soldiers were to seize the entrances and train their rifles on the audience. Reilly and a small group concealed behind the curtains would arrest the Bolshevik leadership. One plan was to humiliate them by marching them half-naked through the streets of Moscow. But the plotters thought it safer to shoot them on the spot. Reilly, Marchand revealed, had promised the conspirators senior positions in the government of a future independent Latvia, to be set up under Allied protection.[21]

Armed with the details of the plot, Dzerzhinsky went straight to Lenin. The problem was how to use Marchand's material. Lenin came up with an ingenious suggestion to protect his source's journalistic integrity. The French journalist was to write a confidential letter to the French president, Raymond Poincaré: nobody could blame a journalist for warning his head of state that his country's spies were planning a ludicrously risky stunt. The letter would then be 'found' by the Cheka during a search of Marchand's flat. Helpfully,

---

* Xenophon Kalamatiano was caught trying to scale the wall of the Norwegian embassy, which represented American interests. His interrogator examined his hefty walking stick and found it stuffed with roubles and receipts from his agents. He survived a spell in the Lubyanka and was exchanged for American food aid in August 1921.

Dzerzhinsky drafted the letter. For a few days, the Bolsheviks were content to watch the plot developing. But the assassination on 30 August of the head of the Petrograd Cheka, Moisei Uritsky (followed in the evening by a shooting that came within a whisker of killing Lenin himself) prompted the communist leaders to spring the trap. On 31 August eight Chekists raided the British embassy in Petrograd, shooting Commander Cromie, who bravely tried to delay the intruders to allow two of his agents to escape from the building.* Lockhart and his assistant as well as the French consul-general were jailed and eventually deported, and 521 hapless Russians were arrested as 'counter-revolutionaries'. Colonel Friede was shot. Reilly was sentenced to death in absentia, but had already escaped.

The fiasco highlighted a central, persistent, and unrecognised dilemma for Western intelligence services in their dealings with the Soviet enemy. Their mission was well described as 'a mixture of intelligence-gathering, disruption, sabotage and assistance to British military forces'.[22] But those elements are inherently incompatible. Watching in the shadows is one thing; twisting arms is another. It is hard for the same spy to do both. The tension between covert action and intelligence nearly cost the life of probably the most able British spy ever deployed against the Soviet regime.

Paul Dukes, a concert pianist from Bridgwater in Somerset, had honed his skills in evasion, deception and persuasion as a schoolboy, faced with the unpleasant necessity of dodging a predatory paedophile who was both a teacher at his boarding school and a friend of his father. A natural linguist, he had arrived in Russia in 1910 as a music student. Rejected for military service because

---

* The Bolsheviks refused to allow the dying man a drink of water, or the embassy chaplain to attend to him. My suggestion to the British consulate in St Petersburg, when it opened in 1992, to name a prize or scholarship after this gallant officer met with a sorry lack of enthusiasm.

of a heart condition, he spent much of the war years working for a government-financed information service called the Anglo-Russian Bureau. In 1917, he was summoned to London for a meeting with SIS, in those days an outfit run by eccentric upper-class men with a dilettantish approach to espionage (cynics might say nothing much changed in subsequent decades). Dukes was told:

> As to the means whereby you gain access to the country, under what cover you will live there, and how you will send out reports, we shall leave it to you, being best informed as to conditions, to make suggestions.[23]

After brief training in invisible ink and cipher, Dukes was dispatched back to the most dangerous place in the world for a foreign spy, to live and work undercover as an illegal – rather as Donald Heathfield and the others were to do in America seventy years later. But whereas they exploited the vulnerabilities of an open society, he had to work in a police state, under the noses of the fearsome Bolshevik secret police, the Cheka. He was an astonishing success: in 1919 he was the most effective, and quite possibly the only, SIS officer inside Bolshevik-controlled Russia. He was running a network of agents in Petrograd,[24] collected in part via a military canteen in which he had installed himself as a part-time pianist (disguised as a tattily dressed and limping tramp). At other times he managed to pass as an official of the Cheka itself, as a member of the Communist Party, and as a Red Army soldier. The result was intelligence of a stellar quality and quantity.[25] Dukes had not only established a network of informers, civilian and military, throughout the city and its great port. He had penetrated the top Bolshevik leadership of Petrograd to such an extent that he was able to transmit to London translations of the highly secret minutes of their meetings in full. But the star spy was in increasingly desperate straits. The tightening Bolshevik bureaucratic controls on movements, food supplies and residency made maintaining his aliases and safe houses increasingly difficult: getting the right papers was tricky and having the wrong ones fatal. The Cheka knew the British spy was at large in the city and had on several occasions nearly caught him. Money could help – but SIS had sent him ineptly forged cash: when the fake banknotes got wet, the ink ran. His priceless intelligence was useless unless it could reach the increasingly frantic politicians in London but getting across the border was difficult: in one two-week period in the summer of 1919 no fewer than six couriers had been captured.[26]

Cumming tasked a young naval lieutenant, Augustus 'Gus' Agar, with rescuing Dukes using lightweight torpedo boats. These contraptions, plywood shells powered by aircraft engines, were the forerunners of the vessels that would be used to send SIS agents to the Baltic states twenty-five years later. The 'eggshells' (when their delicate engines worked, which was not always) could travel at the then astonishing speed of over 40 knots. The mission was dogged by bad luck, communications breakdowns, security breaches, meddling from other officials, and suspicion from Agar's Finnish hosts (who had no desire to provoke the Bolsheviks by supporting madcap British raids and spookery). Agar's main ally against these odds was Admiral Sir Walter 'Titch' Cowan, the commander of a British naval squadron that was helping the Estonians beat off their various foes, though its two light cruisers and ten destroyers were outgunned by Russia's much heavier warships: the *Oleg*, a heavy cruiser, and two battleships, the *Petropavlovsk* and *Andrei Pervozvanni*.* In theory, Agar's mission

---

* Both Russian battleships still had their Tsarist-era names with religious allusions: 'Peter and Paul' and 'Andrew the First-called [apostle]'. A French naval force was also in the Baltic but unable to take part in hostilities against the Bolsheviks for fear that the sailors would mutiny.

was solely the clandestine exfiltration of Dukes from Petrograd. He and his crew wore civilian clothes, and turned up in Helsinki pretending to be speedboat salesmen. But they had also taken a couple of torpedoes (launched in a hair-raising manoeuvre over the back of the craft, travelling in the same direction: the helmsman had a few seconds to turn away from their path). And they had naval uniforms on board, to be donned in the event of real warfare.

Dukes reported that the Russian fleet was riven by disputes between the officers and men loyal to the Bolsheviks, those sympathetic to the Whites, and those with loyalties to other factions. One report, citing a senior Bolshevik, said that the men regarded their officers as 'class enemies' while the officers were a 'mass of spies'.[27] Dukes also obtained a secret transcript from a commission of enquiry following a failed attack on the British squadron. A sailor from the submarine *Pantera* answered with remarkable frankness as follows:

Judge: Will you attack the British?
Sailor: If the commander orders it, we will.
Judge: But will you fire on them?
Sailor: Yes.
Judge: Will you hit them?
Sailor: No.

Following this debacle, Lenin put Trotsky in charge of reforming the navy. He immediately began replacing ideologically sound but useless officers with experienced Tsarist-era ones. He also banned the practice under which committees of 'revolutionary sailors' forced their officers to clean toilets and sweep floors. That restored the fleet's offensive capability. He also ordered the laying of many thousands of mines, making it far harder for the British to attack. Dukes dutifully reported all this, plus a crucial piece of intelligence for Agar: the one-metre depth at which the mines defending the Kronstadt naval base were to be laid. The 'eggshell' boats drew only 2'9" (84cm). With a few inches to spare, they could therefore cross the minefield and use their torpedoes to attack the Bolshevik fleet at anchor.

As Agar waited to rescue Dukes, he watched with despair the Bolshevik fleet pounding the nearby fortress of Krasnaya Gorka (Red Hill) where the garrison had rebelled: this was a tragic miscalculation by its leaders, Ingrian nationalists – ethnic cousins of the Finns and Estonians – who were hoping to make their own bid for freedom. In a daring raid into the heart of Kronstadt harbour, and in defiance of his instruction to concentrate on intelligence work, Agar succeeded in torpedoing and sinking the *Oleg*. It was too late to save the Ingrians, but a second raid with seven more torpedo boats sank both the Bolshevik battleships, ending the struggle for naval superiority in the Baltic and ensuring Estonia's and Latvia's independence – and their lasting, if ultimately misplaced, faith in British integrity and capability. This was to feature in the disasters of the 1940s and 1950s, and in the renewed intelligence ties of the 1990s.

Agar received the Victoria Cross, Britain's highest military honour. But his exploits doomed his mission. Dukes was still stuck in Russia, where Soviet authorities now understood the vulnerability of their defences to the fast British vessels. A later attempt to rescue the master-spy was abandoned under heavy fire. Dukes finally escaped via Latvia, frostbitten, filthy, half-starved and exhausted. SIS showered him with praise – but in a signal piece of mean-mindedness refused to pay his operation's debts. George Gibson, a leading figure in the dwindling British community in Petrograd, had at great personal risk lent Dukes 375,000 roubles* to

---

* Very roughly, around £250,000 or $400,000 in modern money.

make up for the poor forgeries supplied by SIS. But when Gibson returned to London, SIS said his paperwork was inadequate and refused to pay. Only when an infuriated Dukes threatened publicly to renounce his knighthood did SIS back down.

A more famous if less impressive British agent in this era was Dukes's friend Arthur Ransome. To many readers, his name will be inextricably linked with a quite different genre: the 'Swallows and Amazons' children's books. But he was also an expert on Russia, and on the books of SIS as agent 'S-76'. Ransome moved to the Estonian capital in 1918, tasked with gaining information about Soviet Russia. He was also asked by the Estonian authorities to carry a secret message to the Bolshevik leadership expressing their willingness to strike a peace deal. Ransome saw at once that peace with Estonia would be followed by a similar agreement with Latvia. This would help secure the Bolshevik regime in Russia, which, as a left-winger, Ransome broadly supported. It would also end the fighting that was devastating the region. Not for the first time, a British intelligence agent was finding that local allies' wishes clashed with the geopolitical interests of his bosses. For London, the aim of the war was to topple the reds, not to promote democracy or freedom (still largely seen as an eccentric American preoccupation).

The Bolsheviks responded coolly. Undeterred, Ransome crossed the Russian–Estonian front line in a journey that he portrayed as hair-raising (other writers and his biographer reckon it was trouble-free).[28] His aim was not spying but to rescue Evgenia Shelepina, who was his mistress and Trotsky's secretary. It is unclear whether she was using Ransome to snoop on the British, providing him with real intelligence, in love with a glamorous Englishman, or some permutation of these three. During stints in Tallinn and then in the Latvian capital Riga, Ransome spent the next few years in a half-world between journalism and intelligence work. Unable to divorce his English wife Ivy, he could not return to England – his private life was as tangled as his political views. He publicly defended the Bolshevik suppression of the Kronstadt uprising in 1921: perhaps sincerely, perhaps to preserve his personal or professional contacts in Russia.

But Ransome was in tune with the spirit of the times. The anti-Soviet cause was in trouble, doomed from the outset by the Whites' disorganisation and brutality, which alienated even those Russians who disliked the Bolsheviks. By 1919 the British government under David Lloyd George was rapidly losing interest (not least because of a series of naval and military mutinies among war-weary British sailors and soldiers). 'I would rather leave Russia Bolshevik until she sees her way out of it than see Britain bankrupt,' he told the House of Commons in April.[29] The allied intervention wound up in 1920. But as in future years, the instincts of Western spies dealing with Russia were at odds with their political masters' instructions. In the summer of 1920[30] Cumming sent Reilly, Dukes and a former Tsarist secret policeman Vladimir Orlov (known as Orbanski) to establish an 'international anti-Bolshevik intelligence service' in Eastern Europe.[31] They recruited five agents in Warsaw, eleven in Riga, four in Tallinn, two in Kaunas, as well as fourteen in Berlin. The initiative was stillborn. The British government was negotiating the normalisation of relations with the Bolshevik regime, starting with a trade agreement in March 1921. In July, the Warsaw station chief Malcolm Maclaren, a piratical figure who wore gold ear-rings, was instructed to close down the expensively created network; all that remained was a few contacts in the Baltic. Reilly's swashbuckling bunch continued their work, without him or official backing from SIS. But that was enough for the Soviet spymasters to bait their next hook.

In November 1921 an official of the Russian waterways authority, A. A. Yakushev, made contact with an old friend in Tallinn, a former officer in the White forces. Both men were sincere anti-Bolsheviks. The visitor was a member of a genuine if flimsy monarchist organisation in Moscow. His host circulated émigré outposts with an enthusiastic account of what he had heard. Having intercepted one of these letters, the Cheka arrested Yakushev on his return to Moscow. After some persuasion in the Lubyanka he agreed in early 1922 to cooperate with the Soviet authorities. With Yakushev's help, the Cheka steadily began persuading the émigré leadership in the West that a powerful and promising underground movement was developing inside the Soviet Union. The SIS station chief in Helsinki, Harry Carr, a fluent Russian-speaker and fervent anti-communist who was to feature in the even greater debacles of later years, was only too eager to hear this, particularly as the new organisation seemed to have support from the Finnish, Estonian and Polish spy services.[32] He was troubled by its failure to produce any usable intelligence, but accepted that its main purpose was insurrectionary and that espionage activity at this stage would be too risky. That mistake was also to be repeated almost exactly in years to come.

A parallel part of the operation was the infiltration of a band of real anti-communist partisans* in Belarus by a talented Cheka officer called George 'Grisha' Syroyezhkin. Helped by two genuine gunshot wounds from Russian border guards, he succeeded in convincing the guerrillas and their foreign backers of his bona fides. He became firm friends with the émigré leader Boris Savinkov (one of Reilly's co-conspirators) in the movement's increasingly miserable Warsaw headquarters. (Poland had signed a peace treaty with Soviet Russia in March 1921, ending Polish support for a planned anti-Soviet uprising in the autumn). In July 1921 the Soviet secret

---

* It was part of an underground army comprising the remnants of the armed forces of the short-lived Ukrainian republic, anti-Bolshevik Russians based in Poland and others.

police had rounded up much of Savinkov's network inside Russia, using details provided by 'Grisha'.

Dzerzhinsky was careful not to overplay his hand. He left enough embers of the anti-Bolshevik cause smouldering to allow him to play the next round in the game. Savinkov's cause was doomed; it was now time to destroy him personally. Again a purported anti-communist organisation made contact, this time called the Trust. It purported to be democratic, not monarchist, in outlook: this was far more appealing to Savinkov, a radical liberal who detested Tsarist autocracy and communist totalitarianism in equal measure. After some elaborate bits of play-acting involving his emissaries, and the use of a femme fatale with whom Savinkov had begun an affair, the inspirational anti-communist leader was tempted across the Soviet border, arrested, and brought to Moscow. Skilful interrogation by Dzerzhinsky (who regarded physical torture as a crude and unworthy short-cut), eventually brought Savinkov's cooperation in a show trial, after which he was given a light sentence and died in a mysterious fall from a window, possibly in suicidal despair, possibly murdered on Stalin's orders.

The next victim was Reilly. He was no longer formally on the books of British intelligence: SIS records show a series of exasperated telegrams between London and its stations complaining of the masterspy's adventurism. But Reilly retained friends in the service, including Ernest Boyce, his former boss from Moscow days and now the Tallinn station chief. In 1925, Boyce wrote to Reilly asking for his help in investigating what appeared to be a serious underground operation inside Russia. Again a Russian female agent played a central role: this time an attractive woman called Maria Zakharchenko-Shults, who was both sexually voracious and embittered by ill-treatment from her previous lovers. It is not clear whether Reilly became intimate with her, but she certainly exerted a strong influence on him after he arrived in

Helsinki to make contact with the Trust's leaders. The deception soon deepened, with plenty of supporting evidence of the
underground movement's capabilities. The brother of a local SIS
agent, trapped in Russia, was smuggled out. He was a violinist, and
needed his precious instrument to earn a livelihood. Obligingly,
the Trust arranged that too. Carr was a little dubious: it all seemed
too slick for a real bunch of plotters to manage under the noses of
the increasingly all-powerful Russian secret police. Unfortunately,
he stifled his doubts.[33]

The plan was for Reilly to meet Trust leaders in Finland in
September 1925. But at the last minute he was persuaded to come
to Moscow for a meeting of the anti-communist 'government-in-
waiting'. As bait Maria also presented a newspaper cutting with
a photo purportedly showing an emissary of the Trust, Terenty
Deribas, whom Reilly had already met in Helsinki, standing next
to Lenin.[34] What better proof could there be of the organisation's
clout, if it had on board a former lieutenant of the Bolshevik
leader? Unfortunately, the photo was a forgery. As a final incentive, Deribas mentioned the lucrative business deals Reilly would
be able to do in Russia once the communists were out of the way.
The mixture of sex, greed, ambition and adrenalin was irresist-
ible. Reilly swallowed the bait, penned a hasty letter to one of his
wives, and crossed the border.

His hosts did not arrest their quarry immediately. Instead, they
pumped him for information in the guise of allies. Reilly duly
revealed his cupidity, suggesting that the new government could
be financed by selling treasures from Russia's museums and art
galleries: he even offered his own services as a broker in this sordid
deal. At this point the deception ran into political trouble. Those
running the operation thought it would be better to let Reilly
return to the West. This was standard practice with other unsuspecting émigré supporters. Reilly's account of a successful mission

would boost the Trust's credibility, allowing its puppet-masters to play still more games with the Western spy chiefs. But Stalin, by now the Soviet leader, wanted none of it. Even a phoney underground organisation was one too many. The British spy was arrested but gave little away. He probably did not have much to give: he was not on official SIS business, had never worked at its headquarters and his memories of service were several years out of date. He was shot on 5 November.

The ill-fated expedition was just a blip in the British intelligence build-up in the Baltic. As Russia became more isolated, the hunger for information about it grew. Money and men came piling in, with a resulting blizzard of unsatisfactory, confusing and ill-sourced information.[35] Specialisations developed: military intelligence in Tallinn, naval in Helsinki, and political and economic in Riga. Kaunas was said to be rather dull in comparison. Yet enthusiasm was not matched by judgement. The British intelligence officers tended to be Anglo-Russians whose lives had been blighted by the revolution. They found Russian émigrés congenial company and recruited them as sources. This mirrors the same mistakes made by SIS in the years immediately after the war, when again under great pressure to produce results, and facing an all but impenetrable target, it relied on anti-communist refugees and insurgents. They too were ardent allies and willing risk-takers; but die-hard opponents of a regime are unlikely to know its secrets. Hatred uninformed by knowledge and fuelled by wishful thinking is about the worst possible basis for successful espionage. It was not until the late 1950s that SIS was to realise this and concentrate on meticulous recruitment and agent running inside the communist establishment.

Émigré and dissident groups always find it hard to vet new recruits effectively. Any publicly identifiable member becomes an easy target for bullying, blackmail or bribery. Once penetrated, such groups become an asset to their foes, not a threat. Only outfits with small memberships based on close personal friendships have a chance of escaping this fate. That was not the hallmark of the amateurish and feuding Russian diaspora in the 1920s and 1930s, or of the Baltic émigrés in the 1940s and 1950s. Add the extra unreliability caused by affiliation, real or imagined, with the secret world, and it is easy to see how Western intelligence services were ensnared in Bolshevik plots. As the official historian of SIS writes, '1920s Europe was full of dubious White Russian characters representing themselves as secret agents.'[36] They produced little intelligence of any significance[37] but sometimes did real damage: asserting, for example, that the Soviet Union was fomenting insurrection in Ireland and India. Britain issued a thunderous protest, only to be embarrassed when a Soviet response proved that the intelligence, far from being drawn straight from the Politburo (as claimed) was entirely fabricated. SIS bosses complained, and vainly introduced new rules designed to prevent the service paying good money for forged documents. As the British purse strings tightened in the 1930s, many agents began diversifying their sources of income, particularly by offering their services to the *Abwehr* (German military intelligence).

Phoney intelligence particularly affected Riga, the most productive of SIS's stations in the region. Its best agent was a local Russian journalist who supposedly ran a network of eleven sub-sources. An investigation in 1928 concluded that many if not most were bogus: producing entirely imaginary information, for example, about a Russian 'death ray'.* Reporting from Riga also led to one of the greatest howlers in the history of SIS. Published in the *Daily Mail* on 24 October 1924, it purported to be a letter from Grigori Zinoviev, president of the Comintern – the organisation

---

* It is tempting to speculate that this real-life example may have inspired Graham Greene, himself an SIS officer, with the mysterious giant suction device – in fact a domestic vacuum cleaner writ large – depicted in *Our Man in Havana*.

through which the Bolshevik leadership coordinated its activities with foreign communist parties – urging the British Communist Party to lead an insurrection. The story came in the run-up to a general election in which Britain's Labour Party, in office for the first time, in a minority government, was hoping to hold on to power. The letter was not decisive: though the Conservative party won the election, Labour's vote went up. But many suspect that right-wing elements in SIS cooked up the 'leaked' letter, supposedly provided by a sub-agent called FR/3/Moscow, employed in the secretariat of the Comintern (the office which linked the Soviet leadership with foreign communist parties). Riga had filed it to London with a covering note[38] flagging the 'strong incitement to armed revolution' and a 'flagrant violation' of the newly signed Anglo-Russian agreement. SIS also asserted that 'the authenticity of the document is undoubted'. Worse, when the Foreign Office tried to verify the letter SIS claimed (probably falsely) that another agent had corroborated the content. The most elementary checks were missing. Had SIS obtained the letter in English or in Russian? Who exactly was the sub-agent? SIS was unable or unwilling to give firm clear answers and came close to outright lies.[39]

The exceptions to this rather unimpressive performance came from British intelligence links with their local counterparts, especially in Estonia (history may not repeat itself, but it sometimes rhymes). An agent called 'Baron', run by Carr, reported the start of secret Nazi–Soviet negotiations in the spring of 1939, and confirmed in June that they were making good progress. But the desk officer at SIS headquarters in London refused to circulate this intelligence further, believing that the agent could not possibly have had the access necessary.[40] It contradicted the Foreign Office line, that its envoy to Moscow Sir William Strang was making progress on an Anglo-Soviet agreement. The same fate befell another scoop a year later. Although SIS closed its Baltic stations in September 1940 following the Soviet annexation of Estonia, Latvia and Lithuania, many of the agent networks remained, mostly run from Helsinki. A British agent codenamed 'Outcast', formerly run from Tallinn, presented himself to the Helsinki station in September 1940.[41] A Russian émigré living in Berlin (but with no love for the Nazis), he had escaped from Tallinn with German help, in return for agreeing to work for the *Abwehr* against Russia. Now he wanted to spy against them, for the British. In November 1940 he reported to his British case officer: 'German command preparing (June) campaign against USSR.' Sadly, Carr dismissed this as 'incredible' and probably mere propaganda.

Had politicians in London heeded the SIS sources and gained advance warning of the Hitler–Stalin pact, what could they have done? The deal was the culmination of a long period of diplomatic and political failure, in which Britain and France had been outmanoeuvred and Hitler had seen obstacles to his expansion plans melt one by one. It is hard to imagine even the most piercing intelligence insight reversing that. Nor is it easy to see what Britain would have done with the warning of Hitler's assault on the Soviet Union. Stalin had plenty of warnings from other sources: he usually responded by punishing the messenger. Exercises in speculative history are as unrewarding as they are tempting. Yet it is hard not to feel frustration that such accurate intelligence went unnoticed. The wider lesson, if any, is that espionage is valuable only when decision-makers let the results change their thinking. Spies may provide confirmation only that the currents in the depths and shallows are similar. If they offer a different version of events, or prediction of them, officials and politicians must be willing to act on what they are told.

That is one weakness of Western intelligence even in the present day. Readers trying to understand why Russian spymasters so frequently run rings round their Western counterparts will also find it striking that so many other mistakes of the past are replicated so frequently. The tendency to pay good money for bad intelligence is deeply ingrained. Even after the fiascos of the early years, most intelligence from the interwar Baltic was barrel-scrapings, as this downbeat vignette illustrates.

Baltic agent 'BP/24' who was resident in Moscow and had 'connections in Soviet institutions', agreed for a retainer of £50 a month to 'send information three times monthly' about political matters and 'on subject of propaganda'. After his own involvement with OGPU (who blackmailed him over gambling debts) was discovered, he was charged with treason but escaped to Austria, where he continued to peddle intelligence on Russia until the early 1930s. There he was reported to be employed by the Nazi Intelligence Office in Berlin and was offering reports to SIS though a mutual contact in Finland. By 1934 (as SIS discovered in 1946 from captured German documents) he had graduated to the *Abwehr*, was reporting to them on Russia and into the bargain had passed them an SIS questionnaire on Russia received from his Finnish contact.[42]

If the later history of Western intelligence battles with Russia in the Baltic was ill-starred, one can at least say that it was part of a consistent pattern.

9

Between the Hammer and the Anvil

Carelessness, naiveté and wishful thinking were again on ample (and humiliating) display only twenty years later. The episode centred on the doomed underground struggle against communist rule in the Baltic states – one of the least-known chapters in modern European history.[1] The names of the heroes and villains are unfamiliar; so too are the organisations they belonged to and the cause they espoused. But their death and destruction, the moral ambiguity and dilemmas that beset them, and the lethally unhelpful involvement of Western intelligence all deserve recognition. The central paradox was this: the goals of those resisting Soviet rule in the Baltic did not include gathering intelligence for Western spymasters, nor did their aims or origins make them ideal allies. But it was the spy agencies that offered them their only hope of outside support; and for all their faults, they were, at the start of the Cold War, a large part of the slender hand of cards that American and British intelligence could muster.

Intelligence links across the Baltic sea had reconnected during the war, in early 1943. The cooperation was controversial for both sides. The Soviet Union was still officially Britain's ally and many of the Baltic agents were outspokenly anti-communist. Opinion on their side was divided. Many believed that the only hope of staving off another Soviet occupation was to intensify cooperation with the Germans. Others hoped that Britain would ditch its alliance with Stalin and rescue them as it had done in 1920. The first fruits of the connection were bitter. Evald Aruvald, then in the Estonian resistance, recalled: 'We passed to the British . . . details of our strengths and positions at the front, hoping for assistance. The British, in turn, passed on this information to the Soviets.'[2] Colonel Alfons Rebane, a legendary Estonian officer who later worked for SIS, complained: 'This damaged the Estonian people's fight against our slave-masters the communists.'[3]

The story starts with Alexander 'Sandy' McKibbin, born in pre-revolutionary Russia, and then a timber-merchant in pre-war Estonia (and probably on the books of British intelligence)[4]. During the war, he worked for the SIS station in Stockholm: in those days one of the great spy nests of Europe. His main job was spying on the Nazis, who had occupied the Baltic states in 1941 and were now fighting a losing defensive battle against the advancing Soviet forces. Meanwhile the Lithuanian underground, hoping against hope to re-establish the country's independence, was eager to make contact with Western powers. One of its representatives was a regular visitor to Sweden and made contact with McKibbin, who signed him up.[5] (The British spy also contacted an Estonian underground leader, until his capture and torture by the Gestapo in 1944 led to the destruction of his network.)[6]

From the Baltic point of view, the Nazis and Soviets were not hugely different. This perspective will be startling to those who see Hitler's Germany as the fount of all evil and the Soviet Union as a valiant (if ill-led) ally against it. But in the Baltic as in much of Europe the war was a three-way fight. In one corner were the Nazis, with an imperial doctrine based on racial supremacy, in the other the Soviets, who mixed Russian imperialism with the ideology of class warfare. In the middle, bearing the brunt of the bloodshed, were the peoples whose countries the Nazi–Soviet pact had obliterated. As the Lithuanian poet Tomas Venclova notes, the war years offered the Baltics a choice between Hitler, Stalin and death, with one choice not necessarily precluding the others.[7]

By the time of the first tentative contacts between the resistance and foreign intelligence, the damage inflicted by both fighting and invasion was severe. The forcible annexation and Sovietisation of the three Baltic countries in 1940 was followed in June 1941 by the deportation of much of the pre-war elite,[8] typically in the middle of the night, with an hour's notice. The class enemies, loaded on to cattle trucks to freeze, starve and suffer in distant labour camps, included: members of 'anti-Soviet' political parties (whether of left or right), police, prison officers, military officers, political émigrés and 'unstable elements', foreign citizens, 'individuals with foreign connections' such as stamp collectors, senior civil servants, Red Cross officials, clergy, noblemen, industrialists and merchants. These comprised 10,000 people from Estonia, 15,000 from Latvia and 34,000 from Lithuania. They included much of the middle-class Jewish population of all three countries. As the Yale historian Timothy Snyder has pointed out, it would have been little comfort to those Jews to know that they were being persecuted for their class, not their race.

When the Soviet forces returned in 1944, those who had failed to flee and showed any sign of resistance or independent thought were repressed as 'bourgeois nationalists'.[9] This traumatic history is the emotional and strategic backdrop for the espionage debacles of the following years, for the independence struggle of the 1980s, and for the headlong embraces between Western spy services and their Baltic counterparts in the 1990s. Juozas Lukša, a CIA-trained Lithuanian resistance fighter, later wrote:

In 1940, the Russians had come marching into our land to 'liberate' us from 'capitalist and Fascist exploiters.' In 1941, the Germans had marched in after them and thereby 'liberated' us from 'Bolshevik bondage.' And now, the Russians were back again – this time to 'liberate' us from 'the tyranny of Nazi hangmen.' But since we still recalled how they had gone about 'liberating' us the last time, we didn't think we had any cause to rejoice.[10]

Helping the Soviets beat the Nazis made sense from a Western point of view (and was a question of life and death for the region's surviving Jews) but the bungling that followed was inexcusable. British intelligence was keen to find out what was happening in the occupied Baltic states, chiefly to know if the Soviet Union was planning a further push westwards. On 15 October 1945 it sent a boat with four agents from Sweden to Latvia on a reconnaissance mission. Unfortunately, it capsized and the men were caught and tortured to the point of insanity. Their ciphers and radio transmitters fell into the hands of Jānis Lukaševičs, a brainy officer of the Latvian KGB. Here was proof that SIS operations against the Soviet Union had restarted – but how to respond? Waiting for more spies to come and trying to hunt them down was clumsy and risky: far better to lure future British agents into a trap. The operation was labelled *Lursen-S*[11] though it is usually called 'Red Web' – the name of a book in 1989 by the British author Tom Bower, who first unveiled its dark secrets.

In March 1946 Lukaševičs forced a Latvian* who had operated a radio for the British during the war to start sending messages again, claiming that the agents had given him their codes and radio before capture. Perhaps unsurprisingly, the British eventually responded.

---

* Augusts Bergmanis.

A second SIS mission to Latvia in 1946 landed two agents* tasked with finding out what had happened to the previous mission. But the new arrivals' transmitter proved faulty. In an even graver breach of tradecraft, SIS instructed them to make contact with the existing – KGB-controlled – radio operator. That forged a fatal link between the new British operations and the compromised network now controlled by the KGB. With one thread in the web spun, Lukaševičs did not order the men's arrest. He wanted a bigger haul. SIS instructed its agents (now under KGB surveillance) to meet other British agents on the ground. That provided the Soviets with more leads and clues. Other efforts were equally farcical. Two more agents ended up stranded in Latvia and were arrested, along with their networks. Another émigré, Feliks Rumnieks, was instructed to return to Latvia and make contact with the KGB in order to work as a double agent. He was arrested and confessed everything.

Meanwhile the Lithuanian KGB was playing a similar game. It sponsored a rival resistance movement to the main partisan outfit.[12] The bogus organisation's underground leader was a distinguished American-born Lithuanian, Juozas Albinas Markulis, seemingly stalwart, but in fact a traitor since 1944. Such ruses not only divided and distracted the anti-communist cause abroad. They also helped uproot real resistance at home. On 18 January 1947 Markulis summoned a meeting of all the partisan leaders in Lithuania. Though Lukša – a genuine anti-communist of remarkable brains, courage and eloquence – was sceptical, others were trusting: after all, Markulis was in contact with the revered British intelligence service. The Lithuanians walked straight into a KGB ambush. In a similar ruse in Latvia, Lukaševičs arranged for fourteen senior partisan leaders to be summoned for a meeting in Riga with representatives of the 'Latvian government-in-exile'

* Rihards Zande and Ēriks Tomsons.

and a representative of the 'British secret service'. To allay their suspicions, each leader was told to provide a photo, and in return received a valid Soviet ID card – supposedly proof of British prowess in forgery. On 13 October the unsuspecting men briefed the 'British' visitor on every detail of their operations. They were then arrested and never seen again.

Behind the Iron Curtain, trust in the West was still profound. An underground newspaper in Lithuania proclaimed in June 1947:

The world's greatest scholars and most famous strategists – Eisenhower, Montgomery, Adm. Nimitz and scores of others – are gathering weapons and plans from all countries to collectively eliminate criminal-infected Moscow as the sole hindrance of freedom.[13]

That was an overstatement. Britain was ruined by the cost of the war. America was unwilling to face up to the new challenge in Europe. The mood began to change only after the Soviet blockade of Berlin in 1948. On 18 June of that year President Harry Truman signed a fateful order in the National Security Council, tasking the newly created CIA with:

propaganda, economic warfare, preventative direct action, including sabotage, anti-sabotage, demolition and evacuation measures, subversion against hostile states, including assistance to underground resistance movements, guerrillas and refugee liberation groups, and support of indigenous anti-communist elements in the threatened countries of the free world.[14]

The first Soviet atom bomb test in August 1949 and the outbreak of the Korean War in June 1950 stoked interest further. In the days before spy satellites (or even spy planes, which started in 1952) and with Western diplomats in Moscow effectively imprisoned in their embassies, the outside world was acutely short of information about Soviet intentions and capabilities. Panicky politicians put huge pressure on the spymasters to do something. This was something that could be done. So they did it.

Superficially the Baltic states seemed an ideal base for anti-communist activities. The populations were solidly anti-communist. Partisan forces in the forests supposedly numbered many tens of thousands. The region was accessible by boat and plane. It was a forward bastion of Soviet military strength: if an attack on the West were pending, the signs in the Baltic would be unmistakable. The human means were plentiful: émigrés in western Germany, Britain and the United States provided a highly motivated and plentiful source of agents. In short, Estonia, Latvia and Lithuania looked like places where it was possible both to fight communism and spy on it. The disastrous results of this wishful thinking were the SIS Operation Jungle and its CIA counterpart, initially called Operation Tilestone.[15] Failure is an orphan, and nowhere more so than in espionage. When something works, it looks like an act of genius. Had Stalin died earlier and the collapse of the Soviet Union ensued, the operations could have gone down in history as prescient and brave endeavours, worthy successors to the work of SOE in occupied Europe. In fact the disaster that followed was hushed up for thirty years. Secrecy has its uses.

The CIA developed a big training facility for émigrés in Kaufbeuren in Germany. In place of makeshift camps in neutral Sweden SIS set up a spy school for its Baltic recruits at 110 Old Church St, Chelsea (now a luxury townhouse). Among those in charge was Alfons Rebane, who had led a fierce but doomed resistance to the Red Army's re-conquest of Estonia in 1944.* Firearms

---

* His Lithuanian and Latvian counterparts were Stasys Žymantas, an Oxford-educated émigré lawyer, and Rūdolfs Silarājs, an airman.

practice took place in a quarry some twenty miles from London, while parachute training was based at an airport near Abingdon. The trainees practised landing from small boats on the Isle of Wight, learned unarmed combat at Fort Monckton and honed survival techniques at a commando-training base in Scotland near Ben Nevis. The training, ranging from memorisation to Morse code, secret writing, woodcraft and close combat, was excellent. The agents' abilities in communications, tactics, weapons-handling, evasion and escape techniques and other elements of covert operations and spycraft were incomparably higher than their counterparts back home. After the first few years of fighting had thinned the ranks of the veterans, the partisans were mainly farm boys, wise in the ways of the countryside, but no match for the battle-hardened counter-insurgency troops of the KGB. Other bits of the Baltic operations were sloppier. Anthony Cavendish, a former SIS dispatch officer in Germany, recalls:

We took the agents down to the Reeperbahn, the red-light district of Hamburg, to a little bar we had selected beforehand . . . We were soon joined by heavily made-up girls and, as the serious drinking began, I headed back. About 3 am, there was violent banging on my front door . . . Two of our agents had returned but Peter [an SIS officer] and the other agent had got into a fight . . . It was only because of . . . long-standing contacts with the police that we were able to get Peter and the Latvian released into our custody.[16]

SIS seems not to have pondered the lessons of this incident for its selection procedures and security routines. It should also have questioned the flawed assumptions behind the whole operation.

The first of these was that the Soviet Union was indeed

planning a military assault on the West, rather than struggling to deal with its colossal internal problems. Another was that the existing networks were sound. In fact they were a trap. The idea that outside agents would gain useful information about Soviet military activities in the region, let alone any insights into the authorities' decision-making, was far-fetched. That they could engage in combat operations inside the Soviet Union was even more dubious. Were the trainees spies or commandos? Was their job to monitor Soviet troop movements or to sabotage them? From 1949 onwards, SIS tried to downplay the trainees' role in resistance operations and stressed the importance of espionage, but this risked denting their motivation. Going home to fight the occupiers and free the homeland was a powerful incentive, but risking torture and death to snoop around for a foreign power was less compelling.

A second element of treachery was in play too. Until 1947 Kim Philby, the most senior KGB spy in the West, was the head of SIS's Section 9, in charge of all British operations against the Soviet Union. At that point he moved to Washington, DC, to an even more sensitive role: as liaison officer between SIS and the newly formed CIA. As he later wrote:

> In order to avoid the dangers of overlapping and duplication, the British and Americans exchanged precise information about the timing and geographical coordinates of their operations. I do not know what happened to the parties concerned. But I can make an informed guess.[17]

As Britain and America marched deeper into the bog, the KGB became bolder. In October 1948 Lukaševičs organised the bogus 'escape' of a seasoned agent called Vidvuds Šveics, who claimed to be a representative of the Latvian resistance. In retrospect, that seems an obvious dangle and a leading Latvian activist in Stockholm working with SIS was immediately suspicious.[18] But in another grotesque breach of tradecraft, Šveics was put in charge of a six-strong group (two from each of the three countries) trained by SIS. Worse, he was given a list of local sympathisers – just the people that the KGB most wished to catch. When his team landed near the Lithuanian resort of Palanga on 1 May Šveics separated from the others and alerted the border guards, who killed both Estonians and one of the Latvians. The others fled. Šveics sent a cipher message telling SIS that he had made a miraculous escape. By the year-end the entire network was under KGB control, though still, in the eyes of the British spymasters, operating and intact. The next expedition of the beefed-up operation was in October 1949, when a group of the elaborately trained recruits landed in Latvia to be met by KGB agents posing as resistance fighters. In London, SIS celebrated a successful landing.

The Americans were making mistakes too. They were starting from 'virtually empty' files: little more than whatever pre-war reference books and press cuttings could be found in the Library of Congress. Harry Rositzke, a senior CIA officer, noted: 'Even the most elementary facts were unavailable – on roads and bridges, on the location and production of factories, on city plans and airfields.'[19] Incoming intelligence was little help. 'Most of it was trivial, much of it spotty, garbled or out of date.' Amid the ignorance grew panic. Western military planners believed, wrongly, that Soviet forces were capable of reaching the English Channel in a matter of weeks. By late 1949, they reckoned that Soviet bombers could drop nuclear weapons on America. Rositzke recalls a military officer banging the table in the Pentagon and shouting: 'I want an agent with a radio on every goddamn airfield between Berlin and the Urals!' Faced with utterly impractical demands, America's spy chiefs too threw caution (and ethics) to the winds,[20] recruiting hundreds of émigrés for parachute drops into communist-ruled Europe, from the Baltic to the Black Sea. Among them were some notorious Nazi war criminals, including senior Nazis such as Otto von Bolschwing, a close associate of Adolf Eichmann, the architect of the Holocaust.[21] This was not an oversight: German wartime intelligence had been excellent, and retained useful assets and insights in the East. The price was American moral credibility. It became a lot easier for Soviet propagandists to say that the West was crawling with fascists when Nazi collaborators were facing promotion, not punishment.

In the Baltics American efforts centred on the charismatic (and entirely honourable) Lukša, who had returned from Lithuania deeply worried about KGB penetration of the resistance. In January 1949 America flew Lithuanian émigré leaders to Washington, DC, to sign a formal agreement with the CIA, backed by an annual grant of $40,000. Meanwhile the SIS-backed Lithuanians were falling deeper into the KGB's grasp. From being unwittingly under Soviet control, they were now working hand-in-hand with the country's occupiers. Despite warning signals – a failure to answer a trick question and a failed assassination attempt on SIS's top Lithuanian in Stockholm – Britain failed to notice anything amiss. The CIA was misreading the signs too: Lukša's final mission to Lithuania was unsuccessful, because the partisans were by now so weak that collecting intelligence, let alone fighting the Soviets, was difficult. Quite unfairly, the Americans worried that Lukša's lacklustre reporting showed that he had been turned or betrayed. The British-backed agents seemed to be doing so much better. The outcome could hardly have been better for the KGB: the British suspected that the American operation was leaky; the Americans suspected the British. Carr flew to Washington to have it out with Rositzke. The exchange between the two Harrys ran as follows:

R: Do we know which of these operations is already under Russian control?

C: Ours isn't.

R: How can you be so sure that your agent isn't under control?

C: We're sure.

R: But how can you be?

C: Because we've made our checks. Our group is watertight.

R: So's ours, but one group is penetrated.

C: Harry, I think we know our business on this one.[22]

Carr could hardly have been more wrong. Britain was making the biggest bungles imaginable, with a flawed concept, weak operational planning, poor assessment and sloppy compartmentalisation. Worse, the notetaker at this meeting was none other than Kim Philby.* The reaction that his account of this top-secret meeting aroused among his controllers in Moscow can only be imagined.

By 1949, the Baltic resistance was effectively over. Collectivisation of agriculture and the accompanying mass deportations had all but destroyed the partisans' food supplies and support networks. Cruelty against those who continued to resist was extreme:

Extreme forms of torture, quartering, tongue-cutting, eye-gouging, burying heads down in ant hills, etc., were employed to break the fighters. Mutilated corpses were dumped in town squares – and reactions of passers-by were surreptitiously observed in an attempt to identify relatives and friends.[23]

---

* After leaving SIS Philby worked briefly for my employer, the *Economist*, as our Beirut-based Middle East correspondent. Barbara Smith, then one of our Middle East editors, remembers his reporting as excellent but that she had to chivvy him over his lack of productivity. Shortly afterwards we found out the reasons, when he turned up in the Soviet Union.

Western spymasters seemed quite unaware of the disaster. In the spring of 1951, SIS, with Swedish help, sent four new agents to the Latvian coast. Unbeknown to the spymasters in London, one was a traitor planted earlier by the KGB. SIS had prudently ordered the Estonian agent to head straight for his own country rather than make contact with the Latvian group. But nobody in the Estonian KGB was prepared to take the risk of allowing the SIS man to complete even the semblance of his mission there. Instead, they arrested him. He swallowed a cyanide capsule. His code name was 'Gustav' but his real name is unknown. In 1952 more SIS-trained agents came ashore, including one with some excellent forgeries of Soviet passports, which were of great interest to the KGB. With a proper crop of such documents to examine, they could see what errors or omissions to look for. At least according to the KGB museum in Moscow, one such telltale was the high quality of staples used to hold the documents together. In the Soviet Union, these were made of cheap iron which left traces of rust. Western forgeries used staples made with stainless steel. Even if the paper, cover, ink and stamps were perfect, the lack of rust and shiny steel fasteners were a lethal giveaway.

Undeterred, Rebane recruited more agents, speaking of the 'holy duty' of resistance to the occupiers. One such recruit was a hapless young man called Mart Männik. He had been working in a cotton mill in Preston in the north of England – one of the many displaced Estonians, Latvians and Lithuanians starting new lives in the West. Rebane told him:

A resistance organisation has been activated and is operating now, principally on the basis of the forest brothers who conduct an underground struggle against the Russian occupiers with the aim of restoring the Estonian Republic. For us, foreign Estonians, it is a holy duty to support this struggle in every way possible.

Unfortunately, we do not have a link with the motherland so that at any price we need to create this . . . Therefore, we are forced to work together with the English, who on certain conditions set by themselves are ready to assist us materially.

The conditions are: obtaining every type of intelligence information concerning the Soviet Union. We must of course agree with these conditions, all the more so since this does not damage our endeavours, but on the contrary, it will be useful for us. So, the English have now created within their intelligence services a so-called Baltic Group. . .we are totally under their management. . . our only resource [is] brave and enterprising Estonian men who would be ready to carry out this difficult mission.[24]

Männik agreed readily. Rebane explained that he would be posted to Estonia for a year to eighteen months. Equipped with four radios, codebooks, forged Soviet documents, weapons, 2,000 cartridges and 150,000 Soviet roubles, his group successfully landed in Latvia in late September 1951. By now the Estonian KGB was following the example of its Latvian counterparts. It housed the arrivals in an elaborate network of bunkers and safe houses, complete with 'colleagues' from the supposed resistance movement, including an old friend of Rebane's who had been turned by the KGB. On 3 February Männik and his colleague were invited to a party in a Tallinn suburb where he was given drugged vodka and captured.

Despite the brilliance of Lukaševičs and his colleagues, the deception operation was endangered by the feebleness of the intelligence being gathered. Lukša had provided Sweden with extensive information about political and economic conditions[25] and gave the CIA an excellent report about a secret radio installation.[26] To keep the operation credible, Lukaševičs urgently needed to provide more real secrets. But in the paranoid world of Soviet intelligence nobody was willing to take that risk. For example when SIS wanted details of ships docking at the Latvian port of Ventspils, the Soviet defence ministry insisted that the data be deliberately understated. Lukaševičs protested: foreign vessels used the port too so the information could be cross-checked. If the estimates were too low, they would dent the operation's credibility. But Moscow was adamant. Unsurprisingly, SIS analysts in London did notice problems with the data and sent a stern message along with some more demanding tasks.

Compounding the growing unease in some quarters was the absence of trouble. Some seasoned SIS officers had noted that American and British efforts in Ukraine, Albania and Romania had ended in dismal failure. Why was the Baltic operation so curiously successful? An SIS officer of Lithuanian extraction, John Ludzius, was one of those sounding the alarm. But the obsessively secretive Harry Carr, smugly over-confident despite his lamentable failures in the interwar years, enjoyed the personal backing of the then SIS chief, John 'Sinbad' Sinclair. Ludzius was posted to the Far East.

Yet the worries were growing anew. In any clandestine operation, snags signal health and their absence should be profoundly troubling. The new CIA director, General Walter Bedell 'Beetle' Smith became convinced in 1951 that the lavishly financed covert operations against the communist bloc were in urgent need of scrutiny. He charged an old friend, General Lucian Truscott, to re-examine the whole programme.[27] In early 1952, having inspected the training facilities, Truscott was horrified, particularly at the links to the heavily penetrated émigré organisations. An assistant, Tom Polgar, noted that Hitler's 270 divisions had failed to topple Soviet power. How were a ragtag army of lightly armed guerrillas supposed to do any better? All their missions were proving, he scoffed, was the law of gravity. Drop agents out of aeroplanes and they would fall to the ground.

The American spymasters were unmoved. Rositzke thought that the scale of the operation must be causing nightmares in the Soviet leadership: even if they mopped up most of the agents, in a totalitarian system countering the slightest risk of subversion would consume huge resources. 'Those in the Kremlin must be scared shitless,' he said.[*] Caution was out of fashion and money was plentiful.[†] The Baltic operations seemed at least in terms of volume to be the most promising. General Eisenhower himself visited the Baltic agents to assure them of his support. The operation continued, with parachute drops supplementing the midnight naval excursions favoured by SIS. A new American case officer, Paul Hartman, took charge, telling his trainees to ignore 'nationalist rubbish' and concentrate on real spying. Three of his agents parachuted into Latvia on 30 August 1952, with the promise of a $15,000 bonus if they returned safely. Two were caught; one committed suicide, the second surrendered. The third[‡] could have reported the truth: the partisans were defeated and the KGB in full control. Unfortunately, he proved to be an inadequate spy. He tracked down an old girlfriend and spent his operational funds on entertaining her. When he was picked up during a routine document check, the KGB determined that he had not transmitted any substantial intelligence. Armed with his codes and radio, it was able to spin the Red Web to include the Americans too.

---

[*] A CIA officer called David Murphy responded in a similar vein. 'Even if they don't send back good intelligence, we're causing the Russians a lot of headaches.'

[†] The Mutual Security Act allocated $100m to fund anti-Soviet guerrilla warfare.

[‡] Nikolai Balodis.

Increasing political pressure heightened the chances of failure. John Foster Dulles, soon to become secretary of state, had
denounced mere containment of communism as 'negative, futile
and immoral'; it consigned 'countless human beings to despot-
ism and godless terrorism' and enabled the Soviets to 'forge their
captives into a weapon of our destruction'. Over at the CIA his
brother Allen called for a 'spiritual crusade' for the liberation of
Eastern Europe. As Tom Bower notes in *Red Web*:

> At the very moment when the overwhelming majority of the
> CIA's and SIS's covert operations in Russia and the satellite coun-
> tries was proving disastrous, the politicians were clamouring for
> more.[28]

The efforts were producing no usable intelligence and showed
no sign of destabilising Soviet rule. The best agents were dead,
such as Lukša, betrayed and killed in 1951.* Soviet propagandists were regularly publishing gleeful exposés of captured agents,
with details of their training and missions. Meanwhile SIS was
reeling from the news that two British diplomats, Guy Burgess
and Donald Maclean, had been unmasked as Soviet spies. The
case against Philby was unproven, but the CIA had demanded
his recall from Washington. It would have been a good time to
pull back and submit all operations involving the Soviet Union,
émigrés and partisans to cold, clear-headed scrutiny. But Carr and
his colleagues pressed on.

It also would have been tempting for the KGB to use the bogus
networks to plant disinformation – perhaps to scare the West into
wasting resources, or even to give phoney reassurance about the

---

* An American-trained Lithuanian, Jonas Kukauskas, was captured soon after
being parachuted into Lithuania in April. Faced with torture, he agreed to
betray his leader, whose grave has never been found.

benign intentions of the Soviet leadership. But the KGB aim was narrower and deeper: first to distract and then to penetrate SIS and the CIA. The next stage was to send a seasoned KGB officer to the West. The choice was a man named Jānis Ērglis who had long fought the partisans in the forests of Latvia, and was now tasked with impersonating one. He 'escaped' to Sweden, convinced the intelligence service there of his bona fides, and then moved to Germany where, after feigning reluctance, he was recruited by SIS. After training he returned to Latvia, this time as leader of a group of four agents. Thus the KGB not only controlled the activities of the British agents; it was able to stage-manage them too. Flickers of discontent among the unfortunate genuine agents sent to Latvia had no chance of reaching London.

Lukaševičs next arranged for misfortunes to befall two of the genuine London-trained agents. Instead of smelling a rat, SIS decided to send replacements, receiving another phoney partisan, a radio operator called 'Edmundas', as well as a fiery and effective fighter*, whose desire to kill communists had strained the patience of his hosts. The KGB then sent a heavyweight 'ambassador' from the phoney partisans to London, who solemnly negotiated a deal with SIS and the émigré authorities, dividing ministerial portfolios in a putative independent Latvia. He returned home with a colossal cache of money − around a million roubles. Lukaševičs was later to boast that a total of 3.5m roubles from the British taxpayer had financed his entire deception operation. Real agents, such as a brave young Latvian CIA man called Leonids Zariņš, paid the biggest price of these games. He was parachuted into Latvia alone on 14 May 1953. But the CIA shared details with SIS, which took no precautions to keep the information secret from others in the operation. Zariņš walked straight into a trap and perished

---

* Ludis Upāns, cited in Bower as 'Lodis' Upāns.

in a Siberian prison camp. His family, who believed their son was working for Bell Telephone, was told that he had died in an air crash in Austria.

But the KGB was becoming a victim of its own success. London requested a sample of water from the Tobol River, near the site of the reactor that produced the Soviet Union's plutonium. The idea that a partisan, with forged papers or none at all, could emerge from a forest bunker and cross and recross the Soviet Union successfully, via a tightly guarded nuclear installation, was so bizarre that only a spy chief could have conceived it. But the Soviet response was equally incompetent. Told to provide some radioactive water, KGB technicians (presumably poorly briefed) decided to show off. They produced 'river water' of such lethal radioactivity that it could only have been created actually inside the core of a reactor. Once that was analysed in London, it was finally clear that something was seriously amiss. America commissioned an independent investigation and ended its operation in 1954. Operation Jungle limped on for two more years. A final message to the partisans in 1956 read:

> We can no longer help you. Will be sending no further physical or material help. All safe houses are blown . . .This is our last message until better times. We will listen to you until 30 June. Thereafter God help you.

By this stage the real partisan forces numbered only a few thousand. Exhausted and demoralised, with their national identity being eradicated by the occupation[29] and with no sign of the hoped-for Third World War in sight, their mood was bitter. The failure of the West to support the Hungarian uprising in 1956 was the last straw: in the words of the Estonian historian Mart Laar, 'they finally realised that the white ships were not coming'. Elena

Jučiūtė, a Lithuanian dissident deported for fifteen years for her 'anti-Soviet' activities, wrote in her diary that:

> the Western states, which speak so many beautiful words about human rights, the right of national self-determination, freedom, humanitarianism. . .were unwilling to support with a firm word a small nation, heroically fighting for its freedom. None of us had expected such turpitude from the free world; we had a better opinion of them, and for this reason, the disappointment was devastating.[30]

By the end it was only the brutality of the Soviet authorities that kept the spark of resistance alive: if death in battle was bad, capture was far worse. A dry medical account of the wounds on the body of the American-born last leader of the Lithuanian partisan movement Adolfas Ramanauskas, codenamed *Vanagas* (Hawk), finally captured with his wife in October 1956 and tortured for a year before his execution on 9 November 1957, gives an indication of the horrors that awaited the inmates of the KGB's dungeons:

> The right eye is covered with haematomas, on the eyelid there are six stab wounds made, judging by their diameter, by a thin wire or nail going deep into the eyeball. Multiple haematomas in the area of the stomach, a cut wound on a finger of the right hand. The genitalia reveal the following: a large tear wound on the right side of the scrotum and a wound on the left side, both testicles and spermatic ducts are missing.[31]

Probably the last active partisans, the Lithuanians Antanas Kraujelis and Pranas Končius, were hunted down in 1965; a few others continued living illegally in the forests or concealed in family members' houses for years after that. Jānis Pīnups, a Latvian,

lived underground during the entire fifty-year period of Soviet
occupation, emerging from his 'illegal' existence only after the last
Russian troops withdrew from the Baltic in 1994.[32]

In all, Operation Jungle sent at least forty-two Estonians,
Latvians and Lithuanians back to their homelands, usually in the
small hours of moonless summer nights. Not only was their own
fate tragic: their presence was toxic to their cause. If they made
contact with genuine partisans, the result was disaster. It stoked
Soviet paranoia and discredited the West. The bravery of the
resistance proved less inspiring to later dissidents than the legacy
of failure. The demoralisation in SIS, and corrosion of trust with
the CIA, was lasting. For those inside the Soviet empire, the idea
that the West was a reliable ally in the struggle against communism – and even that the struggle was worth waging – had taken
a beating. In the West, the knowledge that the Soviet side had so
easily penetrated the anti-Soviet operation, probably right from
the beginning, was a huge hurdle for anyone suggesting anything
bold in the coming years. That glum mood was compounded
when news broke of the treachery of Kim Philby. It was easy to
think that Western spies, particularly British ones, were worse
than useless.

The great puzzle of Operation Jungle, and of its American and
Swedish counterparts, is who at what stage on the Western side
realised that the operations were blown, and how they reacted.
The conventional account, as outlined by Tom Bower in *Red
Web*, suggests all-encompassing naivety and incompetence. But it
does not quite fit all the facts. One fragment of possible evidence
for an alternative version of events comes from Mart Männik's
memoirs. Confronted by his captors with every detail of his
mission, the resourceful SIS man soon realised that the entire
operation had been a sinister farce from the moment he set foot
in Estonia. Yet he did not despair, instead working out if by any

means he could warn Rebane, thus at least sparing the lives of other Estonians in London. In mid 1953, having spent the intervening months in a prison cell teaching himself Russian from Soviet propaganda books, Männik was instructed to send some messages back to London. After sending seven flawless ones, he claims he carefully inserted a secret code (using the three-dot 'S' in Morse code rather than the four-dot 'H'). This was a signal agreed with Rebane in case he found himself having to make a forced transmission.

He sent a second signal during a meeting with 'Albert', an Estonian partisan unaware of the KGB deception operation who was being sent back to Britain. Männik's job was to reassure him. Instead, risking torture and death, he did the opposite, snatching a chance to whisper: 'Tell Robert (Rebane's code name), and only him, that "H" has been "S" from the very beginning.' It is not clear if the message was understood or got through. In interviews with Estonian officials after 1991 'Albert' maintained that he had not heard any such words from Männik.* But other warnings did get through. Several other SIS men had on their return to London expressed suspicions about their 'partisan' hosts. Ludis Upāns, the real partisan returned to London in 1952 by his KGB hosts because of his excessive zeal, later claimed that he had told SIS that the resistance was bogus.[33] A KGB man sent to London in 1954 posing as a partisan leader was confronted with the puzzle of the radio-active water and suggested that perhaps one group of partisans had been penetrated, while his own was sound. In 1955 Rebane

---

* His real name was Nikolai Urm. He worked until retirement in the electrical department of the John Lewis department store and died in 2005 in the drab London suburb of Neasden, where a rusty horseshoe (characteristic for Estonian homes) over the doorway of his house in Bermans Way is the only remaining sign of his remarkable career. If by any chance his niece, Karen 'Kim' Toley, should read this book I would be most grateful to hear from her.

was alerted personally by a former wartime comrade, turned by the KGB and sent to lure him back to Estonia for a show trial, who confessed his mission during a drunken evening. At least two phoney partisans brought to London had been spotted by chance as communist collaborators by other émigrés.

It is quite possible, as Bower argues, that SIS simply ignored such warnings because self-deception and self-interest overlapped. But continuing with Operation Jungle may have also been a master-stroke of reverse deception. If the KGB could be made to believe it had fooled the British completely, it would greatly increase the chance of running real operations. One piece of evidence comes from Captain Bernhard Nelberg, an Estonian refugee in London, who in August 1950 wrote to his country's ambassador, August Torma (himself on SIS's books) to say that he was going on a dangerous mission during which he might be captured or killed by the Soviets. In that event, he said, he bequeathed his property to the Estonian embassy in London. (This was maintaining a precarious existence on the fringes of official diplomacy. It still had staff and a building, and plenty of work. But the country it represented had been wiped from the map.)[34] Although I can find no trace of Captain Nelberg's mission, it was not part of Operation Jungle.

Harder evidence comes from an operation involving the Estonian Voldemar Kiik, one of the most successful British agents of the post-war era. His story is almost entirely unknown outside Estonia, where he was buried with military honours in the national cemetery, next to Rebane, after his death in 2002. His mission was to reconnoitre the airfield at Tartu, Estonia's second city. Details of his mission remain classified to this day, but it would have been of huge interest to British and American intelligence to know about any hardened hangars, the quality and quantity of air defences, and signs of nuclear weapons storage and transport. Kiik was a medical student in London when Rebane approached him, probably in 1950. He was the ideal recruit – brainy, determined and a cut above the other Estonian young men in London, whose patriotism often outweighed their other talents (they, in turn, found his successful womanising tiresome). He was already battle-hardened. Mobilised by the Red Army in 1940, he jumped off a troop train and hid in a forest before being conscripted by the Germans. Wounded in the head in the battle of Velikaya Luka near Leningrad, he was left for dead during a German retreat, only to be rescued during a counterattack. He detested both occupying powers equally. Rather than exchange the mandatory '*Heil Hitler!*' greeting, he and the other Estonians in his unit would shout '*Ei Ütle!*' (Don't Say!). The pronunciation was close enough to fool the Germans, and gave a pleasant tingle of resistance.

As well as the usual tradecraft, he was schooled intensively in Russian (which he did not speak) and in Pelmanism – the knack of remembering large quantities of data. But in a notable difference from the carelessness that surrounded Operation Jungle, he does not seem to have been trained with the other Estonians. With a cyanide pill sewn into his lip he parachuted into Estonia in the summer of 1952. Though tempted to visit his mother – it would have been his only chance to see her before she died – he concentrated on his mission, perhaps using the remnants of a pre-war British network for support. His route back involved a perilous crossing of the Norwegian–Soviet frontier where disaster nearly struck. Another British agent making the same crossing shortly beforehand had come across some border guards asleep at their post and had shot them, perhaps unaware that he was complicating things for anyone else. The result was a frenzy of border-guard activity. Starving, sodden and fearing capture, Kiik waited in a swamp for two weeks, living off berries. He then took a Benzedrine pill he had been saving for emergencies and crossed the border where his reception party was still waiting, as this previously unpublished picture depicts (Kiik is on the right).* His name did not appear on a list of Estonians wanted by the KGB, and his family was not harassed, showing that the Soviet authorities never got wind of his mission (they believed he had emigrated to Canada). Prematurely grey after his ordeal, he then worked for the British government as an instructor in covert operations (among his pupils, he once said, was the future King of Norway).†

   Kiik's successful mission, the mysterious agent who crossed the border before him, Captain Nelberg's letter and some other evidence of separate, successful missions all support the theory that SIS, perhaps as early as 1950 and certainly by 1952, had reason to continue Operation Jungle as a bluff. If so, the human calculations

---

* I would be glad to hear from anyone who can identify the SIS officer on the left.
† He returned to Estonia for several visits in the 1990s, donating money for a war memorial and enjoying a belated recognition for his efforts. He passed on coordinates for the place near Murmansk where he buried his transmitter. A former Estonian official has the coordinates and plans to retrieve it when practical.

are chilling. Were the agents still inside the Soviet Union counted as good as dead? What of the men being sent to join them? The verdict of sheer incompetence might be moderated by the steel nerves and stunning cynicism that such decisions would involve.

Meanwhile a conflict between intelligence and political objectives was plaguing the other side too. The Soviet authorities wanted to lure a senior Estonian émigré figure – ideally Rebane – across the border for a humiliating show trial. The KGB was more interested in further penetration of SIS and the CIA. But with Rebane belatedly aware of the deception, the hunters had become the hunted. It is unclear how far Rebane and SIS were at cross-purposes in the final years of the operation. The wily Estonian claimed later that even after the closure of the Latvian and Lithuanian operations, he fought to maintain the radio games with the KGB-controlled partisans, in the hope of getting his own agents back. He succeeded in at least one instance, but his career with SIS was over. The once-dashing officer ended up working as a night watchman before moving to Germany and a job in that country's intelligence service. Having dodged repeated attempts by the KGB to entrap him, he died in 1976, having burned his papers; his devoted secretary Liis Dillie Lindre lived to see her country regain independence in 1991, yet continued to sleep with a loaded revolver by her bed (in a suburb of Brussels) even after the Soviet Union collapsed. Rebane's Latvian and Lithuanian colleagues moved to the United States. Carr was shunted first sideways and then out of the service; until his death in 1988 he blamed Philby, not his own incompetence, for the fiasco. Viktor van Jung, a cerebral and charismatic Estonian émigré who had trained two CIA agents[35] who went on a doomed mission in 1954, went on to a high-flying career in the agency. Strong indications are that he was the CIA officer who ran Ryszard Kukliński, a senior Polish officer who passed on invaluable Warsaw Pact secrets to NATO.[36]

According to Rositzke, none of the CIA operatives returned from their missions.[37] But a sprinkling of former agents who survived inside the Soviet Union did crop up after 1991, with embarrassing consequences for their spymasters. One of the most conspicuous cases involved Sweden, a country that had maintained a stony silence over its espionage efforts in the Baltics, which seem to have been every bit as disastrous as those of SIS and the CIA.[38] The activities of the *C-byrån* (C-Agency), renamed in 1946 as *T-kontoret* (T-Office), began during the war and were stepped up in 1948 when a Soviet attack on Sweden seemed all too likely. Using Baltic émigrés and run in close cooperation with SIS, they finished in 1957, after the humiliating public exposure of a Swedish spy ring and a formal Soviet diplomatic protest.[39]

One of the Swedish agents was a young émigré called Ewald Hallisk. His story mirrored many of his generation: conscripted into the German army at the age of sixteen, he had fled to Sweden to escape the Soviet advance. Spurred by a mixture of adventure and patriotism, he volunteered to join the Swedish secret service in 1948 and was sent on a mission two years later. He left behind a fiancée, Margaret, and a toddler son, Peter. For forty-two years after he went missing, his family assumed he was dead. Nobody else wanted to admit that he had existed at all. Swedish authorities covered up the fiasco, citing official secrecy and claiming falsely that even if some such operation had existed all the documents involved had been burned in the 1960s.

On 29 June 1992, Peter Kadhammar, a journalist on the Swedish newspaper *Expressen*, produced a sensational scoop.[40] Far from being dead, Hallisk was living in a modest cottage in Estonia. The 'spy who never was' proved only too happy to talk about his training in firearms, shortwave radio, and invisible ink. He also wanted money: he had, he insisted, been betrayed by the same incompetence that had marred the SIS and CIA operations. The

KGB had picked him up within two days of arriving in Estonia. He had spent two months on death row and then fifteen years in a labour camp in Magadan, one of the harshest parts of the Soviet penal system, and remained under close KGB scrutiny after his release. Swedish officials initially argued that he had been a volunteer and knew what he was getting into. Then they offered him 500,000 kronor (about $80,000 in the money of 2011). He sued, and won a modest top-up of 120,000 kronor. But it was all too late: Margaret had died, and he found little common ground with Peter.⁴¹ After an unhappy stay in Sweden he returned to his humble life in Estonia.

Other survivors were even unluckier. In 1991 I tracked down Klemensas Širvys, parachuted into Lithuania in October 1950 together with Lukša. When I asked him about his mission, he burst into tears. A widower, crippled by a stroke, he lived in dismally poor conditions in a remote part of Lithuania. The botched operation had ruined his life. I was expecting a tirade. But he bore no bitterness towards the Americans or the British: indeed he spoke broken English proudly from his time spent in a British labour battalion in post-war Germany. His one regret was that the Western allies had sent so few people, so late, to fight the communists. It was hard to imagine that this lame, tearful old man had four decades ago come ashore with a Schmeisser MP-32 sub-machine gun, grenades, radios and cyanide tablets. After a year in a bunker he was captured, tortured and sent to Siberia for a twenty-five-year sentence with five further years in exile.⁴² Neither the CIA nor SIS appears to have made provision for him after 1991.* A similarly poignant story concerns Zigmas Kudirka, a bright young Lithuanian émigré recruited by SIS in post-war London and sent in autumn 1952 as a radio operator. In 1956

---

* I shall be delighted if I am misinformed.

he appealed to SIS to get him out, and was told (in his words) 'chin up' and to try to make his own way to Sweden. Speaking in 1989, in fluent English, Kudirka showed unconcealed rage:

> British intelligence is known all over the world as one of the best. Of course I trusted them. I felt elevated to be a member of the British intelligence service and I tried to do my best.

He found the news that he had been a pawn in the KGB's game shattering:

> It was like a blow on the head. I could not understand how an intelligence service like the British could have made such a mistake. It was unbelievable . . . I took the risk but I hoped for normal work. But what happened? I was from the beginning like a blind kitten put into the net of Soviet intelligence. What was the risk for, all the suffering, and all the broken life?[43]

A galling footnote came when Kudirka turned up in London in 1990 in the vain hope of retrieving his belongings, including irreplaceable family photographs, which he had left with SIS for safekeeping. His former case officer, John Ludzius, met him in a pub with the bracing greeting: 'I thought you were all dead.'[44] In the 1990s another Lithuanian SIS man, Anicetas Dukavičius, also tried (apparently unsuccessfully) to gain some compensation from the British authorities. After some lobbying and the publication of Mart Männik's posthumous memoirs, the Männik family on 4 June 2003 received €10,000 from the British government.

Such stingy, tardy or outright hostile treatment contrasts sharply with the efforts made by SIS (and the CIA) to find dependants of dead agents from the more recent era. In one creditable and poignant episode in 1990, a young woman received a startling and mysterious invitation, summoning her to a meeting in the presidential offices in Prague Castle where senior SIS officers and their local counterparts explained what until then had been an inexplicable misfortune in her life. Her father Miloslav Kroča, the head of the British section of the communist secret police, the StB, had died (naturally) of a heart attack in 1976; her mother had some time later became ill after mistakenly taking one of his invisible-ink pills, kept in an aspirin bottle. Puzzled, she took the pills to a pharmacist; an investigation eventually alerted the authorities that the dead man must in fact have been a Western spy. Forced to live in miserable conditions in a remote part of the country, the family was blighted. The mother died, while the daughter was barred from higher education or a proper career. The visitors then handed over a large sum of money, explaining that though her father had spied for the West solely on ideological grounds he had asked that if anything were to befall him his family should be taken care of.[45] Mr Kroča, one of the most important British spies behind the Iron Curtain, was recruited by Richard Dearlove, then a 'First Secretary' (but actually SIS officer) at the British embassy in Prague and later Chief of MI6.

Perhaps the most tantalising loose end comes from Alexander Koppel, who is almost certainly the last surviving agent from Operation Jungle. Tracking him down was rather like finding a pterodactyl alive and well in a bungalow near London (in Mr Koppel's case, Wokingham). A glass-fronted bookcase containing medals and memorabilia is the only sign of his extraordinary past. A sprightly 85 (when I interviewed him in early 2011), he described in matter-of-fact terms his recruitment, training, life in the 'underground', capture, interrogation and eventual release. He came to Britain in 1947, and worked in Dunstable in a cement works, along with many other Estonian, Latvian and Lithuanian young men keen to leave the displaced person camps of post-war

Germany. It was a hard, dull life. News from home was scant: even discovering which family members were alive and which had perished was hard.

In 1952 Mr Koppel was approached by Rebane and asked if he would be willing to go on a mission as a radio operator. He initially declined: his parents were still in Estonia, and would suffer horribly if he were caught. He recalls that Rebane tried to reassure him, in words that seem bizarrely complacent in retrospect: 'Don't worry – it's quite safe, quite nice.' Getting there, he said, was 'as simple as a bus ride'. Mr Koppel moved to Old Church St, and started training. His task was simply to operate a radio, so he received what he describes as 'negligible' instruction in spycraft or combat*. The trainees were taken sightseeing to Stonehenge, and for a boat trip on the Thames. A Lithuanian taught them Russian, which they barely spoke. The evening before his departure, Rebane took him aside to give him a final briefing. 'Take no initiative. You are only the radio operator. Take orders from "Karl" (the partisan commander). Don't drink. Know your place.'

The first hint of trouble came when Mr Koppel arrived in Saaremaa, an island off Estonia's coast that had once been a hotbed of anti-communist resistance. He was met by partisans who – had he known it – were all seasoned KGB officers. They took his carefully packed suitcase, which contained money, arms and other material for the resistance, and returned it with the contents jumbled, claiming that it had been dropped and burst open. His enquiries about the situation in the country got cursory answers. Hidden in an attic in a farm near Viljandi in southern Estonia, Mr Koppel got on with encoding and sending messages to London.

His KGB colleagues made life seem realistic, at one point staging

---

* He had been conscripted in the German army briefly in 1944, but did not serve in Rebane's unit.

1956 Mr Koppel was suddenly taken to Moscow, where
as held in the Lubyanka – the infamous headquarters of the
. No explanation was given, and the treatment was good – at
oint his hosts even took him to the Bolshoi Ballet. 'I am not
ing fingers,' he says. 'They were nice and polite' (this may
be the only time that an imprisoned SIS agent has applied this
ular set of adjectives to his KGB captors). References to Mr
el in KGB files make it clear that his captors believed they
cured his agreement to work in the West. In the small hours
ummer morning, they took him to the coast of northern
ia, and to his huge surprise gave back his gun, and provided
vith a boat, a compass bearing to a lighthouse, and a phone
er in Finland.

Koppel was convinced that this was merely a prelude
murder (it is easy to imagine the KGB-sponsored news
about a 'fascist bandit' being foiled in the act of escape).
ptors' parting words were to remind him that his family
ned in Estonia. As his boat chugged through the twilight, the
dawned. He was indeed being released. As he approached
h territorial waters, a speedboat neared. Fearing that it was
nnish coastguard, Mr Koppel hurriedly dropped his gun
he side of the boat. But the crew of the boat simply waved
assed by. He had returned to the free world. He found
se and made his phone call: Rebane answered. He had
been expecting Mr Koppel's return. Initially, the new
was uncertain what account to give. 'I wasn't sure what to
m – I was in this labyrinth of doubts,' he says. He was also
d that the KGB had a mole in SIS: 'anything I tell them,
tell the Russians'.

r a cursory debriefing by SIS, who appeared distrustful of
then told Rebane the full story – or at least his side of it. But
vas the whole truth? Why had the KGB released someone

a hurried forced march into the forests t
Mysterious lorries came and went in the 1
and delivering teams of KGB watchers,
In the winter of 1954–5, the partisans said
new location in northern Estonia. The g
a villa in Nõmme, a plush suburb of Talli
offered to celebrate – according to 'Karl
the group – a Soviet ID document that t
for their guest.

> I started to feel funny. I said, 'I'm not us
> that I had no time to think. I collapsed.
> movement. When I recovered I was nak
> were Russians, faces looking in. And tw

The KGB was convinced that Mr Kop
pill and had stripped him naked whil
standard procedure had been overlooke
he says, because he had been so seasicl
parents. Unwisely, he had confided to
the bunker that his relatives were alive
for time, but soon realised that every
already known. 'Every cloud has a silv
ing. 'I can't give away anything becaus
It was Mr Koppel's good fortune, per
after Stalin's death, and when the fo
more on counter-espionage than cour
decided to try and use him for their ov
of sanctions against his relatives alwa
moved him to a new location and tol
lar messages to the British, just as befo
than a year. Then followed the great

who would, if he spoke candidly, blow away the cobwebs of deception? One possibility (and to my mind the most likely) is that his release was part of a straight spy swap – the first of the Cold War. Rebane had known for some time that Operation Jungle was blown, and had been in regular radio contact with the bogus partisans. When each side realised that the other no longer believed in the fiction of a serious resistance organisation inside Estonia, it would have been time for straight talking. It may well be that Rebane offered to send back one of the KGB plants in London, in exchange for Mr Koppel.

Another possibility is that the KGB had tried to recruit Mr Koppel. That would explain the hotel-style treatment at the Lubyanka. But he would have been an unlikely plant: with Operation Jungle being wound up, anyone connected with it would be coming under great scrutiny. SIS would be well aware that 'Karl' and his partisans had been phoneys all along. Even if he went along with the KGB plan, the likelihood of anyone trusting Mr Koppel with any more secrets was minimal. Indeed, SIS treated him and the other returning agents with suspicion: some of them complained about regular and intrusive surveillance from counter-intelligence officers. Mr Koppel insists, moreover, that the KGB gave him no instructions or contact in London. His name later appeared on a list of fugitives wanted by the Soviet authorities, which suggests that he failed to follow any instructions the KGB had given him.

Until I outlined them to him, Mr Koppel was apparently unaware of the full extent and nature of the deception surrounding his mission. He had not read *Red Web*. But his faith in Rebane remains undimmed to this day (indeed the legendary Estonian commander was a guest of honour at his wedding in 1960). 'You told me "take no initiative",' he said to his boss wryly. Rebane responded coolly: 'I am a soldier, not a trained intelligence officer.' In any case, espionage was the last thing on Mr Koppel's much-burdened mind. He moved to the countryside, becoming a British citizen, recovering from a near-breakdown and putting all thoughts of Estonia aside. Only in the 1990s did that change. The three surviving Estonians of SIS – Kiik, Koppel and Urm – made themselves known to the newly established Estonian embassy in London. An official there at the time recalls receiving a phone call, in which an anonymous voice asked: 'How does my Estonian sound? You see I haven't spoken it for thirty years.' Along with other veterans of the partisan war, they received military decorations from their reborn country.[46]

After intense persuasion SIS also acknowledged its historical debt, inviting the three men to a champagne reception in 3, Carlton Gardens, where the service entertains foreign guests and the eternal 'Major Halliday' interviews graduate recruits.* It is just a stone's throw from the Ryder St office where their controllers had botched and bungled their mission. In the presence of senior British and Estonian officials, they were given replica statues of the commando memorial at Auchtermuchty on the slopes of Ben Nevis, where the agents of Operation Jungle had trained forty years previously. The figurine shows three men in pre-war battle-dress, bunched together, alert and watching, over an inscription reading 'United We Conquer'.† SIS added 'Never Forgotten'. After Britain's amnesia towards its debts in the Baltic, that could seem like wishful thinking. It is all the more poignant given the efforts that the authorities in Estonia were making to help British intelligence, for the third time in ninety years.

---

* In past years the recruitment interview has been conducted by men of varying build, height and hair colour. All introduced themselves as 'Major Halliday'.
† The statues are available from gift shops, at a price of around £200 (including postage and packing). A solid silver version is also available, but was presumably thought too expensive.

The Upside Down World

In early 1990, an unusual delegation began touring the spy agencies of Western Europe. It comprised the senior security officials of Czechoslovakia – a country where communist power had collapsed only weeks previously. The scruffy trio were more at home in the smoky cafés of the dissident cultural scene than in the taciturn and besuited world of espionage. But the message they bore from their country's new leadership was simple: a request for the greatest possible cooperation. Not only did they want help in building up new security and intelligence services, untainted by the communist past. They wanted defectors to return in glory, and for any of their citizens working undercover for Western spy agencies to come out into the open and receive medals.

The world had turned upside down. Security and intelligence had been both the citadel of communist power and the spearhead of outside attempts to breach it. Now the communist system's spooks were defeated while their Western counterparts blinked bewildered over the silent battlefield. Shortly after the 'Velvet Revolution' in November 1989 I was one of the first outsiders to visit the Prague headquarters of the feared StB secret police.*

---

* For *Státní bezpečnost* (State Security).

I had been the only newsman in Prague for the English-speaking media before the collapse of the regime. The building (a former theological college confiscated by the communists) had long been a source of fascination to me. It lay on the way to the airport, with a roof marked by distinctive antennae; the headquarters of a KGB front organisation was near by. It had a grim air to it: this was where the nastiest people in the country cooked up their witches' brew of blackmail and betrayal, where husbands and wives were set to spy on each other under threats of reprisals against their children, each wracked by guilt but believing that doing so was a necessary sacrifice. I had heard tales of torture in the cellars, and of the ever-present role of 'advisers' from Moscow – the ultimate bosses of the Czechoslovak communist state. Only weeks before any attempt to enter the building would have resulted in instant arrest. Now the regime was defeated; instead of scurrying past, I marched boldly in.

Our glum guide showed little enthusiasm for his task. All other employees, he droned, had been sent home to await instructions. I slipped away from the tour party of other nosy Westerners and roamed the unguarded offices, opening doors at random and browsing through files and card indexes. I hoped, not very realis-tically, to find some trace of the StB officers who in the past year had snooped on me, tried to recruit me, and bullied my friends. But the echoing corridors were not as deserted as they seemed. Around one corner I found an armoured door with an intercom. I pressed it. A peremptory voice asked me to identify myself. 'I'm a British journalist – can I come in?' I replied cheekily. Lucifer in the Vatican would have had a less frosty reception. Seconds later, my hosts crossly whisked me away. 'He was trying to get to the cipher room,' one muttered to the other. I was puzzled. If the service was dead, who was sending messages, and about what? As I was to find out, toppling communism was one thing, uprooting its structures another.

Well before the end of the Soviet empire in 1991, the battle lines had softened. As early as 1986, the CIA and KGB had set up a spooks' back-channel at a meeting in Vienna: the aim was to have a practical, depoliticised way of avoiding crises and misunderstandings, and to explore cooperation on subjects of common interest such as terrorism.[1] It later developed to include agreement about the treatment of defectors and haggling over spy swaps. After the Berlin Wall fell in October 1989, British, American and French spies found themselves hobnobbing with their Soviet counterparts, comparing notes on the troubling prospect of German unity. Milt Bearden, a top CIA man dealing with Eastern Europe, listened sympathetically as his KGB counterpart bemoaned the fact that he would soon need a visa to visit a city that his forebears had liberated from fascism at such enormous cost. In some cases, old foes went into business: setting up security companies or, in the case of two station chiefs from Berlin, KGB and CIA respectively, co-authorship.[2]

As the Kremlin lost its grip, the fringes of the former Soviet Union became a perfect springboard for spying on its core. The borderlands from Tallinn to Tbilisi, formerly a hostile operating environment, were now friendly and rewarding. Moreover, as the stick and the carrot of the Soviet system disappeared, the costs and risks of spying had never been lower. Treachery had once led not just to dismissal and imprisonment, but quite likely to death. The change came quickly. The last Western agent to be executed in the Soviet Union was the idealistic Dmitri Polyakov, a retired GRU major-general, in 1988.[3] But by 1989 the regime had largely lost its power to terrify. It could still blackmail, but the murderous fire in the belly of the system lit by Lenin in 1917 was all but extinguished. The intricate system of privileges used as rewards – access to a better shop, spacious housing, higher education for a child, maybe even a trip to a foreign country – was no longer attractive. With a bit of hard currency, the humblest individual could buy a better lifestyle than the system could offer its most favoured servants.

The ideological climate had changed too. For those with vestigial loyalties to the old regime, it was hard to stay motivated as its day of judgement loomed. Treating the West as a predatory enemy had been a bulwark of the Soviet mentality. Now the 'capitalist camp' was a valued partner, lending money and sending food aid. In the former satellite states, people were positively eager to help anyone wanting to bury the vestiges of the 'evil empire'. Even inside the most senior and sensitive parts of the state, the collapse of morale corroded loyalty.

The Cold War had been an existential struggle, in which ruthlessness generally triumphed over sentiment. The new era provided more complex choices. Was the big prize German reunification on the West's terms? In that case the priority should be to prop up the faltering regime in Moscow while it did the necessary deals. That would mean going easy on aggressive intelligence collection, which might seem like a further humiliation for the Soviet leadership. Others argued that it was futile to believe that the West could bolster the reformists, who might be out of power at any moment. It was better to press home what might be a temporary advantage. Counter-intelligence services in particular argued hard for the latter. The CIA and SIS both suspected that they had been badly penetrated during the Cold War, but had failed to nail the traitors. The Czechoslovak, East German, Hungarian and Polish spy agencies had all been fearsome adversaries. Now they were in friendly hands, offering a trove of clues about their past activities. With even the KGB in trouble, it had never been easier to track down moles, illegals, double agents and other sources. Indeed KGB officers were queuing – in some cases even literally – to offer their services to Western spycatchers, to the point that the CIA office dealing with defector resettlement complained it could not handle any more. In at least one instance, a would-be KGB defector was told to apply for an American visa through the normal channels.

But the spycatchers' needs were only one pile of paper on the desks of the harried spymasters. Their political masters were desperate for more information too. Would the reforms in the Soviet Union continue? What was the likelihood of a coup? Would the USSR break-up? An industry grew up in stealing (or obtaining, depending on your viewpoint) military technology. Electronics, and insights into it, were in particular demand: radar beacons, friend-or-foe identification, encryption technology, nuclear command and control systems, submarine radio systems and the like.[4] Amid the haggling of the arms bazaar were more subtle questions. Who was in charge of the nuclear arsenal, particularly the highly portable tactical weapons, some of them no bigger than a suitcase? Were they properly guarded? What capabilities did the Soviet submarine fleet maintain? And what was the state of Soviet signals intelligence? Could it really listen to phone calls in Stockholm? Or Berlin? Or Washington? The pull-out of the Soviet forces from Eastern Germany and the Baltic was a top political priority until 1994. But so was spying on them. Discipline was ragged and corruption colossal. Everything was on sale, from gadgets such as night-vision goggles to humdrum commodities such as petrol – and also military secrets.

Answering all these questions meant recruiting human assets on a previously inconceivable scale. During the Cold War getting alongside anybody in the Soviet power structures had been a challenge; now even the GRU and KGB were direct targets. Politicians, officials, military officers and spooks were all open to persuasion. Many who had signed up to defend the motherland felt their life's purpose was lost, or could easily be persuaded to

think so. Wages were miserable and paid late; accommodation
was abominable. For most, the offer of money was enough. Senior
officers worried about their retirement. For those with families,
the ability to provide for them trumped loyalty to the motherland. Some found it demeaning to take money, but asked simply
for pharmaceuticals: many readers of this book might betray their
country for a reliable supply of otherwise unobtainable insulin for
a diabetic loved one.

The contrast with the Soviet years was complete. In the years
after the collapse of Operation Jungle and its counterparts, Western
intelligence had fared poorly in difficult conditions. For a start,
its reputation was in tatters. Kremlin propagandists were cock-
a-hoop at the KGB's triumph (and indeed were still publishing
material embarrassing to SIS when the Soviet empire was in its
death throes). SIS and the CIA were depicted, not wholly inaccurately, as cynical, incompetent and infested with fascist collaborators.[5] The dented credibility made it harder to recruit people,
and the KGB's strength made it far harder to run them. Ferrying
agents in and out had been easy when Major Lukaševičs was acting
in effect as the travel agent. Thereafter it was dangerous and difficult. Soviet air defences improved, making parachute drops far
harder too.

With official paranoia fuelled by the subversion efforts that the
West had tried to mount from the mid 1950s onwards, the KGB's
counter-intelligence department commanded colossal clout and
resources. The dangers of penetration and dangles were acute. If
you recruited an agent, how could you run him safely, or know if
he had gone bad? And how could you be sure that the information he passed on to you was sound? According to the best book
on the subject, Nigel West's *The Friends*,[6] SIS gave up trying to
run or recruit agents in Moscow because of the 'impossibly hostile
environment'. KGB surveillance meant that even casual social

contacts with the locals prompted an unwelcome response. Even routine fieldcraft, such as looking for dead-letter drops and clandestine meeting-places, was 'a complete waste of time' thanks to ubiquitous KGB informers. Foreigners were conspicuous, and 'no sooner was one watcher team shaken off, than another appeared in its place'. Nigel West notes that the CIA station in Moscow 'had also concluded that running agents in the Soviet capital was an unprofitable business'. This came after one of its star sources, Piotr Popov, was caught in October 1959 in the act of passing a message to his case officer. The American was released. Popov is thought to be the agent mentioned in the earlier chapter on spycraft: fed into a furnace, with his grisly murder filmed for the benefit of new recruits to the GRU. Viktor Sheymov, the most senior KGB officer to defect to America while living in the Soviet Union, spent months in Moscow simply trying to work out how to meet a British or American intelligence officer in order make his offer of help. He eventually found a means of doing so involving a loose window in a cinema toilet in Warsaw.[7]

If Moscow was difficult, the provinces were even harder to reach. Western spy services maintained a particular interest in the Baltic, which they saw as a potential launch pad for World War Three. Electronic snoopers scoured the airwaves for transmissions to be deciphered and analysed; spy aircraft made high-altitude overflights. Analysts scoured the Soviet media for clues about infrastructure, demographics and public morale (while Soviet censors tried to ensure that even the most innocuous information could not be pieced together to reveal a secret). Human intelligence continued too, using to the maximum the limited opportunities for tourism and commercial travel in the region. Sailors on merchant vessels during shore leave could keep their eyes and ears open, and empty dead-letter boxes or pass on money. Occasional cultural and sporting events let foreigners visit, mingle and discreetly disappear.

But for most visitors, let alone spies, making private contacts was risky to impossible.[8]

In this intimidating climate, the British and Americans did what they could. From the mid-1960s, under the legendary leadership of Harold Shergood (known as Shergy), MI6 focused on recruiting and running Soviet sources in third countries, or non-Soviet ones inside the Soviet Union. Careful operations involving individual agents replaced the leaky, ramshackle networks of the past. After the fiascos of the 1950s, British intelligence dumped unreliable émigrés, and retired incompetents such as Carr. It trained its officers better in practical spycraft, such as meticulous use of dead-letter boxes and brush contacts. The proper use of forged identities evolved too: technical competence is only one element of success; just as important is the context in which the identity is used. Officers and agents were drilled in anti-surveillance and counter-intelligence procedures. Every clandestine meeting involved fall-back plans. Counter-intelligence scrutiny, once a backwater, became more thorough. Spies could expect to be quizzed about anything new or unusual in their lives, from new neighbours to new lovers. SIS also gained a new quasi-academic side: researchers and experts with a far fuller understanding of the intricacies of Soviet bureaucracy than enthusiasts like Carr, able to piece together the careers of opponents and targets from the most fragmentary clues. These efforts over many years did eventually bear fruit, for SIS with the Czechoslovak Miloslav Kroča (whose daughter received her belated reward in 1990); with Oleg Penkovsky (who was executed)[9] and later with Oleg Gordievsky (who was snatched from the KGB's clutches).[10] For the CIA the roll of honour includes spies such as Dmitri Polyakov and the weapons scientist Adolf Tolkachev, executed in 1986.[11] However it is notable that (as far as can be judged from published sources) the vast majority of SIS and CIA recruits in the Soviet bloc – who in the period 1960–1990 numbered at most eighty and perhaps as few as forty that were of any use – were volunteers motivated by idealism, rather than recruits achieved by all the costly and risky efforts to pitch and persuade.

As the Cold War ended, many wondered if this expensive and fairly unproductive espionage apparatus was still needed. CNN, not the CIA, had proved the best guide to the fall of the Berlin Wall and the coup of August 1991.

We didn't have any spies in place who could give us much insight into the plans of the East German government or for that matter the intentions of the Soviet leadership,

recalls Mr Bearden bleakly.[12] Clearly the Kremlin had no desire and little ability to attack the West. It had wound down its involvement in regional conflicts in Latin America, Africa, Afghanistan and the Far East, and was making great efforts to bury past enmities. Particularly in France, Germany and the United States, some political leaders saw their spy services as a troublesome legacy of the bad old days. Friendly countries should not spy on each other, particularly if they wanted to stay friends. The cloaks and daggers belonged in the cupboard. The KGB's aggressive behaviour was simply mirroring the similarly cowboyish behaviour of the Western agencies.

This was a Panglossian approach. Soviet spying continued up to the moment that the USSR collapsed and carried on almost unbroken under the Russian flag. Even in the depths of the collapse, the SVR (as the First Chief Directorate of the KGB was renamed in December 1991) was preparing a new echelon of agents. In May 1992, two Russian illegals were arrested in Finland carrying British passports in the names of James Peatfield and Anna Marie Nemeth (two real people who were bewildered to find their identities being used in this way). The couple's true names were Igor and Natalya Lyuskova, and they were apparently on a training assignment. Under political pressure, SIS and its Finnish counterparts downplayed the affair. Later that year, 'Heathfield' arrived in Canada to start his bogus studies. The most longstanding of the illegals caught in 2010, the 'Uruguayan' Juan Lazaro, had moved to New York in 1985, for a mission that began almost simultaneously with Mr Gorbachev's reforms. Even more worrying for the West would have been the knowledge of the human time-bombs left behind by the KGB in the territory that it appeared to be vacating. As the empire retreated, it safeguarded copies of its most valuable asset: the secret police files showing past collaboration.

Few worried about that in the hectic late 1980s and early 1990s. What kept the spies in business was instability. No sooner had Western leaders grasped that the new rulers in Moscow were friendly than they worried about their fragile grip on power. From its start in 1986 to its end in 1999, the era of openness in Moscow always looked temporary. Western politicians feared a coup, clampdown or electoral reverse that could put an authoritarian regime back in power (though when this turn of events actually came about, with the rise of Mr Putin and the *Siloviki*, politicians stubbornly ignored their intelligence services' warnings).

Some canny Western intelligence analysts had long noticed the growing resentment of Russian chauvinism and raised the unfashionable possibility that 'nationalities' might be the regime's Achilles heel.[13] That notion turned from academic theory to red-hot reality as the Baltic independence movements (and their counterparts in the Caucasus, Central Asia, Moldova and Ukraine) stirred from the shadows in the mid 1980s. But having once tried to subvert communism and free the captive nations, the West's political leadership were unhappy when the supposedly longed-for day loomed close. It seemed much wiser to prop up the Soviet empire for the sake of stability. Analysts who trumpeted the joyful

news of the impending collapse found themselves cold-shoul-
dered. For a generation reared on the idea that the Soviet Union
was a geopolitical fixture, it was also hard to grasp that its component parts were becoming countries in their own right. Though
the Baltics had been countries at least in living memory, others,
such as Georgia, had been off the map for most of the century and
some Soviet republics – such as giant, oil-rich Kazakhstan – had
never been states at all. Similar worries applied to the new Russian
Federation after 1991. Would it stay together, or disintegrate under
the continuing strains of economic hardship and ethno-nationalist
ambition?

The great fear for the West was of a Yugoslav-style confla-
gration. That country – another seemingly permanent entity –
began its descent into war in 1991 in a botched but largely blood-
less attempt to prevent Slovenian independence. Later, around
140,000 people were to die, with more than 4m displaced (I am
glad that Dušan, Olgica's uncle in Oxford, did not live to see
it).[14] A similar conflict in the former Soviet space would not only
be bigger, but could involve nuclear weapons. According to the
conventional wisdom of the time, radical nationalist politicians
were pushing too hard and too fast for independence. An outbreak
of chaos or bloodshed might give hardliners in Moscow an excuse
to declare martial law and end the reform experiment. For countries neighbouring the Soviet Union, another nightmare was of a
lawless, poverty-stricken conflict zone, bringing refugees, terrorism and extremism into the tranquil world that they had preserved
throughout the Cold War. 'There are no good outcomes to this,'
a Finnish official told me glumly in Helsinki in 1991 as I arrived to
spread the joyful news of the impending end of the Soviet occupation of the Baltic states.

But from an operational point of view, the disintegration of
central power was an enormous bonus. The Baltics in particular

were a spies' sweetshop: accessible, target-rich and friendly. After decades when every trip across the Soviet frontier involved elaborate preparation, now all one needed to do was to hop onto a ferry from Helsinki or Stockholm. Within a few hours the foreign visitor could be in a bar near a military base, buying drinks for disgruntled officers and sounding out their availability for some lucrative 'freelance research work' for a 'consultancy'. The spooks were so thick on the ground that their presence in the early 1990s was all too conspicuous. I remember a bunch of crew-cut Americans claiming to be 'television researchers' working on a film about the natural history of the Baltic coast. As a nature-loving former BBC correspondent, I was delighted at the chance of some informed discussion, only to find out that their ignorance of broadcasting was matched only by their indifference to singing swans and other fauna (though they certainly knew the topography of the coastline). Much of this happened under the noses of the nominal authorities, which although pro-Western, had neither the capability nor the interest to deal with foreign intelligence services. A delegation of top Estonian officials driving back from Leningrad in 1990 stopped at a roadhouse for refreshments and was surprised to see a group of taciturn and muscular German-speaking men, in military haircuts and jump suits, accompanying a truck headed in the same direction. Nobody in the Estonian government had any idea about these visitors' presence or mission, and no explanation was forthcoming.

That was soon to change. In early 1992 Estonia set up a spy agency specifically designed to work closely with SIS. Its origins were humble: three young men – a lawyer, a final-year history student and a computer programmer – none of them with any experience of intelligence work, sitting in a small office with a pile of spy books from the library. Their mandate was to build the agency from scratch, without the slightest involvement from anyone connected even tangentially with the KGB. They soon realised that Estonia had a big asset: a ready supply of well-educated and patriotic young men and women who knew the Soviet system from the inside. Once trained as intelligence officers, these people could conduct operations in Russia and other ex-Soviet countries far more easily than any Westerner. They would understand whom to target and how to approach them; they understood everything from body language to security procedures. Their Russian language skills were at a level that few Westerners could ever hope to reach.

It was one thing to recruit such people, another to train them. How were they to learn the advanced spycraft needed to operate effectively? Generating that kind of expertise internally needed scale and time. Estonia was small and in a desperate hurry. The result, in September 1992, was an intelligence classic: a typed ten-page document in a buff-brown folder, with flow diagrams hand-drawn neatly between the paragraphs.[15] Its key points included checks and balances, parliamentary oversight, compartmentalisation of operations, a ban on the use of intelligence for domestic political purposes, and the avoidance of an 'information monopoly'. Spying and spycatching would be separated. And having analysed the other options, it said that cooperation with British intelligence was vital. Past blunders were put aside: the distant shadow of Operation Jungle seemed trivial against the task in hand. 'I was not particularly interested in these historical questions,' says one of the authors. 'What was the alternative?' asks another official of that era. 'The Finns? Too untrustworthy. The Swedes? Too soft. The Americans? Too bossy. The French? Too alien. The Germans? Screwed up here already. It had to be the British'.[16]

The opening question from their first MI6 visitor to his young Estonian hosts was: 'Are you legal?' The British wanted to make sure that they were dealing with a properly constituted government agency, not an enthusiastic bunch of cowboys. What followed was a leap of faith in a normally cautious world. The British decided, in effect, to 'adopt' the newly formed *Teabeamet* (Information Board), and create a close partnership on the lines of those that existed with the 'Anglosphere' countries such as Canada or New Zealand. At a time when most of the world was still trying to find the Baltic states on the map, the first Estonian intelligence officers were starting accelerated training at Fort Monckton. The experiment was a resounding success. The baby spies soon became the darlings of the grizzled veterans of British intelligence.

Russia's spymasters regarded the new developments with intense suspicion. Estonian spies were brazenly approaching any official with saleable secrets, and often walking off with precious pieces of military technology from under the noses of their ill-paid and under-motivated guardians. In the late summer of 1994 Russia delivered what it believed was a severe warning to the Estonian authorities to stop assisting Western special services in stealing military secrets. For the Russians the warning was unambiguous. Passed through diplomatic channels they expected it to be acted on at the highest level. But on the Estonian side it was taken merely as a bit of routine grumbling. The message was not heeded – and possibly never even received in the right quarters. In 2005 a belated Estonian parliamentary inquiry concluded:

Russian equipment was of potential interest to foreign intelligence authorities of various foreign countries and other special services and representatives of private capital military industry companies, possibly for the purpose of industrial espionage. The Committee reached the conclusion that Estonia might have procured . . . special equipment or high technology of the Russian army, which was of great interest to the intelligence services of various countries.

According to the report, this included:

space electronics, high technology directing and surveillance devices (like underwater radio buoys, radars), as well as anti-aircraft complexes . . . and electronic control systems . . . In one concrete case, Estonian military intelligence was officially offered for sale a device of Russian space electronics that enabled military reconnaissance with infra-red cameras . . . In the beginning of the 1990s also other military technology was available in Estonia, like night vision devices for military use. In the opinion of a special-ist of Estonian special services it could have been possible that in the first half of the 1990s also the so-called nuclear briefcases were taken out of Russia . . .[17]

The reason for this remarkable glimpse into Western intelligence activity in Estonia was a tragic one. On 28 September 1994 a civil-ian ferry, the *MV Estonia*, sank to the bottom of the Baltic Sea during an overnight trip to Stockholm, killing 852 passengers. The vessel was sloppily maintained, poorly loaded, and heading into heavy seas for which it had not been designed. But on two occa-sions in previous weeks, on September 14 and 21, the same boat had been used to carry ex-Soviet military equipment to Sweden, under the auspices of MUST, the Swedish defence intelligence service, which was working closely with SIS and the CIA.[18]

At the time officials pooh-poohed speculation linking the trag-edy with any cargo on board. A strange report from a Russian group calling itself 'Felix' claimed that the captain had stopped in mid voyage and opened the bow doors in order to try to send a lorry carrying contraband (cobalt and heroin) to the bottom of the sea in order to avoid an impending customs search in Sweden.[19] That appears to have been pure disinformation. But the idea that Estonia helped the West obtain Soviet technology was not a surprising one. Much of it was on semi-public sale in Russia anyway. As an editor of a Tallinn-based newspaper at the time, I was certainly aware of the trade.[20] However I assumed that the spies in charge of such operations, presumably wily and expert, would use some form of secure and discreet transport – perhaps a private plane or boat. It never crossed my mind that such sensitive cargos would be transported on a civilian ferry.

The puzzling loose ends from the tragedy were partly tied together in 2005 when a Swedish customs official claimed that the shipments of classified material in the weeks before the sinking had indeed taken place under a special arrangement with the defence authorities. Rather shamefacedly, the Swedish authorities confirmed this, claiming that the operation had been authorised by an Estonian official whose name they had forgotten. Some intelligence sources say that the GRU indeed planted a bomb on a lorry carrying stolen Russian military technology on the fatal night. The aim was not to sink the vessel, but to cause a scandal that might stop future operations. By a savage fluke, the explosion on the lorry led to the failure of the *Estonia*'s poorly maintained bow doors. Roll-on, roll-off ferries are inherently dangerous: water in the car decks can quickly render them unstable and prone to capsize very fast. As the water poured in, the ferry listed, turned over and sank, leaving most of the passengers with no time to get to the inadequate lifeboats.

Whatever the cause of the inrush of water, the investigation of the sinking was not a high point for transparency.[21] Official diving expeditions at the wreck suggest an unusual degree of interest in a disaster that supposedly stemmed solely from mechanical failure. Independent attempts to investigate the wreck have been shooed away: it is now out-of-bounds as a marine mass grave, thanks to an international agreement signed (interestingly) by the United Kingdom (which had only one citizen perishing in the accident) as well as by Sweden, Finland, Estonia, Poland, Denmark and Russia. Neither Norway (six dead) nor Latvia (seventeen) signed the treaty. Survivors and the victims' families remain suspicious that they were the collateral damage in a war of nerves between Russia and the West. Limited forensic tests conducted by outsiders have failed to prove any explosion conclusively. Though I am sceptical of conspiracy theories, the official explanation of simple mechanical failure does not fully convince me. If foul play was involved, blame would lie first and foremost with those who placed a bomb on a passenger ferry. Yet at a minimum, the proven fact that ferry passengers were repeatedly used, in effect, as human shields for spy games deserves forthright criticism. A lot more people died in the *Estonia* than in Operation Jungle.

The Traitor's Tale

In the chaotic conditions of the former Soviet Union in the early 1990s, Herman Simm was a reassuringly solid figure. In January 1967 he had taken the standard pledge of the Soviet police force, 'I, a citizen of the USSR, hereby taking the oath of the Soviet *Militsiya*, do solemnly swear that I will serve faithfully to the end the Soviet people, Soviet homeland and Soviet government.' Since then he had a stellar record of competence and hard work. He had forty-four awards, including three medals for exemplary behaviour. At a time when brusque Soviet official manners still plagued public service, he was polite and pleasant. As well as Estonian and Russian, he spoke excellent German with smatterings of other languages. Unlike many officials from the old days, he counted as a patriot. As head of security at Toompea Castle, the country's seat of government, he had masterminded its defence against an assault by pro-Kremlin demonstrators on 15 May 1990 – the closest Estonia came to an armed clash during its struggle to regain independence. By his account, if the defence failed he stood ready to escort the country's then prime minister, Edgar Savisaar, through a secret tunnel to the town below, where a speedboat would whisk him to safety in Finland. Later he claims to have ferried Estonia's hard-currency reserves in suitcases to safety in

Helsinki for the nascent central bank, forestalling a possible Soviet attempt to seize them.[1]

After independence was restored in August 1991 Simm moved onwards and upwards, becoming in early 1993 the regional police chief in Harju County, the area around the capital, Tallinn. That was one of the hottest beats in Estonian policing: as well as dealing with endemic organised crime, toxic waste spills and smuggling, his patch included a Soviet nuclear submarine training base at Paldiski, which was still out of the control of the Estonian authorities and had become a magnet for organised crime. Simm supervised the withdrawal of Soviet nuclear fuel elements and the handover to the constitutional authorities. Two months later, he became the top police officer for the whole country, where he showed a courtier-like ability to ingratiate himself with the powerful and the up-and-coming. In interviews with dozens of former associates, the adjective that comes up repeatedly is 'helpful'. One not particularly close colleague was startled when Simm, having learned of his upcoming wedding, offered the services of a patrol car and two police officers to direct the traffic and organise parking.

In 1995, Simm moved to the Defence Ministry, initially to a low-key job as head of the analysis bureau, where he stood out as an efficient bureaucrat. The then Defence Minister, Andrus Öövel, said proudly that hiring a former police chief for the young ministry was like 'winning the lottery'.[2] Few worried when Simm then added to his portfolio the handling of classified documents. It was an unpopular job: Estonia was plagued by scandals involving missing, supposedly secret, papers. Too many items were classified and the rules for safeguarding them were onerous and badly drafted. Simm's bureaucratic habits, honed in the Soviet era, helped him sort out the chaotic paper flows inside a still half-baked bureaucracy. Estonia's foreign friends, keen to see order prevail over chaos, quickly talent-spotted the new official as someone worth cultivating. Britain's government (noting that his orientation was more towards Germany and Finland than to the Anglophone world) paid for him first to learn English at an intensive course at the Foreign Office language school and then to study security policy and practice at Chicksands in Bedfordshire, the citadel of Britain's Defence Intelligence Service.[3] On his return, he was a natural choice to oversee the ministry's move to NATO's security standards. His efforts received high marks: drills and tests showed Estonia's ability to handle secrets to be first class – and indeed better than in some old members of NATO.

Once Estonia joined NATO in 2004, Simm, by now the ministry's top security official, became a still more regular visitor to its Brussels headquarters. Although slightly handicapped by his stilted English – notably better suited to meetings than social events – his affable manner marked him out as one of the more welcome newcomers. Officials there remember an assiduous networker who used slightly heavy-handed flirtatiousness to good effect when dealing with female colleagues. He was prone to self-importance, seemed to feel that he was under-appreciated in Estonia, and liked to display a vocal anti-Russian streak. At home he oversaw security clearances, promotions and transfers for the country's most important defence and security posts. He recommended people for courses in other NATO countries, and signed off on their requests to take part.

In Brussels, NATO saw nothing unusual. Simm met every criterion for the alliance's top-secret clearance. A similar clearance at home was issued and checked regularly by Estonia's Kapo (Security Police).[4] But Simm's record would have repaid closer scrutiny. Why, for example, had Sweden denied him a visa in the mid 1970s? His background, the result of a brief post-war liaison between a middle-aged lawyer and a young woman, then brought

up by aunts, and having multiple marriages and partnerships in
adult life, could have suggested personality flaws of the kind a
canny intelligence officer can exploit. A Soviet-era police officer
who had travelled regularly abroad could hardly have escaped
contact with the KGB. Yet Simm had declared no such thing.
That should have prompted both thorough scrutiny of the files
and the question of whether he might be vulnerable to blackmail. In fact, he had had his first contact with the KGB Third
Department (which dealt with military counter-intelligence) in
1968, as part of a routine sounding out of all recruits to the law-
enforcement organs. Had the investigators dug deep enough in the
KGB files (as they did later, once Simm was under suspicion), they
would have found that the Soviet secret police formally recruited
Simm in 1985, and that he had brazenly denied this collaboration
in a declaration in 1992.

Even his post-Soviet career was dotted with suspicious pecca-
dilloes. These included a jackdaw-like fondness for trinkets and
souvenirs, collecting caps, pens, badges and plaques and even guns.
He was an inveterate junketer, collaring any foreign travel opportunities available. His political views were unusual by Estonia's
sober standards. He had a conspiratorial and eccentric worldview,
prone to believe that Jews, Masons and shadowy international
organisations wielded huge power behind the scenes. Jüri Pihl
(the then head of Kapo) and others also recall a surprising habit
of bad-mouthing Estonia to visiting foreigners. These included
the late Colonel Michael Scott of SIS, who had been involved
in cleaning up the mess after Operation Jungle, and retained a
deep interest in Estonia, returning frequently after 1992 to visit
old agents and advise on security.[5] Simm cherished photographs of
such meetings, particularly prizing one showing a handshake with
the head of Israel's Mossad. Though not a real intelligence officer,
he was clearly attracted by the glamour of that world, and always

eager for gossip and news of the inner workings of Estonia's spy agency. Indeed, some thought he might move to a senior position there after retiring from the defence ministry. His wife claims that he was even offered a job there.

Close scrutiny of his financial affairs by a suspicious counter-intelligence officer might have followed up gifts from a generous German relative, or his rather heavy use of cash. His lifestyle, in a country where senior bureaucrats are well paid but not wealthy, was on the lavish side, with a big house in a desirable village outside Tallinn, a large Western-made jeep for transport, and a summer house and other properties to his name. (He claimed simply to make good use of his travel allowances and to have regained property confiscated during the occupation.) His unorthodox treatment of official documents should also have attracted more notice. He habitually hand-carried secret papers to NATO HQ in Brussels, claiming that only he had the requisite security clearance. But against regulations, he would stay overnight at a hotel there before delivering them. On occasion, colleagues noticed that envelopes had been opened, unwitnessed.[6] But such incidents were rarely logged and never followed up. As head of security, Simm made the rules – and if he chose to break them, presumably he had a good reason for doing so. To most people, Simm was not an impressive or mysterious figure, but a friendly and amenable bureaucrat, doing a dull job well. 'I never thought about him as the National Security Authority,' recalls Indrek Tarand, then a senior official and now a member of the European Parliament. 'It was just Uncle Herman doing something funny.'

Even his earlier role in the defence of Toompea Castle in 1990 was not universally seen as heroic: some Estonians there at the time believe he gave himself a nosebleed as a sign of valour. Mr Savisaar recalls: 'He was brought before me red in the face and shivering. He gave me the impression of a coward. So we fired him.'[7]

Jüri Pihl, who worked closely with Simm, describes his ability to deal with organised crime as 'zero'. It was the steely young officers of his service (including one who later masterminded Simm's arrest) who cleaned up organised crime in post-Soviet Estonia, not the then oafish and bungling officers of the uniformed police. In 1995 Mr Savisaar — then the Interior Minister in a coalition government — again crossed swords with Simm. He recalls a 'somewhat theatrical' red uniform ordered just for the force's most high-ranking officers. 'Like something out of an operetta,' he says disdainfully. Simm was loyal, almost fawning. 'Every morning he was sitting in my secretary's office eager to report — but he could not cope.' For a few months Mr Savisaar pondered how to dismiss his unwelcome subordinate. Then he summoned him and spoke of a 'serious problem', while laying his hand on a large file labelled 'Herman Simm' which was actually full of old newspaper. To his relief, Simm immediately resigned. 'I was a little surprised that he then got a job at the Defence Ministry,' says Mr Savisaar drily.*

To be fired twice by a hate-figure is a strong recommendation. The hawkish officials of the defence and security establishment had long loathed Mr Savisaar, seeing him as a cynical and greedy machine politician with unhealthily close ties to the Kremlin. If Simm was their enemy's enemy, his foibles were irrelevant. Behind the scenes, some did worry. Security officials at the Foreign Ministry made a point of refusing to let him see diplomatic telegrams. The Defence Ministry's internal counter-intelligence service clashed with Simm on occasion, but its efforts to constrain his unorthodox habits were undermined by a conspiratorial and bungling approach: it once attempted to put several senior figures in the ministry under surveillance, supposedly as an exercise. It

---

* Mr Savisaar had found some evidence of Simm's misuse of public funds, in a complicated story involving a dentist's chair bought for his then wife's clinic.

was easy for the self-assured Simm to arrange for such jumpy and troublesome junior officials to be fired, transferred or ignored.

Simm was a happy man as his career peaked. From his bleak and humble upbringing in the Stalinist era, he had made a successful career not only in the Soviet system, but in the one that had replaced it. On 20 November 2006 a press release marking his retirement (one of several documents mentioning him still on the Estonian Defence Ministry's website in mid 2011)[8] gives a ghostly reminder of the esteem in which he was then held. It praises the organisation he built up as 'effective and efficient'; and notes that he signed agreements on the protection of classified information with nearly twenty countries. The Defence Minister added that without doubt Simm had shown 'excellent professionalism'. He also received praise from the then director of the NATO Office of Security, Wayne Rychak. Yet had any of his colleagues known the truth, they would have arrested him on the spot – for nearly thirteen years the avuncular, dependable Simm was an agent of the SVR, Russia's foreign intelligence service.

Simm was one element in the human minefield left behind in the former Soviet empire amid the collapse of communism. The nature of these devices varied widely. One kind were former dissidents, often now in influential positions, who had been protected from their own countries' secret police by their KGB connections. Some also had sincerely cultivated ties with the Soviet authorities in the belief that Mr Gorbachev's reforms offered the best chance of bringing change to their own stagnating societies. Another component was people who feared German hegemony in Europe, or who were sceptical of American intentions. Such feelings – as in Simm's case – were sometimes compounded with jealousy at the rise of smooth young Atlanticist types to senior positions. A big latent category was officials from the old regime with undeclared KGB or secret-police connections. Many of the files containing such details were destroyed after the collapse of communism (typically as part of energetic efforts by the new leaders to conceal their own collaboration). What was left behind was deliberately muddled, so that it was unclear even whether the names listed were victims of the totalitarian system, or its accessories. This created a false sense of security for many who moved on to good jobs in the new system. They did not know that before communist power collapsed the KGB had removed its own records, and copies of the most important files belonging to other agencies.

As a result, the KGB ensured that even after the Soviet empire collapsed, it, and only it, had an accurate record of who had collaborated and why. This has provided Russian spymasters over the past two decades with a unique ability to blackmail and pressurise seemingly impeccable figures in post-communist public life, who believed that their guilty secrets were forgotten or buried. Suspicions in some countries swirl around household names – heads of government or of state, ministers, newspaper editors, academics and tycoons. But the fact that such connections are even rumoured makes them less dangerous. For someone in the public eye, cooperating with the secret service of a foreign power is risky and conspicuous. Russian spymasters may gain some secrets from them, but they can exert little influence through them. More damaging are senior second-rank figures out of the public spotlight, especially in the security world like Simm. They not only know secrets, but are also in a position to cover their tracks. They are thus archetypal targets for Russian intelligence.

A 141-page classified NATO report calls Simm the 'most damaging spy in the alliance's history'. He unveiled the alliance's innermost secrets, from the content of meetings to the details of its most important codes. He gave accounts of the arguments that raged inside the alliance about Russia, about the relative strength

and weaknesses of different countries, and psychological assessments of its senior officials.

The real harm, though, was less in the actual secrets he revealed
during his time as a spy, as in the breaches of trust with the NATO
alliance that arose after he was arrested. For many of the old
members, Simm's treachery confirmed their worst fears about its
eastwards expansion to countries that had so recently been under
the Kremlin's thumb. To them it seemed that the new member
states were simply untrustworthy, riddled with Russian spies
and incapable of keeping secrets. The idea of a 'core NATO' of
seasoned West European members able to work closely together
had never been fully buried during the alliance's expansion to the
ex-communist East. The news of Simm's work for the Russians
revived the discussion. For the new member states themselves the
sense of distrust was different. Simm's parallel work for German
intelligence (of which more later) confirmed fears of big-country
machinations over their heads, not just in Estonia but also in other
countries. Were German agents also at work stealing secrets in
Warsaw, Prague, Budapest or elsewhere? Before Simm's arrest the
idea would have seemed preposterous: Germany had presented
itself as a solid ally for the ex-communist countries, always at pains
to stress that its special relationship with Russia did not undermine
its commitment to its immediate neighbours' security. The new
members now came to believe that was a lie.

Simm's ability to operate undetected in the heart of Estonia's
much-prized new security system also raised painful questions about
the competence and integrity of those who should have checked
him. What had the NATO spycatchers been up to? How come they
had not asked Simm properly about his career in the Soviet Union?
Someone of his age and background, however affable and competent, should have been a candidate for special scrutiny. Yet the checks
had always been superficial. With little more than bluff, Simm had

been able to escape the tightest security in what is supposedly the world's most formidable military alliance. And what about Estonia, which prides itself on keeping its security establishment free of any ex-Soviet taint? Simm was quite unlike the bright, clean-cut, English-speaking young officials who hold most of the top jobs in Estonian public service. During the 1970s and 1980s, they were only children. Simm was already a grown man then – and necessarily more vulnerable to KGB pressure. That should have raised hard questions, which the incomplete and misleading 'official version' of the case leaked by Western officials fails to address. Did Simm have a powerful protector? Was his escape from scrutiny mere incompetence, or perhaps something more sinister? How was he recruited? What did he betray? How was he caught? And why did it take so long? These questions are corrosive and troubling, and have remained unanswered to this day. The answers involve not only secrets, but lies and blunders. Even Simm himself does not know the full truth, and would not (or could not) speak frankly to me about what he does know. But without his account, mine would be incomplete.

It is rare for an outsider knowingly to meet a spy, and almost impossible to meet a jailed one. Once the interrogators have squeezed their subjects dry and damage-control officers have done their work, the traitor is left to a life behind bars. Spycatchers may be proud of having hunted down their quarry, but it is also their fault that the breach happened in the first place. They may worry too that the convict will try to send a coded signal to his former masters: perhaps that he has successfully concealed some vital piece of the puzzle, or has planted a particular piece of disinformation. From the authorities' point of view, the less said to the outside world, the better. So getting to see Simm took some doing. Arrested in 2008 and jailed in 2009, he is serving a 13-year sentence in a maximum-security prison in Tartu, Estonia's second city. Many Estonians hope he dies there. Even my close friends in Estonian officialdom were worried by the idea that an outsider with no security clearance, writing a book that would not be vetted by the Estonian authorities, could visit the country's most notorious prisoner. Simm had outsmarted his colleagues over a period of many years. Maybe he would have some more tricks still to play. Another reason for Estonian caution was embarrassment. Simm's conviction was a brilliant piece of work by the country's spycatchers and their foreign colleagues. But the sooner the affair was forgotten about, the better for Estonia's reputation.

My counter-argument prevailed. Estonia aims to be the epitome of clean and open government. It should deal with the Simm case according to principle, not convenience. But practicality played a role too: concealing Simm would stoke conspiracy theories and look defensive. Sooner or later a Russian author or newspaper would be able to make contact with him and write him up as a victim, or hero. My book would put Simm's treachery in a broader and more informative context. The result of some hard haggling was exclusive, repeated access to Simm. An official of Estonia's security police, whom I agreed not to name, sat in on our meetings and interrupted if we strayed on to topics he regarded as sensitive (Simm seemed frustrated by this, but when I reached him later by telephone, he remained reluctant to provide any significant further information, claiming to be too frightened). I insisted that I would write what I wished: I provided no guarantee that I would submit any portion of the manuscript to any outsider; nor did I promise any veto on its contents (though I have of my own volition omitted a few names and blurred some dates).* The only big point on which I failed to reach agreement, despite repeated requests, was to be allowed to make a recording of the meetings.

---

* I have no desire to reveal details that will mean little to the reader but perhaps make life easier for Russian intelligence.

of classified information, procedures or intergovernmental cooperation. Simm's agenda was partly self-aggrandisement and partly
to get money for his wife.[9] Distinguishing fact from fiction in
his account was hard. It featured confident, conspiratorial and
eccentric assertions on everything from the prevalence of homo-
sexuality in Britain to Freemasonry in Estonia. He habitually
overstated his own role and denigrated that of others. Checking
his veracity is hard. A lot of the material is secret. Some events
are long ago. Other people involved have their own reasons for
keeping silent, or can simply contradict Simm's version: after
all, who will believe the word of Estonia's most-hated prisoner?
Repeatedly and without exception, he skirted over any personal
wrongdoing. He portrayed himself partly as a victim of the
machinations of great-power politics; but also (quite contradic-
torily) as a man of destiny, who made the world safer by keeping
everyone informed.

His descent to treason began, according to him and to Estonian
officials, during a summer holiday in the Tunisian resort of Sousse
in July 1995. A familiar figure approached him in the street. It
was Valeri Zentsov, a former official in the Soviet Estonian KGB.
Casually dressed in a T-shirt and shorts, he introduced himself,
pressing Simm to join him for a vodka. This meeting was no coincidence: when an intelligence officer pitches to a potential agent,
every aspect is worked out in advance. What are the target's weaknesses? What happens if he threatens to report the encounter to
his authorities? What mixture of bribery, threats and flattery will
work best? That the Russians had identified Simm, and knew his
movements well enough to approach him when he was on holiday, in between jobs, and following the end of his relationship
with a much younger girlfriend, suggests a thorough knowledge
of the comings and goings of Estonian society. Simm himself
believes that a Russian mole elsewhere in the defence or security

It was therefore with pen and notebook that in Ju took the bumpy train from Tallinn to Tartu to meet Sin face for the first time. The prison underlines the progr has made in the past twenty years. Soviet prisons v smelly and dark. Tartu's clean, light design, with smoot walls and yellow doors, could be anywhere in the Nor Male prisoners were exercising in the yard, with Est music blaring from loudspeakers. The sight was oddly took me a few seconds to realise why. In the days of th economies, clothing was hideous in both colour and inmates' baggy brown tracksuits, with orange stripes, sort of apparel you might have found in a Soviet departn in around 1985. Then it would have been the height o Now the garb is designed to make escaped prisoners con Yet nothing short of a military attack would spring Simu reaching the interview room in the high-security win prison, we passed eight doors, all opened only with ca two passport checks and a metal detector.

For a man who prided himself on his personal groomin cut a sorry figure: pasty-faced, ill-shaven and with a faint sweat. Only his oily quiff of silvering hair seemed to have the indignities of his imprisonment. He claimed, belligerei he was expecting his lawyer, not an author. His first wor set the tone: 'So, you work for MI6.' Lecturers at his co security at Chicksands, he maintained, had told him that ing British foreign-affairs journalists are in the spooks countered that if so, I would not need to be asking him questions, as I would know everything already. He gru accepted that. But the multi-dimensional battles of wit many hours that followed were the most challenging of m years in journalism. My object was simple: to get from Sin real story. The minder's job was to forestall any detailed dis establishment had 'spotted' him as a likely prospect. That may well be true. Yet it is also possible that the story is in whole or in part a fake. No external corroboration for it exists. The real truth may be that Simm needed not to be recruited, but just reactivated.

Zentsov greeted him (at least according to Simm's version of events) with pleasantries. Simm recalls:

I knew it was not a chance meeting. I thought we might be observed. But I was afraid my career would be over if I said no. Also I thought about the future – who would help me? My salary was low.

Simm claims that the approach came at a time when he had survived bruising encounters with organised crime gangs in Tallinn. He recalls:

I wore a bullet-proof vest . . . Life was cheap . . . a killer cost just $300 . . . Russian intelligence has more than 500 poisons, for ladies and for men. If they could find me in Tunisia they could find me anywhere. Who could I trust?

Zentsov assured Simm that Russia had no hostile intentions to Estonia, dismissing the (then only occasional) outbursts from Moscow as a mere 'political game'. But he said his superiors were worried that NATO would use the small country as a base for an attack on Russia. That concern, Simm says, was a hallmark of Russian demands for intelligence over the next thirteen years. 'Even at the last meeting, they were worried about NATO bases in Estonia.'

The natural thing for a patriotic Estonian to do – even a nervous and unemployed one – would be to listen politely and then report this encounter immediately to the authorities. Simm did

not, apparently because Zentsov threatened to expose his collaboration with the KGB in the 1980s. Yet the threat was matched by
an appeal to Simm's self-importance, and his dislike of Estonia's
young, pro-Western, English-speaking security elite. He says
elliptically of his decision to commit treason:

> It was a very hard question right until the end. But there had to
> be a little balance. I know the Russian mentality. They needed
> information because if they believed they were being attacked,
> they would attack Estonia.

Traitors typically salve their consciences with the idea that they
are playing a great role in geopolitics. Simm seems to have been
no exception. The Russian also played skilfully on Simm's troubled psyche, presenting himself as a similarly apolitical colleague.
'He was a patriot and I was a patriot,' Simm says, without irony.
Zentsov stressed a common disdain for politicians, bemoaning the
sleaze and abuse of power of the Yeltsin era, while also under-
mining Simm's view of Estonian statehood. Did he know, asked
Zentsov, that Estonia's pre-war military leader, General Johan
Laidoner, had worked for Soviet intelligence? And that the country's then president Konstantin Päts had been on the Kremlin
payroll too? Most Estonians would regard these ideas not just as
fanciful but outrageously insulting. President Päts died in a Soviet
mental hospital in 1956, where he was incarcerated because of his
persistent belief that 'he is a president of Estonia'. Laidoner died in
a Soviet prison in 1953. Comparably absurd allegations would be
to say that Winston Churchill was a Soviet agent, that FDR took
money from the Nazi Party, and that General Douglas MacArthur
had been in the pay of Chinese intelligence during the Korean
War. But they chimed with Simm's weakness for conspiratorial
explanations.

With a classic mix of money, blackmail and flattery, the pitch worked. Simm agreed to cooperate with Russian intelligence, not as traitor but (he insists) as an officer, with a clandestine rank, salary and pension. That played on a grudge: that the Defence Ministry had never given him the military rank – equivalent to his position as a police general – that he believed he had been promised on joining. Simm claims he also insisted that he would never work against Estonia's interests (as defined by him). The offer and promise alike were delusions, but Simm's value for the SVR was all too clear: a trusted, well-connected source, in the heart of the country's burgeoning defence establishment. Running the new agent was easy. With his KGB background obscured by his status as a 'military pensioner', Zentsov had no difficulty in visiting Estonia, though most of the contact with Simm took place in third countries.*

Everyone involved in Simm's rise through the Defence Ministry bureaucracy is eager to blame someone else. But the new recruit's experience at the outset was of profound disappointment. Used to the established bureaucracy of the police force, he found only empty desks, bare walls, intrigues and chaos. He was also unconvinced about the whole idea of defending Estonia by military means. British advisers, he recalled, told him that resistance to a Russian attack would last 'just four hours' – the time it would take for tanks to get from the border town of Narva to Tallinn.

Simm's initial haul of Estonia's defence information was correspondingly scanty. Estonia in 1995 had practically no armed forces, slender military relationships with other countries, and seemingly

---

* It is worth noting that Estonia experienced extreme international pressure in the 1990s to be softer on military and security personnel from the former occupation regime who did not wish to return to Russia. Had the authorities been allowed to adopt tougher rules, it would have been far harder for Zentsov (and perhaps others like him) to ply their trade.

scant chance of joining NATO. The biggest target for the Russians was Western intelligence cooperation, about which Simm could make only informed guesses. What he could offer were insights into the Estonian elite: who was up, who was down, who was facing a financial or marital problem; who was being trained in what specialism by which friendly country, how deeply, where and when. In one security exercise, supposedly to help the ministry get ready for NATO membership, he grilled staff with sixty questions covering private hobbies, plus possible weaknesses ranging from sex and alcohol to cars. Although he did not have access to the full 'confessionals' of Kapo's counter-intelligence interviews, in which senior officials have to explain the details of any sexual or other entanglements that could make them vulnerable to blackmail, he would have had a good idea about their conclusions. His knowledge of crisis management plans was also damaging. The Estonian elite is small, with perhaps two hundred people in the key decision-making roles. Many have served in senior positions in several different ministries or agencies – defence, interior, security, the police, the diplomatic service and intelligence. Many of them are trained to stand in for colleagues in an emergency. These carefully made plans were laid bare to Russia. Should it want to decapitate Estonia in future, it knows where to strike.

Simm's tradecraft instructions were straight out of the Soviet KGB's playbook. He placed films, and later memory sticks, into small juice cartons of a particular brand and colour and threw them away in rubbish bins in designated parks. Each dead-letter box was used once only. By his own estimate, he met Zentsov sixteen times in ten different countries. But here arises one of the big mysteries of the case: the exchange of information. Simm insists, in multiple interviews, that the relationship with Zentsov was not a one-way street: 40 per cent of information flowed from him to Zentsov, 60 per cent the other way round. But what was that incoming

information? And what did Simm do with it? During my interviews with Simm, the Estonian minder resolutely kept that subject
out of bounds, and Simm himself subsequently claimed to be too
scared to discuss it when we spoke on the phone.

That is rather tantalising. If he truly passed on information,
Simm would inevitably be quizzed about its source. Any intelligence service would wish to double-check it. Any counter-intelligence agency would be deeply alarmed by a senior official meeting
a known spy from a hostile country; it would allow such contact
to continue only under the closest scrutiny. Simm claims that he
would have liked to confide in British or American intelligence
but was too scared to do so. 'I did consider telling someone,' he
says, while insisting: 'But I used that material and passed it on.' But
what material, and to whom? Whether Simm's claim of a 'two-
way street' is self-delusion, mischief making, or a fragment of a
bigger story remains one of several unsolved puzzles. Others are
even more intriguing.

Zentsov was an old-style spy: a hardened KGB veteran from
Soviet-occupied Estonia. While he was guiding Simm into the
heart of the Defence Ministry, a new Russian intelligence presence was developing in the region, in the form of Antonio Graf, a
plump, bearded man from Madrid. Apart from his slightly exotic
middle names (de Jesus Amorett) he cut an unremarkable figure in
the Baltic states. A Portuguese citizen, born in Brazil and working
in Spain, he was one of thousands of consultants and go-betweens
getting to know the continent's new eastern frontier lands. Until
1989, West European businesses had been almost wholly igno-
rant of the markets and suppliers behind the Iron Curtain. Dealing
with the communist bureaucracy involved marathon negotiating
sessions, best conducted with strong government support. Shortage
of hard currency made customers stingy; NATO controls on the
export of sensitive products meant that the deals that looked most

promising were probably illegal. When communism collapsed, most businesses were initially deeply sceptical about the new markets. Would bills be paid? What was the work ethic? Could the communists come back? Would civil war and chaos spread from the Balkans? What about organised crime? And corruption? Even the most basic data about household income, family structure, education levels, property rights, currency regulations and the like were unknown.

So Antonio (as he was known to his many acquaintances and contacts) sounded completely plausible in his many trips to the Baltic states, which seem to have started in the mid 1990s. He assiduously collected information about business conditions and the political and economic outlook, apparently spending some years building his 'legend' as a regular and credible visitor before engaging in any spying. His mission seemed anodyne and convincing. One contact recalls:

He told me that he was representing Portuguese businesses. He said: 'It appears you guys are going to join the European Union – we want to know more about your countries.'

People who met him recall nothing suspicious, and little that was even distinctive, except possibly his odd choice of tipple: a revolting mixture of Campari and tonic. Anyone suspicious about his motives or background would have found it hard to check them. Spain and Portugal, and their languages, were all but unknown in the Baltic states in the 1990s. If his Spanish sounded faintly accented, that would be because he was Portuguese. If a Portuguese speaker noticed a stray syllable, the answer was that he was born in Brazil – which from a Baltic point of view could have been the far side of the moon. The idea that he was in fact a Russian intelligence officer named Sergei Yakovlev, working under an elaborately constructed illegal identity, would have seemed paranoid fantasy.

When Zentsov retired, it was Antonio who took over as Simm's case officer. Relations were poor from the start. Zentsov had excellent tradecraft and good people skills. Antonio did not. He was already known to Simm as a postman, handling the huge amounts of classified material that the Estonian was passing to the Russians. They had met once at a suburban railway station outside Tallinn. But Yakovlev was a curious choice of case officer for a source of Simm's importance. He appears to have broken several cardinal rules of Soviet spycraft. The cost of establishing a fully fledged illegal in a NATO country is considerable. Creating an identity for Antonio involved obtaining the birth certificate from Brazil, using that to obtain a Portuguese passport, and then establishing a convincing pattern of activity that would take him to the Baltic states when necessary. In the austere world of the KGB, his only task would have been to run Simm: meeting him in carefully chosen locations either with proper clandestine preparation, or openly in a way that fitted both men's natural pattern of activity.

But the Russian was clearly being used for other purposes too. A good illustration of his approach comes from Ivar Tallo, a distinguished Estonian official who has helped make the country a world leader in 'e-government' – putting public administration online. Mr Tallo recalls meeting Antonio rather reluctantly in 2001, as a favour to a friend and colleague in high office. That was nothing unusual: foreign visitors were flooding into the Baltic states as the reborn countries' economic and political importance grew. Senior officials could not possibly meet them all, and a persistent Portuguese consultant would be quite likely to be farmed out to someone less important. At any rate, Mr Tallo chose an expensive Italian restaurant in Tallinn, on the reasonable assumption that he would at least get a decent meal in exchange for his time. Two more meetings followed. Antonio quizzed Mr Tallo on Estonia's politics and economics, showing no particular interest in his specialty of e-government or associated questions of cyber-security. At the third meeting he suggested formalising the coop-eration on a commercial basis. He suggested that Mr Tallo set up a company offering political and economic forecasts, for which his clients in Portugal would be prepared to pay handsomely; to underline the point he pressed an envelope of cash on Mr Tallo as an advance payment. The Estonian politely declined. He did not want to be obligated to the persistent Portuguese and found the offer of money slightly disconcerting. Truthfully, he explained that he was simply too busy to take up the offer. His interest was in e-government, not business information. Antonio never contacted him again.

The approach is straight out of an intelligence playbook. First hook the fish, then reel him in. Money creates a relationship, then an obligation. At some point the material asked for becomes less anodyne and more sensitive. Before the victim is fully aware of what has happened, he is enmeshed. Then comes the offer of still more money for really interesting information, and perhaps the threat of exposure in the case of non-cooperation. Mr Tallo was never close to that danger, and reported the encounter to the Estonian authorities as soon as news of the spy's real identity broke. Fatefully, Antonio tried a similar approach with a senior Lithuanian public figure a few years later, arousing the interest of that country's then formidable counter-intelligence service.[*] It remains unclear where else he tried his persuasive tactics, and with what result. As late as 2010, Latvia's spycatchers were still follow-ing up leads dating from his regular trips to Riga. Yet Antonio was failing in his primary duty: to run Russia's key Estonian source securely and efficiently. Simm instantly distrusted his new case

---

[*] It has since been crippled by political wrangling and corruption scandals.

officer, referring to him as a *soplyak* – a derogatory Russian word for an incompetent beginner that translates roughly as 'snotnose' or 'wet behind the ears'.

After a botched first meeting with Simm in Cyprus, distrust turned to loathing. Simm says his case officer was 'lightweight and arrogant': snooty, rude and worst of all careless. The Russian was greedy too. 'When we met I would eat a small fish dish. He would have steak and red wine,' Simm recalls in a characteristically petulant aside. He assumed that Antonio was fiddling his expenses and doubted that the Russian was a fully trained illegal; his cushy job, Simm suspected, stemmed from connections not talent. That is consistent with the theory that nepotism is rife in Russian intelligence (a theory also supported by the way the lightly trained Ms Chapman gained a plum posting in the West). In his last meeting with Zentsov, Simm had complained about the new man, only to be told that Antonio was the best available: the SVR, Zentsov maintained, had only a couple of illegals in all of Western Europe.

A more tough-minded agent might have gone on strike at this, demanding a serious handler. Astonishingly, given the risks he was taking for the SVR, Simm settled for a stipulation that meetings with his case officer should be held only outside Estonia. Communication between the agent and source was simple. Simm continued to hand over his material via dead drops, using a more sophisticated digital camera, flash drives and memory cards, sometimes concealed in a pill container with a false bottom. He received, in cash, a 'salary' of €1,000 a month, plus expenses. The two men met fourteen times in total, mostly in the Baltic region but sometimes farther afield. By Simm's account, only Germany, Norway and Britain were off limits. They arranged their sessions via a Prague-registered pager account, with simple numeric codes to send and receive messages. The number could be dialled from a public phone box. In retrospect, that might seem sloppy too. A central principle of spycraft is to make the source do nothing unusual. That would mean exchanging messages through means that seem like random variations in ordinary life: for example by using particular combinations of coloured ties, shirts and scarves. That would be necessary for Western spies operating in a police state like Russia; in the open environment of the European Union, Russian spymasters may have considered such precautions unnecessarily elaborate.

Simm's productivity rocketed as Estonia joined NATO. He was party to the inner counsels of the alliance, attending scores of security-related meetings in Brussels and elsewhere. His own clearance was impeccable. 'The Americans checked me, the UK people checked, the Norwegians, Germans, Denmark, Finland – all services checked me,' he recalls. A big area of Russian interest was cryptographic security. Simm duly provided details of NATO's top-secret Elcrodat network, a heavy-duty encrypted communications network used for secure messaging and scrambled voice traffic. During the Cold War, with a military conflict a real possibility, such a breach would have been catastrophic. But in peacetime, with the Soviet threat long gone, it is more embarrassing than damaging: most of the secrets that Elcrodat carried were non-secrets before and after they were fed into the system. Moreover, a key principle of cryptographic security is that if one encryption key is compromised, another can be used in future. An analogy is the combination to the lock on a safe: knowing it is useful only if something valuable is inside; and once the breach is known, the combination can be changed.

In short, it would be wrong to overstate the effect of Simm's treachery on the overall balance of power between Russia and NATO. In an alliance of more than two dozen countries, security is never as tight as it seems. Among other NATO members are countries such as Greece, which have in the past proved leaky on issues of interest to Russia, and more recently Bulgaria. Given the activity of the GRU and SVR stations in Brussels and elsewhere, it is a fair bet that Russia was receiving plenty of other information about NATO too. Simm may have been a big source, but he was certainly not the only one. By Simm's own account, he gave his SVR handler only 'two or three things that were really important' (he declines to say what they were). Paradoxically, Simm's biggest betrayal in this regard may have been to reveal that NATO (at least at the time that Simm was spying) itself had so few secrets about Russia. When the alliance expanded eastwards, it did not draw up formal contingency plans to defend its new members, on the grounds that this would be provocative to Russia, and also unnecessary, as Russia was a friendly country.* America, with the support of Germany and other countries, explicitly barred MC-161, the top-secret NATO committee that draws up the threat assessment, from considering any potential military dangers from the East. When Poland protested about this in 2007, NATO chiefs reluctantly agreed that a threat assessment could be drawn up – but only for an invasion from Belarus, a country roughly a third of Poland's size. NATO military commanders also quietly engaged in what they called 'prudent planning' – sketchy desktop exercises about how in an emergency the alliance might respond to a Russian threat.

All this would have been interesting for Russia – and valuable in the (almost inconceivable) event that it planned a military attack on the new member states of NATO. But it was not what the spymasters in Moscow wanted to hear. Their interest

---

* The logical absurdity of this was not properly teased out: if Russia was friendly, then why would drawing up defence plans for its weak and vulnerable neighbours be provocative? And if Russia was so easily provoked, could it really be counted as friendly?

was in portraying the West as aggressive and intrusive, justifying the xenophobic rhetoric and paranoid worldview that allowed them keep a tight grip on power and its spoils. Consistent with that would be secret bases in NATO's new members, with plans to attack Russia. Yet the harder that Simm's taskmasters urged him to find evidence of nefarious NATO intent, the less successful was his search: the secrets he was seeking simply did not exist.

Simm also provided Russia with damaging insights into the weakness of NATO's counter-intelligence efforts. These are severely hampered by political constraints: in particular Germany dislikes the idea of hunting Russian spies inside the alliance, and puts pressure on NATO Office of Security to soft-pedal investigations and not to act on the results. Details of that were most interesting for Russia's spymasters. Simm attended two NATO counter-intelligence conferences, according to the damage control report. The German magazine *Der Spiegel* asserts that:

At the conference held in the Dutch town of Brunssum in 2006, a CD* containing the names of all known and suspected Russian NATO spies, as well as detailed information on double agents, was distributed to attendees. [Antonio told Simm that] the CD 'landed directly on Putin's desk' and 'caused quite a stir' in Moscow . . . For the coup, Simm received a €5,000 bonus and was reportedly promoted to major-general.[10]

---

* I find that implausible, as even a national intelligence agency would hesitate to compile such information in a single list and distribute it internally, for fear of the damage done if it leaked. The risk of sharing such sensitive material with twenty-plus other agencies of varying trustworthiness would be huge and such a step unlikely. It is possible that this CD was a list of past Russian agents, rather than active or suspected ones. That would still be useful information for the SVR.

Simm's other betrayals were more clearly damaging. The sixty-point security questionnaire he circulated inside the ministry, ferret-ing out officials' hobbies, weaknesses and guilty secrets, would have been valuable information for a Russian intelligence officer looking for other potential targets. But even more interesting than this kind of information may be the rules that govern its collection. In the run-up to Estonia's admission to NATO, Simm obtained the alli-ance's procedures for issuing security clearances. An application is submitted, and either rejected, accepted, or (sometimes for a reason, sometimes at random) referred for further investigation. No expla-nation is offered. This basilisk-like stance is essential in preserving the integrity of the system. If you don't know what to lie about, it is much harder to lie about anything. NATO at the time was deal-ing with many clearance applications from officials in the former Soviet bloc, and had decided that it would be unreasonable to say that former membership of the Communist Party was an automatic bar. For applications from Western Europe, such political activity, except possibly as a temporary student affectation, would have been an instant bar. NATO decided that a key disqualification for appli-cants from behind the old Iron Curtain would be attendance at a Higher Party School. These elite courses in the communist system's internal university were attended by the ambitious and brainy, and thus a prime recruiting ground for the KGB. For a Russian spymas-ter trying to work out how an agent could penetrate NATO, that would be most useful information: those with Higher Party School education should either not bother to apply for a clearance, or else should see if this part of their past could be concealed.

Another use for Simm concerned Estonia's help for Georgia and Ukraine, which for much of the last decade had hopes of joining NATO. The alliance was publicly cautious about their chances, which eventually flopped at a disastrous NATO summit in Bucharest in 2008. But a strong lobby in America had tried hard to boost their chances, not least by helping them reorganise their defence, security and intelligence services along Western lines. It soon became clear that advice from Estonia (and to some extent the other Baltic states) was particularly effective. American and British advisers knew the theory, but not the practice. Estonia had first-hand experience in judging which parts of Soviet administration were incorrigible, and which could be successfully transformed. An influential cabal of advisers in Georgia gained the nickname of the 'Estonian kitchen', after a senior Russian official complained publicly 'we know this kitchen'. Russia could not stop the burgeoning cooperation between Tallinn and Tbilisi. But thanks to Simm it knew a lot about it.

Simm was also useful in keeping an eye on the relationship between Estonia's intelligence agency and its NATO counterparts. The most sensitive operations were run on a purely bilateral basis. But NATO wish lists and some intelligence obtained did cross Simm's desk. Clearly, the SVR was thrilled with their agent. As well as receiving a medal in 2006, Simm also met a senior officer – he believes a deputy director – of the SVR, in a carefully staged meeting in the western Czech spa town of Karlovy Vary. The two men walked in a park together, with Antonio keeping a discreet distance. This is standard practice in Russian spycraft when a source becomes particularly important: it allows the service to be sure that the case officer has indeed recruited the person he claims, and provides a check against embellishment, or the use of a double agent.

But long-term espionage operations, when successful, contain the seeds of their own destruction. Information obtained must be used, or the effort to obtain it is pointless. And using it creates clues for the other side. If you regularly see your opponent is forewarned, you wonder why and start taking measures to plug the leak. Simm's case was no exception.

Indeed unease had been growing for years in Western capitals about Russian penetration of NATO. Initially, at the end of the Cold War, the guard had dropped. The prospect of a Soviet conventional assault on Western Europe, giving a few panicky days to decide between nuclear war and surrender, had shaped thinking for a generation, but with the military threat gone, and Russian forces in retreat from their former empire, thinking about security relaxed. That led to blunders – for example in the NATO operation in Yugoslavia in 1998, when a French officer at the alliance's HQ, Pierre-Henri Bunel, leaked its military plans to Belgrade (and was jailed for it). As NATO tried to befriend Russia and treat it as a partner, it became easier for Russian spies to pitch to NATO officials: passing on a bit of information was no longer treason, it was just oiling wheels that were already turning. Russian espionage attempts played skilfully on jealousies and rivalries within the alliance. Some of those recruited by the Russians resigned quietly when caught, rather than face prosecution: nobody at the top in NATO wanted to seem too hawkish or provocative when the message from their political masters was to promote reconciliation and trust. That was annoying for NATO's spycatchers. So too was the difficulty of screening officials from new members of the alliance (though attention focused on countries such as Hungary and Bulgaria, rather than the Estonians, who were seen as star pupils). But more troubling than all this were the agents the spycatchers could not find. Russia was clearly devoting considerable resources to penetrating the alliance, at a time when NATO's counter-intelligence services had neither the capability, nor the political backing, to deal with it.

Similar worries were soon to be felt even more sharply at the top of British and American security establishments. Western human and electronic sources inside the Russian defence and security establishment suggested that huge quantities of documents, as

well as details of cryptographic security and of high-level policy
discussions on issues such as cyber-warfare and missile defence,
were making their way into Russian hands. This was far more
than the piecemeal collection of small leaks, gossip and chance
disclosures that could be expected from normal espionage activity:
the explanation could only be a major breach. Close scrutiny of
the evidence suggested that the leak was in some way connected
with the Baltic states. The finger of suspicion pointed either at a
senior official in the region, or to one posted to Brussels. At the
same time Western intelligence appears to have had a separate
lucky break, recruiting a source in the heart of the SVR, closely
involved in the illegals programme. The information was initially
fragmentary and incomplete. But it still marked a breakthrough
– the biggest, perhaps, since Vasily Mitrokhin's archive – in finding Russia's most elusive spies in the West. The spycatchers' net
was beginning to close at two ends: one around the blundering
Antonio and his colleagues, and the other around the disgruntled
Simm.

At this stage, Western spy chiefs took no action. It was more
important to identify the leak than to try to catch the traitor. Once
they knew the person or people involved, the time would then
come to decide whether to prosecute, to hush the matter up, or
to try some ruse in return. This reflects a paradoxical feature of
counter-intelligence: that the seemingly most difficult business, of
identifying a suspected spy, is in practical terms the least demanding. Collecting the evidence, especially if a prosecution is planned,
is far trickier. The surveillance needs to be comprehensive but
invisible, and must be conducted against targets trained to spot it.
The slightest slip may end in disaster. Simm's watchers knew that
it would be all too easy for Russia to bundle their quarry into the
back of a van and spirit him across the border. For MI6 to rescue
Oleg Gordievsky under the noses of the KGB had been a hugely

complex and risky operation. For the Russians to do the same from a Western country is easy. Antonio could board a plane from Madrid and never be seen again. Without enough evidence, you cannot stop a suspect escaping. But gathering the evidence is just what may prompt him to escape.

The spycatchers of the CIA's counter-espionage division and a tiny group of trusted foreign partners took enormous care not to show their hand. Their aim first was to hunt down the prize catch of a Russian illegal, based on the tentative clues available. Where was he based? How had he gained his illegal identity? What was he up to? Who were his agents? Who was his controller? Would it perhaps be possible to 'turn' him and run him as a double agent within the SVR? Patience and subtlety would bring a reward: haste and carelessness would mean catastrophe. Then Antonio's blunder forced the pace; the Russian's attempt to solicit information from the Lithuanian alerted that country's counter-intelligence service. Initially, they found the Hispanic-seeming visitor a puzzle. Was he perhaps a Western intelligence officer on an undeclared mission? Or from Israel's Mossad? Or from China? The initial hypothesis was that he might be from the intelligence service of neighbouring Belarus. Then they observed him meeting Simm. That seemed to explain the affair: the mysterious visitor was clearly being run by those clever Estonians. But enquiries in Tallinn drew a blank. Discreetly, the Americans and Lithuanians compared notes and over a weekend in April 2008 separately briefed their Estonian counterparts: Simm, the most trusted official in the Defence Ministry, was a Russian spy.

A nerve-wracking period of ultra-discreet observation and analysis followed, involving at its peak counter-espionage officers of more than a dozen countries. One avenue was electronic: trying to snoop into the Russian's computer in Madrid. Another was the paper trail: discreetly checking up on his documentation and aliases. A third was to obtain his DNA and compare that with databases of other known agents. Only a handful of people in Estonia knew the truth: their tricky task was to maintain absolutely normal relations with a man they once trusted, but now detested. An operational headquarters for the spy-hunt was established at a CIA base in a converted riding stable in Antaviliai, 20km outside Vilnius.[11]

Simm claims that 'one and a half years' before his arrest he had picked up signs in NATO that the information he was passing to Moscow was attracting attention in the West. He sensed a change of atmosphere in Tallinn. And he believed (rightly) that he and Antonio had been under observation at a meeting in the Latvian capital, Riga. He says he tried, but failed, to make discreet contact with a Western secret service, presumably with an offer to be a triple agent: for whatever reason, this approach was rebuffed. In January 2008 Antonio reported to Moscow that his source was 'in a panic'.[12] At the penultimate meeting in Stockholm later that year, Simm began to suspect that his Russian handlers were hanging him out to dry. While continuing to urge Simm to seek a job in Estonia's foreign intelligence service, Antonio responded to his tales of woe with a blunt 'that's your problem'. He turned down his agent's request for emergency exfiltration to Russia, and informed him that the colonel's rank he had been promised when recruited was no longer available, let alone the major-general's rank to which he believed he had been promoted. The system, Antonio explained blandly, had changed.

The disillusion was not sudden. Simm claims that he wanted to stop spying as early as 2005. After stepping down as the National Security Authority in 2006, he had worked as an adviser on special projects, such as organising NATO meetings in Tallinn, and handling Estonia's contribution to the war in Afghanistan. He had made this career move – he says – without consulting Antonio,

who had been furious when he heard. In his final meeting with
Antonio in June 2008, Simm gave him a blunt message to pass to
Moscow: 'that I was retired, had no access, was not working'. He
received no response, returning to Tallinn crestfallen and worried.
Far from facing a comfortable retirement as a general in the SVR,
he was a mere paid traitor, and a clapped-out one at that. His
access to important secrets was gone; he was on the brink of retirement, and at risk of discovery. On 16 September 2008 Antonio
then inexplicably compounded the danger by telephoning him
on his mobile phone and cancelling a meeting, claiming to be
ill. Simm's phone was already tapped by the spycatchers of Kapo,
which had secretly opened a criminal case on 26 May 2008, and
had been collecting the evidence necessary for a treason trial. The
trap was ready to be sprung.

The Rõõmu (pleasure) shopping centre in Keila is like many
others in small-town Estonia. The supermarket boasts a good
selection of wines (Estonians are fond of beefy New World reds),
automatic checkouts (Estonians like gadgets) and a well-stocked
cake shop. On 19 September 2008 Simm and his wife headed
there to collect a three-kilogram *kringel* (iced cinnamon pastry)
they had ordered to celebrate his mother-in-law's upcoming
birthday. As the couple emerged from the building carrying their
shopping, they looked like any married couple preparing for a
comfortable and untroubled family weekend. In the bustle of a
Friday afternoon, neither of them noticed a black VW minibus
parked discreetly near by, or the ambulance waiting around the
corner in case Estonia's most-wanted man violently resisted arrest,
collapsed, or took poison. The Kapo officer* who placed them
there was a seasoned veteran of the service's toughest operations

---

* I am withholding his name, in accordance with the sensible convention that
serving intelligence and security officers should not be identified.

against Russian organised crime. But this arrest was to be the most important event of his career. It had been meticulously planned, in close cooperation with counter-espionage officers from friendly foreign services. Simm's treachery was humiliating: a flawless arrest and prosecution would go some way to redress the balance. 'We wanted it quiet, no conflicts and the goal was immediate cooperation,' recalls the Kapo officer. The first moments would be crucial: 'You cannot rewind if you make a mistake.' Showing his badge, he approached his target: 'I need a couple of words.' Simm seemed unbothered: he knew the Kapo officer and assumed it was some minor query to do with security at the ministry. In a few seconds, Simm was sitting in the minibus, with his wife whisked away to a nearby car, where she was told 'just wait quietly'. She assumed it was a mistake: her husband had not worked full-time in the Defence Ministry since April.

In the minibus came the thunderbolt: 'Mr Simm – you are under arrest on suspicion of treason.' Simm was familiar with handcuffs, but not with the sensation of being handcuffed. He started sweating, as he was searched for poison or other incriminating evidence. 'I will speak. You won't,' continued the arresting officer. He produced a pile of papers, at the top of which were three pieces of evidence. One was from Simm's KGB file, showing that he had promised cooperation in the Soviet era. Another was a picture of Simm making a phone call (in fact to his case officer's pager) from a public telephone in the coastal resort of Pärnu. The arresting officer then informed him Kapo knew that Antonio was a Russian intelligence officer called Sergei Yakovlev. Simm cracked: 'It had to happen sometime,' he mumbled, 'I didn't expect you would come so soon.' The prisoner and his captors went directly to Simm's home. They found cipher pads (presumably used in radio messages), lists of dead-letter boxes and piles of classified papers (Simm claims that these were not for espionage, but material for a book of memoirs that he was planning to write). Simm also gave details of the memory cards he used to transfer information. The interrogation that followed by Estonian and foreign counter-espionage officers remains secret. But Simm appears to have put up little resistance. He pleaded guilty at his trial in February 2009 and has contested only the authorities' attempts to seize his property.

A big puzzle in this is that an inviolable rule of Russian spycraft is that a second source, run by a separate case officer, must back up any important agent. The people involved are not (in espionage jargon) 'inter-conscious'. They may know that their behaviour and intelligence product is being compared with a rival, but they do not know who, where, or how. This provides a powerful cross-check. If a source is tempted to embellish his material, it will stand out. If a case officer takes a short cut or exaggerates a difficulty, his report will be compared with that of a counterpart. This technique helps to deal with everything from fiddling expenses to a full double-cross. So where was the other Russian spy? The answer to this question depends on whether Simm's prime target was Estonia, the Baltic states in general, or NATO as a whole. Matching his access to NATO documents would not be too hard, in an alliance of (now) twenty-eight members. Finding a similarly highly placed agent in Estonia, however, would be harder. Plenty of rumours surround this: according to one, Russia had another agent in the heart of Estonia's security establishment, whose code-name was *Kask* (silver birch). If this agent existed, what happened to him? He clearly was not prosecuted. I can find no convincing trace of a senior Estonian (or Latvian or Lithuanian) official having defected, disappeared, retired prematurely or emigrated mysteriously. Perhaps the evidence for prosecution was insufficient. Perhaps the person concerned made a full confession, switched sides, or decided to brazen out any enquiry. My own hunch is that the parallel agent was in a big West European NATO country and was unearthed around the same time but eased into discreet early retirement to avoid embarrassment. This agent could well have been run out of Brussels by one of the Russian intelligence officers later expelled from the Russian mission to NATO.[13]

Shortly after the excitement of Simm's capture, another scandal broke: Simm had been not only a spy for the Russians but for the Germans. This aspect of his life is shrouded in secrecy. A handful of leaks to the German magazine *Der Spiegel* have painted a sanitised version of his cooperation, claiming that it dated from his days as a policeman, rather than in the Defence Ministry, and concerned chiefly Russian organised crime, rather than intelligence matters.[14] Yet fragmentary clues suggest a darker picture. According to other officials in a position to know, Simm's cooperation with the German BND spy service was deep and long-lasting, stretching at least up to Estonia's membership of the European Union and NATO in 2004, and possibly even longer. In retrospect, the BND's misbehaviour is less of a puzzle. After Estonia restored its independence, the absence of good ties with German intelligence was conspicuous. Some countries such as France were annoyed that the British had got their feet under the table so quickly and hurried to catch up. Sweden and Finland were the quickest to regularise their activities, with 'declared' intelligence liaison officers taking up postings at the new embassies in Tallinn. America too built up a large CIA station, which enjoyed correct if sometimes aloof relations with its Estonian counterparts. As well as with these countries, Jüri Pihl, head of Kapo from 1993 to 2003, recalls the excellent ties that his service built up with partner agencies in Austria, Norway, and later the Czech Republic and Poland.

Germany was the notable exception. The Baltic region had historically been Berlin's shared backyard with Moscow. Relations with Russia, on everything from energy to migration, were vital.

It is easy to see that senior German politicians would find it annoying that devious and interfering spooks from London were hooking up with a bunch of zealous and youthful Estonians, to the detriment of far more important East–West relations. Though Germany's intelligence cooperation with Estonia was cool, its interest in what the spy agency there was cooking up with the British was keen. Simm declines to discuss this in detail, reverting only to his formulaic 'I helped lots of people'. I can reveal, having heard it from multiple sources, that Germany apologised officially to Estonia in 2008, shortly after Simm's arrest. If the BND had recruited and run an agent there in the late 1980s or early 1990s, when Russian organised crime was a serious problem for Germany, and the Estonian constitutional authorities were in no state to provide effective help, few would object. Continuing clandestine operations after 1992 was another matter. Estonia is not just a friendly country. It is one to which, since the Nazi–Soviet pact, Germany owes a historic debt. Most Germans would be horrified at the idea of running hostile intelligence operations against Israel. Those officials in charge of Simm (and presumably of other agents in the Baltics and Central Europe) may have neglected to consider Germany's other historical baggage. It is easy to see why Berlin was interested in burgeoning Anglo-American defence cooperation with a new country in Germany's Baltic backyard. But running a senior official there as a secret agent was no way to slake that curiosity.

Simm's importance as a BND agent grew just as Germany's relationship with Russia was intensifying. The friendship between Gerhard Schröder (federal chancellor from 1998 to 2005) and Mr Putin was notorious. It culminated in the German leader taking a retirement job as chairman of the board of a joint Russian–German gas pipeline, built on the Baltic seabed against the strenuous objections of the other littoral states, who saw it as a direct attack on their energy security. Some officials close to the case suggest that Simm was run on the direct instructions of the security coordination office in the Federal Chancellery under Mr Schröder, and against the judgement of the BND chiefs, whose attitudes to Russia were considerably more hawkish (and to Estonia, more friendly). That is hard to prove: everyone involved declines any kind of comment. All Simm will say is that he turned to the Germans as a 'protection' against the Russians. This suggests strongly that he was recruited by the BND after 1995, not before.

What is clear, however, is that Simm's cooperation with Russia and Germany overlapped. That raises an interesting question. Did the SVR know that Simm was working for the BND? And did the BND know that he was working for the Russians? The former is more likely. The BND has long been something of a laughing stock among other secret services, because of the degree of Russian (and now Chinese) penetration. In Cold War Berlin in the 1980s, a senior intelligence officer from an English-speaking service told me derisively: 'If we want Gorbachev to know something and take it seriously, we give it to the BND and tell them it's top secret. It'll be on his desk in the Kremlin the next morning.' Little suggests that security has improved since then.

It is possible that Simm told the BND that he was under pressure from the Russians in the hope that they would rescue him were he exposed. At least one senior official close to the case says that Simm indeed played this card when he was arrested. The BND responded quickly by saying that Simm was a former agent, not a current one, and that the Estonians were welcome to try him for spying for Russia. At any rate, the Estonians have gone to great lengths to conceal evidence of Simm's work for the BND. No questions to Simm on this subject were permitted during my face-to-face interviews, and he was also deeply reluctant to address the subject on the phone, or via intermediaries. 'If I tell you that, I will be dead in my cell tomorrow,' he said dramatically. In another interview he said elliptically, 'I had to make sure that the pigs were fed but that the wolves did not go hungry.' One reason for Estonia's unwillingness to raise Simm's BND connection was that it would have required another criminal trial. Another was the excellent relations that now exist between Estonia and Germany under Angela Merkel. The normally ultra-cautious Germans showed strong support in the crucial meetings that decided Estonia's application to join the euro zone in 2009 and 2010. Some have suggested, plausibly, that this was a quid pro quo for Estonia's willingness to hush up the unpleasant question of Simm's work for the BND. The prime minister, Andrus Ansip, is fond of saying: 'What is good for Germany is good for Estonia.' But the result of the Simm case has been to dent trust – not only in Estonia – that Germany is an honest partner for its smaller neighbours in NATO and the EU.

The overlap raises a still more intriguing question: whether Russia knew that Simm was spying for the BND, and if so whether it tried to exploit this. It would certainly explain its remarkably unpleasant treatment of its once-prized agent in the final year of his service to them, which is only really consistent with a case officer who actively wants his source to be exposed. If the SVR did know – perhaps from Simm, perhaps from a source in Germany – that it was dealing with a double agent, then an elegant way of ending the affair would be to stage this denouement. Simm was of no further use to the SVR. Antonio himself needed to be recalled to Russia before he was arrested. Under interrogation, Simm would certainly mention his BND link, in the hope of invoking powerful outside help. Any outcome would then be good for Russia. Perhaps Estonia would hush the whole affair up, in which case it would spare the SVR's blushes. It would certainly have a private or public spat with Germany, weakening NATO and underlining the isolation and fragility of the Baltic states' security arrangements.

This is an elegant but not wholly convincing explanation of Russian sloppiness towards Simm. Anyone considering treachery naturally worries about how he will be treated. A reputation for callous carelessness does not help. Simm's treatment damages the SVR brand. A better explanation is that Antonio himself was recruited by the Americans and helped set up Simm's prosecution. This fits rather more of the facts. It would explain, for a start, the mysterious disappearance of Antonio following his clumsy and revealing phone call to Simm's mobile. It is hardly likely that its spycatchers would succeed in nailing Simm but fail to gain the much bigger prize of a fully fledged Russian illegal. It is interesting to speculate when the double-dealing started: was Antonio already under Western control when he made his clumsy pitch to the Lithuanian? It would be nice to imagine that the Western intelligence services were using the Russian illegal for their own purposes, testing weaknesses in NATO members' security and gaining a revealing picture of the SVR's wish-list, sources and methods. Perhaps not only Simm but also other Russian agents run by Antonio have now been rounded up.

At any rate, the official story of simple SVR sloppiness looks incomplete. Retrospective analysis of intelligence operations is always skewed by their outcomes: the successful ones appear to have been run brilliantly; the failed ones look doomed from the start. But in all of intelligence history, it is hard to find an example of an illegal blown solely because of bad tradecraft. They normally trip up on one of two fronts. One is a spouse or lover who becomes suspicious of a pattern of activity that only he or she is in a position to notice. The other is penetration. But Antonio did not have a woman in his life. Rumours swirl around Tallinn and other cities about his whereabouts now, and the means used to recruit him. He was supposedly detained in Turkey around the time of Simm's arrest, but has not been heard of since. One version is that the

Western secret services planted child pornography on his computer, and told him that he would face a lengthy sentence in a Spanish
jail unless he cooperated. Another account is that he was offered
a large sum of money for his help, which he initially spurned. He
returned to Moscow in a panic and alerted his controllers – only
then to think better of his decision and slip out of Russia to the
West where he then defected.

A final puzzle is the relationship between the Simm case and the
American illegals such as Anna Chapman and Donald Heathfield.
According to the Russian authorities, a senior SVR officer,
Aleksandr Poteyev, defected to the United States in June 2010. In
June 2011 a military court in Moscow sentenced him in absentia
to a 25-year jail term on charges of treason and desertion. Aged
58 at the time of his trial, Mr Poteyev was a decorated intelligence
veteran of the Soviet war in Afghanistan, who was then posted
first to Washington, DC and then to New York in the early 1990s
to service the illegals network. During that posting, he appears
to have been spotted by the CIA as a potential recruit, with the
initial approach being made via his daughter, who worked for
an American academic exchange outfit in Moscow. A decisive
psychological nudge – according to Russian news reports – came
with a CIA-staged burglary at his flat.[15] This supposedly under-
lined the weakness of the Russian state and the omnipotence of
the Americans.

From 2000 Mr Poteyev worked as deputy director of the North
America division of the S-Department (dealing with illegals). It
is hard to imagine a more useful asset for the CIA, at least from a
counter-espionage point of view. Mr Poteyev was able not only
to give details of the identities of his agents in North America,
but also to keep an eye on their missions, tasking and intelligence
results.[16] According to Russian news reports (which as officially
sanctioned leaks must be taken with a Siberian salt mine's worth

of scepticism), Mr Poteyev was able to evade a lie detector test and also get his daughter and son outside Russia before he himself defected. He is said to have feigned illness, travelled to Belarus on a false passport provided by the Americans, and then to Kiev, where he was exfiltrated to Frankfurt. A text message to his wife read: 'Mary, try to take this calmly: I am leaving not for a short time but for ever . . . I did not want this but I had to. I am starting a new life. I shall try to help the children.' If true, the whole episode reflects sloppiness by the SVR's once-fearsome internal counter-intelligence.

Mr Poteyev's recruitment would have been the third blow to Russian espionage in North America in twenty years. The Mitrokhin archive, when analysed in the early 1990s, produced details of many illegals planted in the United States and Canada in the Soviet era. Almost all of them appeared to have become inactive when followed up by the FBI: they had settled into a quiet suburban routine, with the undemanding long-term tasks that would be needed only in time of war. (One illegal in Europe was provided with a carefully constructed false identity in order to get an unremarkable job at a car factory. His sole intelligence-gathering task was to inform Moscow of any sign of its switching to military production). The second blow came with the defection of Sergei Tretyakov, the deputy head of the SVR station based at the Russian mission to the United Nations. He was passing secrets to the United States from 1997 until his defection in 2000.[17] His duties also included some support for illegals' networks. Mr Tretyakov died, apparently of choking on a piece of meat, on 13 June 2010, on the eve of the spy scandal. Nobody has alleged foul play, although the coincidence is certainly striking. On top of that came the reported breach from Mr Poteyev.

Making sense of all this is tricky. The all-embracing conspiracy in which one side masterminds every twist and turn of a story is rarely a satisfactory explanation. History suggests that real answers to intelligence puzzles invariably include large doses of incompetence and misjudgement. Assuming that Antonio did indeed defect to America, Simm's career in the Defence Ministry still remains mystifying. Why did he rise so quickly? Why did nobody note his KGB past? The truth is, I fear, that Simm had developed an unofficial relationship with Kapo, which was concerned about the growing Russian interest in Estonian defence, the scope for provocations and penetrations, and the weakness of the ministry in dealing with the threat. Soon after Simm's arrival, Kapo picked up his sloppy behaviour. But instead of having him fired, it made him the agency's unofficial eyes and ears, providing a stream of gossip, innuendo and other information. Kapo felt it had the weaknesses of the ministry under excellent scrutiny. And so they did – except the one that mattered. This theory is denied by all concerned, but I believe it to be true. As I shall argue in the conclusion, our complacency towards the mediocre is Russia's deadliest weapon.

Conclusion

Simm's treachery exemplifies the central point of this book: the need to defend an open society at its weakest points, against people who appear to be no threat to it. Annoying though it may be to NATO's security officials charged with protecting the thousands of documents that Simm passed on to his handlers, the transfer of these papers did little lasting damage to the alliance. Nor did he manage to crack the innermost secrets of Estonian intelligence cooperation with countries such as Britain and America. Though he did give Russia a damagingly accurate inside view of the Estonian elite, even that country's greatest fans could not call that a geopolitical earthquake. The real cause for alarm about Simm and Antonio is the same reason as for Donald Heathfield and Anna Chapman. Rather than the secrets they may have stolen, it is the vulnerabilities they exposed that matter. Catching spies is hard enough. But when they use weaknesses that are intrinsic to our society, the real question is how many more are playing the same tricks now, and may do so in future. Nothing has changed to stop other Russian agents such as Ms Chapman – perhaps much better trained and more determined – following the same path into the heart of Western business, social and financial life. Nor have we any idea how many more Herman Simms may lurk in the

fifty-plus generation that holds top jobs in the new member states of the EU and NATO, but conceals dark secrets from earlier careers in communist-run countries.

Russia would never countenance such tactics in reverse. At a think-tank meeting in London, one of Britain's most seasoned Russia-watchers bumped into Ms Zatuliveter and asked who she was: she readily explained that she was a Russian, working for Mike Hancock MP. My friend was thunderstruck. He knew Mr Hancock was on the defence committee; a post in his office would be the perfect vantage point for a talent-spotter, recruiter or agent-runner. (He would have been even more concerned had he known that Ms Zatuliveter was also planning to move on to one of Britain's leading defence companies, or that she was dating a NATO official dealing with Russia.) He asked drily if it would be possible for a British citizen to have a similar job working for a member of the Russian parliament, the Duma. 'Of course not,' tittered Ms Zatuliveter. She is not the only one laughing. For the *Siloviki* in Moscow, Western society is a spies' paradise. Despite the tedious metal-detectors and identity checks that burden daily life, we are astonishingly, almost suicidally, trusting when it comes to real security – protecting our secrets and our decision-making. To worry about Russian spies still counts as almost comically paranoid. The popular assumption is that we have no secrets worth stealing; and that even if we did, Russia has no interest in or means of obtaining them.

As I have tried to show in this book, that is untrue. We do have secrets. Our countries and alliances make decisions vital to our welfare. Russia is interested in these for reasons of its own. So are other countries – as I have noted earlier, spying is always a grubby business. But Russia is not like other countries, as the case of Sergei Magnitsky demonstrates. It uses its intelligence agencies as part of a broad and malevolent effort to penetrate our

society and skew our decision-making. We do little to protect ourselves.

These Russian agencies are indeed incompetent, nepotistic, corrupt, blinkered and wasteful, like the state they serve. On occasion we have penetrated them and gained important victories – such as the arrests of the illegals described in this book. But they have crucial assets that we lack. One is determination: they really mind about besting us, whereas we do not take them seriously. Another is long-term thinking. For Western intelligence, spying is a demand-driven business. If the political customers want to know something, you invest. If they don't, you move resources elsewhere. Russian spymasters think differently. They are willing to spend large amounts of time and money building up long-term assets, with little concern for the immediate payoff. The fact that the illegals arrested in America may not have done much spying does not mean that they were failures: it just means that their missions were incomplete. Russia's third advantage is the ability to mount deception operations. As I have shown in the book, Western intelligence is fooled time and again by such ruses. Whether it was the Lockhart plot, the Trust, Operation Jungle or trusting Herman Simm's security clearances, the story is the same: complacency and delusion on our side, ruthless ingenuity on theirs.

Despite our spycatchers' recent successes, the rules of the game have not changed, and are in Russia's favour, not ours. The Russian illegals were spies who looked like us, swimming effortlessly and invisibly through suburbia, nightlife, think tanks and consultancy, exploiting the natural trust and collegiality of an open society. Without a lucky break, they would still be there now. Nothing on our side has changed to make such missions harder, or on theirs to make them less likely. Everyone in such worlds needs to be more careful in who they deal with. The lesson of the 'Spies in

suburbia' headlines should be that, however unlikely it may seem, and whatever their passport, background or career, a friendly new colleague, customer, supplier or business partner could, just possibly, be a Russian illegal, perhaps along the deep-cover model of Antonio or Heathfield, more likely resembling Ms Chapman. We will never return to the security-consciousness of the Cold War. But in any society that thinks its values are worth defending, those in professional or public life need to be wary about the questions people ask, and particularly of any offer of money for information.

We also need to rethink the comforting conventional account of European history after 1989. For many people the years that followed the Soviet collapse represented the longed-for 'rollback': the reversal of the gains made by Stalin in the years 1944–49. From this viewpoint, 1989 marked the belated culmination of John Foster Dulles's ringing promise forty years earlier:

> We should make it clear to the tens of millions of restive subject people in Eastern Europe and Asia that we do not accept the status quo of servitude aggressive Soviet Communism has imposed on them, and eventual liberation is an essential and enduring part of our foreign policy.[1]

Too many in the West projected their own sense of triumphalism onto the countries of the former Soviet empire. The gains there were indeed huge: political pluralism, prosperity, the rule of law and the chance to make sovereign decisions about security. Visible Russian influence diminished sharply. Hundreds of thousands of military personnel left the region as its occupation finally ended. The days when every government ministry had a senior Soviet official as a minder were gone. But in retrospect, the West (and many locals) over-estimated the scale of the Kremlin's retreat. What looked like roll-back from one point of view was a stay-behind operation from another.* It is not just that a whiff of Putinism is now noticeable in many countries between the Baltic and the Black Sea, where politicians taste the pleasures of a close overlap between business and politics, and the use and abuse of officialdom against opponents. Amid the ruins of old structures, the KGB established new networks and assets that were to serve it well in the years ahead. Coupled with the inability of the new member states to carry out thorough counter-intelligence screening where it is most needed, the Soviet legacy created, in effect, a cohort of Trojan horses welcomed by Western alliances, states, services and agencies with open arms.

It is hard to know how far this was a deliberate operation, and how far the accidental dividend of precautions taken during the Soviet withdrawal. But the upshot is the same. From the Russian point of view, the outcome of 1989–91 has proved far less damaging and humiliating than it seemed at the time. An expensive, brittle and unruly empire has gone. Today these countries are the West's problem. It is not Russia that pays for their modernisation, but the EU and international lenders.† That barely costs the Kremlin coffers a kopek (indeed Russia benefits from some of this largesse too). Growing prosperity in the ex-captive countries makes them better neighbours and trading partners for Russia. But more importantly, the continuing penetration of their societies, state structures and business by Russian intelligence gives the Kremlin an influence in Europe far more useful than it enjoyed in Soviet days. Recruiting

---

* Stay-behind operations were a staple of NATO planning during the early years of the Cold War, and envisaged well-organised networks of saboteurs and spies working to disrupt Soviet rule after an invasion of Western Europe, with access to secret arms caches. They included the notorious Operation Gladio, which degenerated into political mischief-making in Italy.

† Chiefly the European Bank of Reconstruction and Development and the European Investment Bank. If things go badly wrong, the International Monetary Fund and European Central Bank provide bailout packages.

and running Simm was child's play compared to conducting a similar operation during the Cold War. Not only does NATO provide comfortable, well-lit office space and official passes for the Russian intelligence officers who spy on it, but the bureaucracies of a dozen new member states are full of potential targets for recruitment.

These human time bombs will not tick for ever. People who were in their early thirties in the late 1980s (and thus already tainted by collaboration) are in their fifties now, and at the peak of their careers in officialdom. Within another decade, they will retire. Already for many officials in the ex-communist world, the days of totalitarianism are a childhood memory, not a reality of adulthood. Yet the tainted generation can leave plenty of damage behind it – for example in discreetly advancing the careers of other younger officials willing to cooperate with Russia, or blocking those who seem obstinately honest.

I want to stress that these concerns do not mean writing off the new member states as allies or lessening ties with them. A deplorable result of the Simm case has been to weaken trust between the old West and new East in NATO. If even the Estonians, star pupils in the new order, can blunder in this way, what basis is there for trusting other countries with bigger and more shambolic arrangements? Although more realism and better counter-intelligence procedures are long overdue, to take this standoffish approach is in my view patronising, self-satisfied and hypocritical. It risks handing Russia just the victory that it seeks, in further weakening and demoralising European and transatlantic solidarity. The lesson of the Simm affair is that we need deeper, closer and more effective security cooperation among countries threatened by Russia, not less. A key point is that for all its earlier shortcomings, Estonia did at least catch, prosecute and jail the worst traitor in its history, and did so unflinchingly and conscientiously. It did not allow him to escape to Russia, or to retire into convenient obscurity. That is more than can be said for some other countries in similar circumstances, which have chosen easier and more convenient options. As I have shown, the old West's record on espionage and security in the course of the last hundred years is far more badly blotted than any of the new member states, which have had far harder challenges to overcome, with far fewer resources. Kim Philby, Guy Burgess, Donald Maclean and Anthony Blunt came from the heart of the British establishment, not from Estonia. Lockhart, Reilly and Carr had only themselves to blame for their blunders. Ames and Hanssen passed every security clearance. Antonio stole a Portuguese identity and lived in Spain; Heathfield studied in Canada, worked in France and lived in America; Ms Chapman gained a British passport. The painful lessons from that are at home, not abroad.

Gullibility towards Russia and snootiness towards allies are two of the problems I have highlighted. A third is that the Western mindset tends to try to fit Russia's activities abroad into mistakenly neat pigeonholes. More than ten years ago James Woolsey, a former CIA director, characterised the problem thus:

> If you should chance to strike up a conversation with an articulate, English-speaking Russian . . . wearing a $3,000 suit and a pair of Gucci loafers, and he tells you that he is an executive of a Russian trading company . . . then there are four possibilities. He may be what he says he is. He may be a Russian intelligence officer working under commercial cover. He may be part of a Russian organised crime group. But the really interesting possibility is that he may be all three and that none of those three institutions have any problem with the arrangement.[2]

Since 1999, the Russian intelligence threat has morphed further, posing a daunting task for Western spycatchers. The adversary is a shape-shifter: in one manifestation it is a legitimate energy company, then a curious student apparently from a NATO country, then a pushy official from the Russian embassy, then a supposedly independent charitable outfit offering a large donation to anyone who conducts the right research, then a hard-working secretary, then a Portuguese business consultant. For Russia the 'natural capacity' of which the CIA can only dream is already in place. It exists not only in Russian business abroad, but via foreign businesses with investments or offices in Russia. The people they take on as local employees and then send on foreign postings may be loyal workers for the company, or they may have been assigned to it by the authorities, perhaps for nepotistic reasons, perhaps with clandestine work in mind, perhaps for both. If that fails, the Russian diaspora provides a rich fishing ground for whatever catch is needed.

Russian misbehaviour abroad can seem a problem solely for the criminal justice authorities: they deal with gangsters, forgers, people-traffickers, cyber-crime and assassins. Blink and the problem seems instead one for the authorities that supervise the financial system, and have to deal with Russia's many strange business-like entities. Alert to every loophole, these are moving vast quantities of murkily obtained cash into the respectable world's banks and stock exchanges. Curbing that could prevent the people who swindled the Russian taxpayer and murdered Mr Magnitsky from enjoying their loot. Then again, the Russia files seem destined for the visa authorities: it is their job to cordon off our societies from ill-wishers and malefactors. Sometimes the regime in Moscow seems like a matter for diplomats, who with luck and skill may coax it into cooperative relationships with its neighbours, and defuse the misunderstandings of the past.

The grave weakness of the Western approach is that it regards spy-catching, criminal justice, financial supervision, lobbying disclosure and media-ownership rules as quite separate areas of decision-making. Yet given the multi-faceted threat they face, the agencies involved in these fields need to work in concert, not separately. It is troubling that the British and Irish authorities have not, for example, followed up the case of Steven Sugden. Because no money seems to have been stolen, it is below the radar of the police. From the spy-catchers' point of view, it is a 'cold case'. They are too busy stopping things that may be going to happen to worry about events that took place a few years back. Moreover, even if techniques of Russian spycraft were used, the aim falls outside their remit. MI5 catches spies, not criminals. Yet finding out if, how and why an imposter purloined the real Mr Sugden's signature, and what really happened with the addresses in Rossmore Grove, deserves proper investigation. The culprits are still at large; they and their accomplices are unpunished. The loopholes are still open. Someone may try the same trick again. If your own name, your address, your signature and your date of birth were used in such a manner, it would be of little comfort to know that the case fell between the cracks of a bureaucracy designed for another age.

A guiding principle in the West's dealings with Russia should be to listen to those people there who share our values, and to sustain and encourage them rather than demoralising them. In February 2011 the four leaders of the main opposition party, the Party of People's Freedom, wrote a sharply worded newspaper article, berating the Western countries for their role in facilitating the misrule and looting of Russia.

We urge Western leaders to discontinue their kisses-and-hugs 'Realpolitik', which has failed, and to stop flirting with Russian rulers – behaviour that has not brought any benefits to the West and produces in Russia an impression that Putin's system is a decent one, like any other in the democratic world.

It means the West should cease greeting Russian rulers as equals, providing them with legitimacy they clearly do not merit. It means the West should start exposing corrupt practices by the Russian establishment, whose ability to find havens for stolen funds and leave Russia for comfortable lives in Western nations is one of the regime's pillars of stability. It means Western nations should introduce targeted sanctions against the officials directly abusing the rights of their compatriots.[3]

Sanctions of this kind do not mean isolating Russia as a whole, which would indeed be futile and counterproductive. But it is worth stating bluntly that the current approach, of engagement without willpower, is certain to make matters worse, not better. The West hardly realises that it is dealing with an adversary that understands us better than we know ourselves, whose goals and methods are mysteries to us, and whom we barely recognise when we see him. He is determined; we are divided. He is resentful and paranoid; we are complacent and trusting. We want to like him. We hope he will like us, and eventually be like us. He wants nothing of the kind. As Don Jensen points out: 'Those who keep calling for an engagement that will eventually transform Russia cannot see that it is the West, not Russia, that is being transformed.'[4] I hope this book can help the West to avoid that fate.

Notes

Links cited here are available at www.edwardlucas.com

INTRODUCTION

1 *Miss Fire: The Chronicle of a British Mission to Mihailovich 1943–1944* by Jasper Rootham (Chatto & Windus, 1946). *Petar. A King's Heritage; The Memoirs of King Peter II of Yugoslavia* (Cassell, 1955). Three Yugoslav-centred books that shaped my childhood are Lawrence Durrell's neglected classic spy novel, *White Eagles over Serbia* (Faber & Faber, 1957); the masterly 'Sword of Honour' trilogy by Evelyn Waugh (Chapman and Hall, 1955, 1951 and 1961); and Rebecca West's *Black Lamb and Grey Falcon* (Macmillan, 1941).

2 *Smiley's People* by John le Carré (Hodder and Stoughton, 1980). Colonel Alfons Rebane, the Estonian officer who played a leading role in SIS's Operation Jungle, was the model for le Carré's 'General Vladimir', an Estonian émigré whose murder brings George Smiley back into the spy world.

3 See for example this report on the suicide of Nikolai Kruchina: 'Soviet Turmoil; New Suicide: Budget Director', *New York Times*, 27 August 1991 http://www.nytimes.com/1991/08/27/world/soviet-turmoil-new-suicide-budget-director.html and also 'Desperately Seeking Rubles' by Susan Tifft and Yuri Zarakhovich, *Time*, 4 November 1991 http://www.time.com/time/magazine/article/0,9171,974181–1,00.html

4 The Cheka (formally the *Vserossiyskaya Chrezvychaynaya Komissiya* or All-Russian Extraordinary Commission) was itself in some senses a successor to the Tsarist-era Okhrana (*Otdelenie po Okhraneniyu Obshchestvennoi Bezopasnosti i Poryadka*, or Department for Protecting Public Safety and Order). Successor organisations were the OGPU (*Obyedinennoye Gosudarstvennoye Politicheskoye Upravleniye*, or State Political Directorate,

the NKVD (*Narodnyy komissariat vnutrennikh del* or People's Commissariat for Internal Affairs) and the KGB (*Komitet gosudarstvennoy bezopasnosti* or Committee for State Security). The FSB (*Federalnaya Sluzhba Bezopasnosti* or Federal Security Service) is the main successor organisation to the KGB. The SVR is the much smaller *Sluzhba Vneshney Razvedki* or Foreign Intelligence Service. It used to be the First Chief Directorate of the Soviet-era KGB. By contrast the GRU (*Glavnoye Razveditelskoye Upravleniye* or Main Intelligence Directorate) is the military-intelligence service. Much diminished in recent years, it has changed neither its title nor its structure since Trotsky established it in 1918.

5 See '*Delo Poteyeva: predatel nanes ushcherb v 50 mln dollarov no ne smog obmanut nachalstvo ukrainskoy lyubovnitsey*' (The Poteyev case: the traitor cost $50m but couldn't fool his bosses about his Ukrainian mistress) http://www.newsru.com/russia/28jun2011/poteev.html (this and all other links accessed July 2011).

6 'Spying Suspects Seemed Short on Secrets' by Scott Shane and Benjamin Weiser, *New York Times*, 29 June 2010 http://www.nytimes.com/2010/06/30/world/europe/30spy.html 'Russian Spies Too Useless, Sexy to Prosecute' by Dan Amira, *New York* magazine, 7 July 2010 http://nymag.com/daily/intel/2010/07/russian_spies_too_useless_sexy.html 'Spy swap: Viennese Waltz' *Guardian*, 10 July 2010 http://www.guardian.co.uk/world/2010/jul/10/spy-swap-russia-us-editorial 'The Russian spy scandal that nobody much cared about' by Alexander Chancellor, *Guardian*, 2 July 2010 http://www.guardian.co.uk/commentisfree/2010/jul/02/russian-spy-ring-scandal

7 'Spy Swap' by John le Carré, *Guardian*, 9 July 2010 http://www.guardian.co.uk/world/2010/jul/09/spy-swap-john-le-carre The Harry Lime reference is to the 1949 film *The Third Man* (later a novella by Graham Greene, who wrote the screenplay) of espionage in post-war Vienna.

8 *Call For The Dead* by John le Carré (Penguin, 1965). The first chapter is online. 'A Brief History of George Smiley', *Guardian*, 22 May 2009 http://www.guardian.co.uk/books/2009/may/22/le-carre-call-for-the-dead

9 http://charlescrawford.biz/blog/more-on-russian-illegals-and-sleepers (accessed 4 July 2010).

10 The central character in thrillers by Robert Ludlum, later made into films such as *The Bourne Identity* (2002).

11 An excellent fictional account of this comes in Vasily Grossman's wartime classic *Life and Fate* (tr. Robert Chandler, Vintage Classics, 2010). The NKVD's wartime role through the eyes of Soviet soldiers, is well portrayed

in *Ivan's War: Life and Death in the Red Army, 1939–1945* by Catherine Merridale (Picador, 2007).

12 The home page for this programme (in Russian) is here http://www.ren-tv. com/pages/tayny-mira-s-annoy-chapman

13 The author Yulian Lyandres (1931–93), under the pen name Yuliam Semyonov, published his first book *Semnadtsat mgnoveniy vesni (The Seventeen Instants of Spring)* in 1968. Unusually, it portrayed Nazi German officials as real people, not caricature monsters. Known as Colonel Maxim Isayev to his KGB colleagues, Stirlitz disrupts Nazi efforts to conclude a separate peace with the Western allies. After the war he hunts fugitive Nazis in Latin America, and is imprisoned at the height of the Stalinist post-war purges.

14 *The New Cold War: How the Kremlin Menaces Russia and the West* (Bloomsbury, 2008). Published in America as *The New Cold War: Putin's Russia and the Threat to the West* (Palgrave, 2008).

15 For details see http://russian-untouchables.com/eng/

16 Mr Mitrokhin made contact with an SIS officer in the British embassy in Riga on 24 March 1992. The CIA had previously turned him down. SIS brought him and his family to Britain in November and later retrieved a large amount of material, said to be six aluminium trunkfuls, copied from the KGB archives and hidden in his dacha garden. Some of it appeared in a series of books that he wrote with the historian Christopher Andrew (Allen Lane 1999–2005), *The Sword and the Shield: The Mitrokhin Archive and the Secret History of the KGB; The World Was Going Our Way: The KGB and the Battle for the Third World; The Mitrokhin Archive: The KGB in Europe and the West.* A parliamentary inquiry criticised some aspects of this: http://www. archive.official-documents.co.uk/document/cm47/4764/4764.htm

17 Though this reflects a rise of one-third from the 3 per cent spent in 2008/9 to 4 per cent in 2009/10. It is a larger slice of a larger cake too: the Security Service has twice the staff and three times the budget it had in 2001. http:// isc.independent.gov.uk/committee-reports/annual-reports

18 *SB a Lech Wałęsa. Przyczynek do biografii (The SB and Lech Wałęsa: A Biographical Contribution)* by Sławomir Cenckiewicz and Piotr Gontarczyk (Institute for National Remembrance, Warsaw, 2008) http://www.ipn. gov.pl/portal/pl/229/7615/SB_a_Lech_Walesa_Przyczynek_do_biografii. html

1 LOOTING AND MURDER

1 Extensive documentation on this is available at www.russian-untouchables. com and www.lawandorderinrussia.org. A film telling the story is available at http://www.youtube.com/watch?v=2aj2NLFL-lE and (full-length rental version) at http://vod.journeyman.tv/store?p=4455. A thorough legal presentation of the Hermitage case can be found here http://www.scribd.com/ doc/20910344/DECLARATION-OF-NEIL-MICKLETHWAITE   A much more critical account is 'Sergei Magnitsky, Bill Browder, Hermitage Capital Management and Wondrous Metamorphoses' http://marknesop. wordpress.com/2011/01/19/sergei-magnitsky-bill-browder-hermitage-capital-management-and-wondrous-metamorphoses/ but Mr Browder rebuts this criticism, to my mind convincingly.

2 An accurate but unflattering account of Mr Browder's approach comes from my successor in Moscow, Gideon Lichfield. 'A Russian Odyssey', *Stanford Business*, November 2006. http://www.gsb.stanford.edu/news/ bmag/sbsm0611/feature_browder.html

3 http://hermitagefund.com/about/hermitageeffect/

4 http://hermitagefund.com/about/hermitageeffect/Harvard%20 Business%20School%20—%20Hermitage%20Case%20Study.pdf

5 An excellent account of this comes in *Putin's Oil: The Yukos Affair and the Struggle for Russia* by Martin Sixsmith (Continuum, 2010). Yukos was bankrupted by bogus tax demands and its assets handed over to Kremlin cronies; its owner was sentenced to lengthy jail terms after successive farcical court hearings, at which he has denounced the regime and the lawlessness it stokes and thrives on, for example in the statement he and his co-defendant Platon Lebedev issued during their trial, on 2 November 2010 http://www.khodor-kovskycenter.com/mikhail-khodorkovsky-full-transcript-his-final-words

6 'Bewilderment As Browder Barred As Security Threat' by Catherine Belton, *St Petersburg Times*, 21 March 2006. http://www.sptimes.ru/index. php?action_id=2&story_id=17062

7 The clip can be seen here http://www.youtube.com/watch?v=lcnF0Cu8 Wtc *'Putin ne smog obyasnit, pochemu v Rossiyu ne puskayut samogo predannogo zarubeznnogo invevestora'* ('Putin can't explain why Russia won't let in the most successful foreign investor'), unsigned article, 17 July 2006 http:// www.newsru.com/arch/finance/17jul2006/browder.html

8 The attorneys' names are Ekaterina Maltseva, and a husband and wife team: Andrei Pavlov and Yulia Mayorova. In other cases related to the same fraud, this couple has represented claimants against Hermitage. But on this

occasion they were claiming to represent it. http://russian-untouchables.com/eng/240m-theft-from-budget/

9 A video giving an account (critical – and to me unconvincing) of Hermitage's activities can be found (in Russian) here http://www.mk.ru/video/politics/1013-skeletyi-uilyama-braudera-.html

10 http://www.assembly.coe.int/documents/workingdocs/doc09/edoc11993.pdf

11 An excellent account of Mr Magnitsky's treatment in prison can be found here in Russian http://www.rb.ru/inform/127947.html and here in English 'Report of the public oversight commission for human rights observance in Moscow detention centers: Review of the conditions of the detention of Sergei Magnitsky in the pre-trial detention centres of the City of Moscow' http://online.wsj.com/public/resources/documents/WSJ-20091229-MagnitskyReport.pdf. The extracts from Mr Magnitsky's own writings can be found here: http://russian-untouchables.com/docs/Prison-Diaries-Magnitsky-General-Prosecutor-Complaint.pdf

12 Ibid. Medical care in Russian prisons is generally lamentable, but high-profile prisoners seem to have a particularly bad time. A lawyer for Yukos, Vasily Aleksanyan, contracted HIV and tuberculosis while in prison, lost his sight and got cancer, before he was released thanks to a ruling by the European Court of Human Rights.

13 http://russian-untouchables.com/docs/Alekseyeva-Complaint-Eng29Mar2010.pdf

14 http://russian-untouchables.com/eng/2011/07/russia-blames-medics-for-hermitage-lawyer-death/

15 The video is available on Mr Browder's website http://russian-untouchables.com/eng/ or at http://www.youtube.com/watch?v=H7yBOEPYJTc

16 A list of all sixty can be found here http://www.csce.gov/index.cfm?Fuseaction=Files.Download&FileStore_id=1744 The criteria for inclusion on the list is that the person signed a document associated with the case.

17 These purported terrorist attacks created a climate of panic in which the then unknown new prime minister, Vladimir Putin, rapidly became the most popular politician in the country thanks to his seemingly tough response. A botched attack on an apartment block in Ryazan turned out to have been the work of the FSB, which explained its actions, deeply unconvincingly, as an anti-terrorist drill. Those brave Russians who have tried to investigate this mysterious affair have ended up dead. See *The New Cold War*, chapter 2.

2 THE PIRATE STATE

1 A thorough and lively account of these and other abuses is in Luke Harding's *Mafia State* (Guardian Books, 2011). It also details the persistent harassment campaign mounted against him and his family.

2 World Report 2011: Russia http://www.hrw.org/en/world-report-2011/russia

3 See my article 'Licence to Loot', *The Economist*, 17 September 2011 http://www.economist.com/node/21529021

4 See 'Frau Fixit: Germany, Central Europe and Russia' *The Economist*, 18 November 2010 http://www.economist.com/node/17522476

5 *The Return: Russia's Journey from Gorbachev to Medvedev* by Daniel Treisman, (Simon Spotlight Entertainment, London, January 2011), published in America by Free Press.

6 'Neo-Feudalism Explained' by Vladimir Inozemtsev, *The American Interest*, March–April 2011. http://www.the-american-interest.com/article.cfm?piece=939

7 http://wikileaks.ch/cable/2010/02/10PARIS170.html

8 http://wikileaks.org/cable/2008/10/08LONDON2643.html

9 http://wikileaks.ch/cable/2009/11/09MOSCOW2749.html._ A similarly worded but slightly different version of the cable can be found at http://www.cablegatesearch.net/cable.php?id=09MOSCOW1051

10 http://www.cablegatesearch.net/cable.php?id=10MOSCOW317

11 'The Concealed Battle to Run Russia' by Amy Knight, *New York Review of Books*, 13 January 2011 http://www.nybooks.com/articles/archives/2011/jan/13/concealed-battle-run-russia/

12 *The New Nobility, The Restoration of Russia's Security State and the Enduring Legacy of the KGB* by Andrei Soldatov and Irina Borogan (Public Affairs Books, 2010). The authors run the www.agentura.ru website, a magpie's nest of news and analysis, mostly in Russian, all of it well-informed, about the inner workings of the secret state.

13 Ibid. p. ix.

14 Quoted in ibid, p. 5.

15 The draft 'de-Stalinisation' programme from the President's Human Rights Council can be found here http://www.president-sovet.ru/structure/group_5/materials/the_program_of_historical_memory.php
See for example *Natsionalnoye primireniye nevozmozhna bez suda i pamyati* (National Reconciliation is impossible without a trial and memory) http://www.rg.ru/2011/04/08/repress.html

16 'Stalin against Putin' (unsigned) *Vedomosti*, 28 April 2011 http://www.vedomosti.ru/newspaper/article/259344/stalin_protiv_putina

17 'Reading Russia: The *Siloviki* in Charge' by Andrei Illarionov. *Journal of Democracy*, Vol. 20, no. 2, April 2009 http://www.cato.org/pubs/articles/andrei_illarionov_the_siloviki_in_charge.pdf

18 Inozemtsev, op. cit.

19 'The mindset of Russia's security services', Andrei Soldatov and Irina Borogan, 29 December 2010 http://www.agentura.ru/english/dossier/mindset/

20 An English version can be seen here http://www.viddler.com/explore/Eastculture2009/videos/4/ The script (in English) can be found here. http://www.pravoslavie.ru/english/080211155439.htm

21 Soldatov and Borogan, 'The mindset'.

22 See for example: http://www.telegraph.co.uk/finance/newsbysector/energy/oilandgas/8244470/Gazprom-held-back-by-its-corrupt-nature.html; http://www.iie.com/ppublications/papers/aslund0508.pdf; and http://www.europeanenergyreview.eu/data/docs/Viewpoints/Putin%20and%20Gazprom_Nemtsov%20en%20Milov.pdf

23 Mr Navalny's site is www.navalny.ru; Mr Nemtsov's is www.nemtsov.ru; Mr Milov's is http://www.milov.info All are in Russian only at the time of writing.

24 '*Olga Kryshtanovskaya: Putin vernetsya kak don mafii*' ('Olga Kryshtanovskaya: Putin returns like a mafia don') by Andrei Polunin, *Svobodnaya pressa*, 8 February 2011 http://svpressa.ru/politic/article/38451/

25 '*Nelzya dopustit, chtobi voini prevratilis v torgovtsev*' ('We must not allow warriors to become traders') *Kommersant*, 9 October 2007 http://www.kommersant.ru/doc/812840

26 The episode was well analysed here by the Jamestown Foundation's Jonas Bernstein, 'Shvartsman's Description of Siloviki Business Practices – Truth Or Fiction?' *Eurasia Daily Monitor*, 7 December 2007 http://www.jamestown.org/single/?no_cache=1&tx_ttnews%5Btt_news%5D=33224 and in 'Former Russian Spies Now Prominent in Business' by Andrew Kramer, *New York Times* 18 December 2007 http://www.nytimes.com/2007/12/18/business/worldbusiness/18kgb.html

27 The survey is by the INDEM thinktank and available (in Russian) here: *Sostoyanie bitovoi korruptsii v Rossiiskoi Federatsii* (State of Domestic Corruption in the Russian Federation) http://www.indem.ru/corrupt/doklad_cor_INDEM_FOM_2010.pdf

28 See for example 'A Stain On Mr Clean' by Christian Caryl and Mark Hosenball. *Newsweek*, 3 September 2001 http://www.newsweek.com/2001/09/02/a-stain-on-mr-clean.html

29 *Die Gangster aus dem Osten (The Gangsters from the East)* by Jürgen Roth
   (Europa Verlag, 2004). It urgently needs updating and publication in
   English. Also worth reading is *Red Mafiya: How the Russian Mob has Invaded
   America* by Robert Friedman (Berkeley, 2002).

30 In the course of another investigation, I tracked down a foreign engineer
   who had been involved in a commercial court case against one of the 'four'
   – in those days much less powerful – involving a broken contract. In the
   course of the litigation, he had uncovered compelling evidence of links
   between this individual and organised crime. This led to a prompt settlement of the case when he threatened to disclose it. When I approached him,
   he was long retired and running a provincial hotel. He said that it was more
   than his life was worth to share his research with me. A good example of the
   tangled, fascinating but inconclusive investigative reporting surrounding the
   regime's business interests comes from 'Factories, tanks, offshore firms
   and neighbours' by Roman Anin, *Novaya Gazeta*, 22 April 2010 http://
   en.novayagazeta.ru/data/2011/042/02.html

3 DEADLY GAMES AND USEFUL IDIOTS

1 For example my article 'Walk on the dark side' about the criminal Russian
  IT company RBN. *The Economist*, 30 August 2007 http://www.economist.
  com/node/9723768

2 'Reset Regret: Moral Leadership Needed to Fix US–Russian
  Relations' by Ariel Cohen and Donald Jensen, 30 June 2011.
  http://www.heritage.org/Research/Reports/2011/06/
  Reset-Regret-Moral-Leadership-Needed-to-Fix-US-Russian-Relations

3 http://www.guardian.co.uk/world/us-embassy-cables-docu-
  ments/247712   and   http://www.guardian.co.uk/world/2010/dec/01/
  wikileaks-cable-spain-russian-mafia

4 A well-sourced account of this comes from the Jerusalem-based journalist
  Gil Yaron, writing (in German) in the *Salzburger Nachrichten*. http://search.
  salzburg.com/articles/5847190. A Finnish connection in the story remains
  to be investigated.

5 See for example this speech by Jonathan Evans, director of the Security
  Service (MI5) here http://www.societyofeditors.co.uk/page-view.
  php?pagename=TheKeynoteSpeech and the German *Verfassungsschutz*
  (Office for Constitutional Protection) annual reports, for example (in
  German) http://www.verfassungsschutz.de/download/SHOW/vsbericht_
  2009.pdf '*Putins Konjunkturprogramm: Russische Agenten spionieren deutsche*

Energie-Unternehmen aus' ('Putin's growth programme – Russian agents spy on German energy companies') by Dirk Banse, *Welt am Sonntag*, 21 June 2009. http://www.welt.de/wams_print/article3965455/Putins-Konjunkturprogramm-Russische-Agenten-spionieren-deutsche-Energie-Unternehmen-aus.html

6 Chiefly in chapter 3.

7 *Londongrad – From Russia with Cash; The Inside Story of the Oligarchs* by Mark Hollingsworth and Stewart Lansley (Fourth Estate, 2009).

8 The official Air Accidents Investigation Branch report can be found here http://www.aaib.gov.uk/cms_resources.cfm?file=/Agusta_A109E,_G-PWER.pdf with a small but interesting correction here http://www.aaib.gov.uk/cms_resources.cfm?file=/Agusta%20A109E,%20G-PWER%20Correction%209-05.pdf

9 A comprehensive summary can be found here 'Russia's intelligence attack: The Anna Chapman danger', by Peter Hennessy and Richard Knight, 17 August 2010. http://www.bbc.co.uk/news/uk-10986334 A link on the site plays the programme.

10 In mid 2008 I became aware of this story and made persistent enquiries about it. Britain's Ministry of Defence press office repeatedly denied that any such incident had taken place. The story was then leaked. 'Russian Nuke Jet Buzzes Hull' by Tom Newton-Dunn, *Sun*, 30 August 2008 http://www.thesun.co.uk/sol/homepage/news/article1749464.ece

11 'Fighter jets intercept Russian bombers after flying into Dutch airspace' 8 June 2011 http://channel6newsonline.com/2011/06/fighter-jets-intercept-russian-bombers-after-flying-into-dutch-airspace/

12 This WikiLeaks cable gives a flavour of the subsequent discussion at NATO http://www.cablegatesearch.net/cable.php?id=09USNATO581

13 *Rosja ćwiczyła atak atomowy na Polskę* ('Russia practises a nuclear attack on Poland') by Michał Krzymowski, *Wprost* (Warsaw), 31 October 2009 http://www.wprost.pl/ar/176722/Rosja-cwiczyla-atak-atomowy-na-Polske/ See also *Sõnad ja Teras* ('Words and Steel') by Kaarel Kaas, *Postimees* (Tallinn), 19 September 2009 http://www.postimees.ee/165608/kaarel-kaas-sonad-ja-teras/ and 'Russian Military Thinking and Threat Perception: A Finnish View', by Stefan Forss http://www.ceri-sciencespo.com/ressources/n5_13112009.pdf

14 See for example 'Russian Subs Patrolling Off East Coast of US' by Mark Mazzetti and Thom Shanker, *New York Times*, 4 August 2009 http://www.nytimes.com/2009/08/05/world/05patrol.html and 'Russian subs stalk Trident in echo of Cold War' by Thomas Harding, *Daily*

Telegraph, 27 August 2010 http://www.telegraph.co.uk/news/uknews/defence/7969017/Russian-subs-stalk-Trident-in-echo-of-Cold-War.html

15 No documentary evidence exists for the promise. If it was made (or understood) orally, it was to a state that no longer exists, under duress and without consultation with the other countries concerned. Moreover, Russia can hardly argue both that it is no threat to its neighbours, and that it has a right to veto their security choices. See *Opening NATO's Door: How the Alliance Remade Itself for a New Era* by the late Ronald Asmus (Columbia University Press, 2002).

16 A *Washington Post* investigation in 2010 'Top Secret America' highlighted the unmanageable size and complexity of the nation's intelligence agencies. http://projects.washingtonpost.com/top-secret-america/

17 'Polish FM in WikiLeaks: Germany is Russia's Trojan Horse', by Andrew Reitman, *EU Observer*, 16 September 2011 http://euobserver.com/24/113652

18 *Welt am Sonntag*, ibid.

19 'Time to Shove Off', *The Economist*, 10 September 2011 http://www.economist.com/node/21528596

20 This is actually the wrong acronym, as FAPSI has been incorporated into the FSB. http://www.fas.org/irp/world/russia/fapsi/index.html

21 http://www.panoramio.com/photo/38125772 by P. King.

22 As reported here: 'Seen from on high', Europe.view column, *The Economist* 3 April, 2008 http://www.economist.com/node/10950261. The Inmarsat satellite was repositioned in 2009. Russia could in theory have built the station in the Kaliningrad exclave – but any data sent back to the rest of Russia would have been vulnerable. Modern interception technology is able to obtain not only microwave and radio transmissions, but also data carried on seabed fibre-optic cables, by means of a 'collar' placed at a point where the cable curves.

23 Russia is now a participant in the Wassenaar Arrangement, which restricts the export of sensitive equipment to so-called rogue states. http://www.wassenaar.org/guidelines/

24 This is an archaic bit of legislation dating from 1974 intended to put pressure on the Soviet Union to allow Jewish would-be émigrés to leave the country freely. It is routinely waived by the Senate, but remains an irritant. See http://www.cfr.org/trade/jackson-vanik-amendment/p18844

25 Discussion of this case is difficult for legal reasons. For some years Mr Deripaska, an aluminium tycoon, has had difficulty gaining an American visa because of what officials described as 'concerns about his business

practices and associates'. The FBI is believed to have an audio recording in which he discusses some business difficulties and a planned solution in robust terms. He recently received a visa in exchange for a lengthy interview with officials from the criminal-justice system who sought his help in areas of interest to the US government. Nothing concrete resulted. See 'FBI Lets Barred Tycoon Visit US' by Evan Perez and Gregory White, *Wall St Journal* 30 October 2009 http://online.wsj.com/article/SB125685578903317087. html and also Mr Deripaska's response http://online.wsj.com/article/SB125687000832717809.html

26 http://valdaiclub.com/ gives a flavour of the lavish nature of this event.

27 Other papers which have swallowed this include *European Voice* (published by the *Economist*), where I write a weekly column; *Le Figaro* (France); the *Economic Times* and the *Times of India* (India); *Duma* (Bulgaria); *Folha de São Paulo* (Brazil); *la Repubblica* (Italy); *Clarín* (Argentina); *El País* (Spain); *Süddeutsche Zeitung* (Germany) and *Geopolitika* (Serbia). http://russianow. washingtonpost.com/about/ and http://www.telegraph.co.uk/sponsored/russianow/

28 On 8 September 2007 it printed a commentary claiming that the Katyń massacre of Polish officers in 1940 was not the work of the Soviet secret police, but of the Nazis. The original article is available here http://i1159.photobucket.com/albums/t147/apamyatnykh/GAZETA01s.jpg?t=1191101536 See also http://katynfiles.com/content/pamyatnykh-sabov-strygin-shved.html

29 http://www.youtube.com/watch?v=ipGjIs3ovIc

30 Such as complaining about the language and citizenship laws in Estonia and Latvia: see for example 'Latvia and Estonia discriminate against non-citizens' by Yevgeny Kryshkin, *The Voice of Russia*, 26 February 2010 http://english.ruvr.ru/2010/02/26/4852056.html Both countries have substantial, though declining, populations of Soviet-era migrants who have so far declined to learn the national languages or take the test that would entitle them to citizenship. Estonia's non-citizen population dropped below the symbolically important 100,000 mark in April 2011; in Latvia the Russian-speaking population is better integrated socially but more active politically (partly as a result of Latvian state weakness, and partly because of Russian state interference).

31 See http://www.siac.tribunals.gov.uk/Documents/zatuliveter_substantive_29Nov11.pdf

4 REAL SPIES, REAL VICTIMS

1 'Russian Spy Has Defected to Canada' by Jim Bronskill and Mike Trickey, *National Post*, 9 March 2001. Not available online directly but copied at http://lists101.his.com/pipermail/intelforum/2001-March/004354.html

2 Snapshots of the site are available at http://www.domaintools.com/research/screenshot-history/ for subscribers, or via the Wayback internet archive.

3 AIA listed its contributors as follows: Michel Elbaz – general coordinator; Allister Maunk – administrator and editor; Can Karpat – Turkish and Balkan section; Simon Araloff – European section; Anders Asmus – regional and international politics of Baltic states; Pavel Simonov – Russian section; Ulugbek Djuraev – Central-Asian section; Asim Oku – Turkish section; Sami Rosen – Israeli section; Alexander Petrov – webmaster.

4 One oddity was that on 13 May 2009 the privacy-protection had slipped. The registrant's email was now listed, with an Israeli postal address: m_falkov@yahoo.com Ha-Ela 16, Bene Ayish 79845. Whoever had been so keen to protect the site's identity was now either careless or carefree.

5 'WikiLeaks cable: Russian leadership viewed Lieberman as "one of its own": Message from US embassy to State Department shows FM was treated as an "old friend" during a 2009 visit to Moscow' by Barak Ravid, *Haaretz*, 29 November 2010 http://www.haaretz.com/news/diplomacy-defense/wikileaks-cable-russian-leadership-viewed-lieberman-as-one-of-its-own-1.327694

6 'Intelligence war breaks out in Israel's Foreign Ministry' by Joseph Fitsanakis, 20 July 2009. http://intelligencenews.wordpress.com/2009/07/20/01-188/

7 According to the German security service http://www.verfassungsschutz.de/download/SHOW/vsbericht_2009.pdf p. 331 (in German).

8 A prominent semi-retired officer, Anton Surikov, died mysteriously in late 2009. In his last interview with a Western journalist a few weeks earlier, he said that Russia was run by 'bandits from St Petersburg'. They, he said, were trying to push the country towards an authoritarian, Chinese-style model of political and economic development. The GRU director Valentin Korabelnikov retired in 2009 to avoid sacking, amid semi-public disagreement with his bosses over Russia's military reforms. 'Last Cake with a Russian Agent' by Ben Judah, *Standpoint*, January/February 2010 http://www.standpointmag.co.uk/node/2580/full

9 Viewable at http://www.youtube.com/watch?v=RFnsqivNW6A

10 '*Polska broń w służbie gruzińskiej armii*' ('Polish weapons in the service of the Georgian Army') by Michael Majewski and Pawel Reszka; *Dziennik*, Warsaw, 10 August 2008. http://wiadomosci.dziennik.pl/polityka/ artykuly/156916,polska-bron-w-sluzbie-gruzinskiej-armii.html

11 An excellent account of the conflict is *A Little War That Shook The World* by the late Ron Asmus (Palgrave Macmillan, 2009). Another is *The Guns of August 2008: Russia's War in Georgia* by Svante Cornell and Frederick Starr (eds.) (M. E. Sharpe, 2009).

12 *Georgia's South Ossetia Conflict: Make Haste Slowly*, Crisis Group Europe Report No. 183, 7 June 2007, p. 16 http://www.crisisgroup.org/~/media/ Files/europe/183_georgia_s_south_ossetia_conflict_make_haste_slowly. ashx

13 My source for this is a Georgian government non-paper and interviews with senior Georgian and Western officials. See also 'Tbilisi Says Evidence Links Russian Officer to Blasts', *Civil Georgia*, 8 December 2010. http://www.civil.ge/eng/article.php?id=22940 and 'Georgia accuses Russia of bombings, warns on talks' by Stephanie Nebehay, Reuters, 7 June 2011 http://www.reuters.com/article/2011/06/07/ georgia-russia-talks-idUSLDE75622520110607

5 SPYCRAFT: FACT AND FICTION

1 They may have some self-defence training and will often be excellent drivers. Those who have joined after a previous career in the military, particularly in special forces, are different; so are the dodgy characters often recruited as auxiliaries. For gossipy details of CIA training, see *Blowing My Cover: My Life as a CIA Spy* by Lindsay Moran (Putnam, 2005).

2 Search warrant for 35b Trowbridge St, Cambridge MA. http://www. thebostonchannel.com/download/2010/0715/24272005.pdf

3 See (in Swedish) http://www.forsvarsmakten.se/hkv/Must/ and *Sveriges hemligaste rum* (Sweden's most secret room) by Emelie Asplund and Ewa Stenberg, *Dagens Nyheter*, 3 October 2005 http://www.dn.se/nyheter/ sveriges-hemligaste-rum Next-door Finland is even lower-profile. It has a domestic security agency (SuPo), which is part of the police, and a military intelligence agency. Any capability for foreign human intelligence is admirably hidden.

4 See 'Factbox: Who are the spies Russia plans to swap?', Reuters, 9 July 2010 http://www.reuters.com/article/2010/07/09/us-russia-usa-spies-factbox- idUSTRE6681DG20100709 The others were Igor Sutyagin, who had

worked at a think tank; Aleksandr Zaporozhsky, a KGB colonel who spied for America and helped unmask Ames and Hanssen, but unwisely returned to Russia; and Gennady Vasilenko, about whom little is known. See *Stranny srok 'shpiona' Vasilenko'* (The strange life of the 'spy' Vasilenko), Rosbalt, 13 July 2010 http://www.rosbalt.ru/moscow/2010/07/13/753359.html

5 Sources differ on whether the man concerned was Oleg Penkovsky, the West's highest-ranking agent-in-place in the Soviet Union, or Piotr Popov, the first GRU officer to be recruited by the West, who was betrayed by the SIS officer George Blake. The account comes from *Aquarium – The Career and Defection of a Soviet Military Spy* (Hamish Hamilton, 1985) by Viktor Suvorov (the pen name of Vladimir Rezun).

6 The same 'spotlighting' was experienced in 1996 by Norman MacSween, the then SIS station chief in Moscow, who was the case officer for Platon Obukhov, a 28-year-old foreign ministry employee. He was shown waiting vainly on a park bench in Moscow. See 'British Diplomat Linked to Spy Case' by Owen Matthews, *The Moscow Times*, 31 July 1996. http://www.themoscowtimes.com/news/article/british-diplomat-linked-to-spy-case/320742.html

7 'The cold war is over, but rock in a park suggests the spying game still thrives' by Nick Paton Walsh, Richard Norton-Taylor and Ewen MacAskill, *Guardian*, 24 January 2006 http://www.guardian.co.uk/world/2006/jan/24/russia.politics; and 'Spy-rock Russian faces 20 years' jail' by Mark Franchetti, *Sunday Times*, 29 January 2006 http://www.timesonline.co.uk/tol/news/world/article722212.ece

8 *The Big Breach: from Top Secret to Maximum Security* was originally published in Moscow in 2001, with the help of Russian intelligence. It is now available in the UK from Cutting Edge Press.

9 'Spies Among Us: Why Spies, Why Now?' 10 July 2010 http://www.psychologytoday.com/blog/spycatcher/201007/spies-among-us Mr Navarro can be reached through www.jnforensics.com

10 His real name is still classified, according to a CIA spokesman. The document can be read at http://www.scribd.com/doc/515327/ciadeepcover

11 'What's wrong with America's spies', April 2003, *Middle East Intelligence Bulletin* http://www.meforum.org/meib/articles/0304_me1.htm Mr Carroll's website is http://www.tpcarroll.com Another useful primer on espionage is this course syllabus http://www.csus.edu/indiv/c/carrollt/site/welcome_files/gov't%20139g%20class%20notes%20fall%202006%20-%2024%20oct.pdf

6 SPIES LIKE US

1 Available at http://www.justice.gov/opa/documents/062810complaint2. pdf and http://www.justice.gov.opa/documents/062810complaint1.pdf

2 'Russian Spy Suspects Were Suburbia Personified' by Manny Fernandez and Fernanda Santos, *New York Times*, 30 June 2010 www.nytimes. com/2010/06/30/nyregion/30couples.html

3 Interview with author, December 2010.

4 Mr Patricof, a prominent New York-based financier, was a donor to President Bill Clinton's campaign and a friend of Mrs Clinton's. He admitted that he knew Mrs Murphy but insists he never discussed anything of a political or sensitive nature with her. He is believed to be the person referred to in the Department of Justice initial complaint (section 85a, p35). Available at http://www.justice.gov/opa/documents/062810complaint2. pdf Complaint 1 is available at http://www.justice.gov/opa/ documents/062810complaint1.pdf

5 'Busted Russian Spy Wants Old Life Back' by Richard Boudreaux, *Wall St Journal*, 7 August 2010 http://online.wsj.com/article/SB1000142405274870 3309704575413600124475346.html

6 See Complaint 1, section 40.

7 One might start by sparing a thought for the children involved, such as the Murphys' daughters. For them, their parents' foray into international espionage meant a painful and bewildering upheaval, ending in a return to Russia, a country they did not know with a language they did not speak. Children trust their parents above all and find even minor deceptions upsetting. The revelation of a double life will leave deep scars. Spouses can suffer quite badly too. A whiff of the hurt and distrust caused by the affair came in February 2011 with an interview given to *Caretas*, a Peruvian magazine, by Ms Peláez, who insisted that she had no idea that her husband of twenty years was not who he claimed to be. 'Not even when we fought would I hear a word in Russian . . . not even in intonation. Such was his preparation.' Ms Peláez, who was handcuffed and put in prison uniform before the initial court hearing, shows some sympathy with her husband's cause, suffused with the grandiloquent rhetoric of Soviet-era solidarity with the Third World. She describes him as the 'last Soviet hero' and an 'unseen warrior', who told her: 'I was brought up as a revolutionary, as an internationalist.' In a column for *Moscow News*, where she began as a regular contributor in August 2011, she says he is 'sad' about how much life has changed in the thirty years since he left the Soviet Union. Her own

son from a previous relationship and her younger son Juan (fathered by Vasenkov) have remained in New York. She said her husband 'suffers for the lack of his son, to whom he dedicated his best hours and whom he now can't see'. She said she does not want to stay in Russia, where she is receiving a $2,000 monthly pension, but wishes to return to either Peru or Brazil eventually. Some doubt about Ms Peláez's eloquently expressed disappointment comes from the criminal complaint against her husband, in which FBI eavesdroppers say they overheard him talking to her about his family's wartime experiences in the Soviet Union: 'We moved to Siberia . . . as soon as the war started.' It is conceivable, if unlikely, that she believed that he was a Uruguayan (perhaps of communist parents) who had spent the war years in the Soviet Union. Perhaps she knew he was spying but thought it was for another country, such as Cuba. The Peruvian authorities queried her marriage and birth certificates. See 'Vicky Peláez to face corruption charges in Peru' http://www.livinginperu.com/news/13009 and 'La "Espía" que Volvió del Frío' ('The "Spy" who returned from the Cold') http://nuestragente2010.wordpress.com/▶-vicky-pelaez-regresa-al-peru as well as 'Mystery surrounds alleged spies' children – With parents behind bars, kids' lives likely in turmoil' by Elizabeth Chuck and Ryan McCartney, msnbc.com, 30 June, 2010 http://www.msnbc.msn.com/id/38021300/ns/us_news-security/

8 www.bostonredcarpet.com and the seemingly identical www.foleyann.com, accessed 7 September 2010 (now defunct).

9 http://www.futuremap.com/conversion-pages/strategic-leadership/future-challenges
The website gives no clue about the number of people working at Futuremap, and blurs the distinctions between the 'institute' and the 'company'. Heathfield's name appears only once on the entire site. Both futuremap.com and myfuturemap.com are written in Russified English, with a notable absence of definite and indefinite articles.

10 'Records show alleged Russian spy graduated from York' *Ylife* 5 July 2010 http://www.yorku.ca/ylife/index.asp?Article=3260

11 *Scenarios for Success: Turning Insights into Action* (John Wiley & Sons, 2007). Heathfield's chapter can be downloaded here http://www.futuremap.com/Portals/56527/docs/book%20chapter-%20don%20heathfield-fm%2070124.pdf

12 Interview with the author, February 2011.

13 Interview with the author, February 2011. For reasons of commercial confidentiality, this source wishes to remain anonymous.

14 http://www.linkedin.com/profile/view?id=24934901   Another   of   the
spies, Cindy Murphy, had a LinkedIn profile but has not updated it. http://
www.linkedin.com/pub/cindy-murphy-cfp%C2%AE/10/a27/6a6

15 Interview with the author, 1 March 2011.

16 Appendix B (p.61–63) includes a couple of screenshots of the software.
http://www.forwardengagement.org/storage/forwardengagement/docu-
ments/fall_2006_final_report.pdf

17 The intern, then aged 20, was one of Leon Fuerth's students. I have with-
held his name at his request. His main job was to input data into the software, such as forecasts for China's growth. He resigned when Heathfield
declined to accept his suggestions for improving the software. Nobody from
the FBI has contacted him, or Mr Glenn (who still has a copy of the software), or four of Heathfield's other associates that I tracked down during
research for this book.

18 Interview with the author, March 2011.

19 Heathfield, p. 19.

20 Email to the author 25 February 2011. Mr Fuerth adds: 'Forward Engagement
is in any event not a business, but a concept I have used for teaching and also
for advocating a closer integration of foresight processes and public policy-
making. All elements of Forward Engagement are to be found at www.
forwardengagement.org.'

21 See paras 79a and 79c in http://www.justice.gov/opa/documents/062810
complaint2.pdf

22 Interview with the author, 23 February 2011. For more details of Techcast,
see www.techcast.com

23 http://www.soft-technology.org/html/menu/about-us-en.html

24 www.chinagreenfuture.com

25 Email to the author, 22 February, 2011.

26 'Anticipatory   leadership'   http://www.fccsingapore.com/fileadmin/
template/images/news/Future%20Map_AnticipatoryLeadership_
FCCS091118.pdf

27 http://myfuturemap.com/Donald_G4So.html

28 Global Partners declined to respond to requests for comment about
Heathfield's time there.

29 Interview with the author, 1 March 2011.

30 Who wishes to remain anonymous – in itself a telling sign of the climate in
Russia.

31 The best biography of Harold Adrian Russell ('Kim') Philby is *Philby: KGB
Masterspy* by Phillip Knightley (André Deutsch, 2003).

7 THE NEW ILLEGALS

1 http://www.linkedin.com/profile/view?id=21028567 It now lists him just
   as 'Mikhail' to non-subscribers.

2 Complaint 1, Para 8.

3 For an account of Semenko's activities at a think-tank meeting, see 'My
   spy story – *Washington Times* writer meets Putin's agent' by James Robbins,
   Washington Times, 30 June 2010 http://www.washingtontimes.com/
   news/2010/jun/30/my-spy-story/

4 His book on the subject is *Secret Empire: KGB in Russia Today* (Westview
   Press Inc, 1994).

5 For salacious coverage of Ms Chapman, it is hard to beat the former
   British Sunday tabloid the *News of the World*. Its website no longer
   works, but the story from 5 July 2010 called 'Mile High Sex Games
   with My Spy in the Sky' is available at http://patdollard.com/2010/07/
   naked-pictures-of-sexy-russian-spy/

6 http://www.linkedin.com/profile/view?id=26221285

7 A rough cut of a television interview with Ms Chapman can be seen here
   http://www.mirror.co.uk/news/top-stories/2010/07/01/russian-spy-suspect-
   anna-chapman-exclusive-video-beauty-talks-about-uk-links-115875-
   22373084/#ixzz0sRiPh5Nm

8 I have seen extensive email correspondence between Ms Chapman and a
   potential investor in her company, who has asked me not to identify him in
   order to uphold the implicit commercial confidentiality of the exchanges.

9 http://www.scribd.com/doc/33836446/NYC-Rentals-Business-Pitch

10 http://www.youtube.com/watch?v=js_6-UwdkyU

11 www.elliotsblog.com/domain-investor-connection-to-alleged-russian-
   spy-4992

12 'Red-hot beauty Anna Chapman snared in Russia "spy" ring' by Bruce
   Golding, Andy Soltis and Cathy Burke, NYPOST.com, 29 June 2010
   http://www.nypost.com/p/news/local/spy_ring_qzWW8bImf9y
   EDTbtXcQnUL

13 The FBI in October 2011 released some surveillance footage of the meeting: http://www.youtube.com/watch?v=z7-SCKuvxqo

14 An English version of the story is available at http://www.sovlit.com/
   miltarysecret/militarysecret01.html

15 http://www.youtube.com/watch?v=nVpqiRD_fCA

16 103 Gibson Gardens, London N16 7HD.

17 Quoted in 'Anna Chapman: Diplomat's daughter who partied with
   billionaires' by Amelia Hill, Rajeev Syal, Luke Harding and Paul Harris,

Guardian, 1 July 2010 http://www.guardian.co.uk/world/2010/jun/30/anna-chapman-russian-spy-ring

18 The claim is examined at 'Here's The Real Role Anna Chapman Actually Had At The Hedge Fund Navigator' by Courtney Comstock, 1 July 2010 http://www.businessinsider.com/anna-chapman-navigator-asset-management-advisors-nicholas-camilleri-2010-7

19 'Agent Anna the Man Hunter: London flatmate reveals how she and Russian spy used sex to prey on string of oligarchs who were enemies of Kremlin bosses' by Richard Pendlebury, *Daily Mail*, 25 September 2010. The story implies that Ms Chapman had an intimate relationship with a fugitive Russian oligarch, and that she was separately in contact with Mr Berezovsky.

20 'Security services "foil plot to kill Berezovsky at the London Hilton"' by Richard Beeston, *The Times*, 18 July 2007 http://www.timesonline.co.uk/tol/news/world/europe/article2094719.ece

21 08HARARE1016, REGIME ELITES LOOTING DEADLY DIAMOND FIELD http://213.251.145.96/cable/2008/11/08HARARE1016.html

22 The only company Lindi Sharpe was associated with was called Nexgen Builders, dissolved in 2002. She was company secretary; the sole director was her daughter, Rychelle Sharpe.

23 Some news reports have described Southern Union as a charity. It is not registered on the UK Charity Commission website. The companies mentioned here have no connection with Southern Union Money Transfer Ltd of Dagenham, established in 2011.

24 'Redhead Russian spy linked to money smuggling ring' by Barbara Jones (pseudonym), *Daily Mail*, 18 July 2010 http://www.dailymail.co.uk/news/article-1295606/Redhead-spy-linked-UK-money-smuggling-ring.html

25 I have talked extensively to Mr Sugden. For an example of the media coverage, see 'MI5 probes link between Russian spy and Zimbabwean businessman' by Daniel Boffey, *Daily Mail*, 4 July 2010 http://www.dailymail.co.uk/news/article-1291828/MI5-probe-links-Russian-spy-Anna-Chapman-mysterious-Zimbabwean-businessman.html
'Caught up in a spy ring scandal' by Mary Harris, 9 July 2010 http://www.thisiskent.co.uk/news/Caught-spy-ring-scandal/article-2394123-detail/article.html A possibly related company with a similar name was dissolved on 8 November 2005.

26 www.hi5.com/friend/p41744008—sugden+steven—html (defunct). In order to try to exclude him from the story, I contacted all the friends listed on the social-networking site. One replied, confirming that Sugden existed. The others did not answer.

27 http://namesdatabase.com/people/SUGDEN/STEVEN/14248266 (defunct)

28 Southern Union Money Transfers Limited was incorporated on 19 August 2003. It was also registered at a misspelled address, 3 Gold Street Muse [sic], Northampton.

29 'Russia's Anna Inc' by Owen Matthews and Anna Nemtsova, *Newsweek*, 21 February 2011, http://www.newsweek.com/2011/02/13/russia-s-anna-inc.html

30 Described as a 'new Mercader' in a reference to Ramon Mercader who murdered Leon Trotsky with an icepick in Mexico in 1940. See http://rusinfotoday.com/news/kto-sdal-rossijskuyu-zvezdu-annu-chepmen.php/#more-1253

31 *Volgogradskyi musikant napisal pensyu ob Anne Chapman* ('Volgograd musician writes song about Anna Chapman') http://v1.ru/newsline/302348.html

8 THE COCKPIT OF EUROPE

1 A brief list would include the First World War, during which the front line ran through the territory of what later became Latvia, displacing around a third of the population; Bolshevik-backed insurrections in Estonia and Latvia, both put down by armed force; the Russian civil war; the rise and fall of the German *Landeswehr* and *Freikorps*; a communist insurrection in Estonia in 1924; the Soviet occupations of 1940 and 1944; the intervening Nazi invasion; and a decade-long partisan war. A definitive history has yet to be written, but I recommend *The Baltic States: the Years of Dependence* by Romualdas Misiūnas and Rein Taagepera (Hurst & Co., 1993).

2 Kremlin propaganda presents all opponents of the Soviet Union during the war and after as *ipso facto* 'fascists', 'war criminals', and perpetrators of the Holocaust. The vast majority of the Estonians, Latvians and Lithuanians who fought the Red Army did so not as Nazi sympathisers but because they wanted their countries' freedom. Westerners wrongly hold faraway peoples to a much higher standard than they apply to themselves. The atrocious treatment of Jews (and others) by Nazi collaborators in places like Lithuania rightly attracts condemnation. But it must be proportionate to the blame applied to (among others) Flemish, Dutch, Danish, French and Norwegian collaborators, whose countries were lucky enough not to end up in Soviet hands after the war. Hitler's killers found willing henchmen in every occupied country and among every nationality (not least among Russians).

It is particularly unfair to argue, as did Gordon Brown, the former British prime minister, that 'unlike in Germany, Lithuanian society has never gone through a period of reconciliation and repentance of its Nazi past'. Lithuania was not willingly part of Hitler's monstrous empire. It suffered huge human and material losses at the hands of its German occupiers. For someone writing from the comfort and safety of a country that has not been invaded for nearly a millennium, to lecture a country that experienced hardship on a scale unimaginable to any modern British citizen is not just patronising, it is outrageous. Placed under foreign occupation, people will collaborate, either to save their own skins, or out of opportunism, or to protect family members, or perhaps because they think they are choosing the lesser of two evils. 'Women of courage: Rachel Margolis' by Gordon Brown, *Independent*, 9 March 2011 http://www.independent.co.uk/news/people/profiles/women-of-courage-rachel-margolis-2236081.html See also *Nazi/Soviet Disinformation about the Holocaust in Latvia* by Andrew Ezergailis (Occupation Museum, Riga, Latvia, 2005).

3 The first in the series is *Swallows and Amazons*, set in the Lake District in northern England. Subsequent books are set in the Norfolk Broads; near Shotley in East Anglia; in the Outer Hebrides; and (in two more fancifully written books) on the coast of China and in the Caribbean. Close scrutiny of the text reveals many clues to Ransome's past. I was rereading the entire canon (out loud to my daughter Izzy) during the writing of this book, and (I beg the indulgence of readers here) found the stories to be full of clandestine infiltrations and exfiltrations, deception operations, escapes, pursuits, surveillance, codes, disguises and what the children call 'Indianing' and 'sleuthing'. A short list would include: Titty's surveillance of the burglars in *Swallows and Amazons*; Nancy and Peggy's escapes from the Great Aunt in *Swallowdale*; the use of Bill the cabin boy as an unwilling surveillance agent in *Peter Duck*; the use of codes in *Winter Holiday*; Tom Dudgeon's evasion of the Hullaballoos' pursuit in *Coot Club*; the use of clandestine photography and a dangle in the *Big Six*; the deception of the Dutch harbour pilot in *We Didn't Mean to Go to Sea*; the kidnapping of Bridget in *Secret Water*; the escape in *Missee Lee*; the elaborate and misguided surveillance operation against the hapless Timothy in *Pigeon Post*; the burglary and close cover operation in *The Picts and the Martyrs*; and the elaborate deception, disguise and surveillance operations mounted against the sinister Mr Jemmerling in *Great Northern*.

4 The best is *The Red Web: MI6 and the KGB Master Coup* (Aurum Press, 1989) and a film of the same name, broadcast on the BBC's 'Inside Story'. Perhaps

because the other events of that year were so dramatic, Tom Bower's extraordinary scoop did not receive the attention that it should have done. I am deeply grateful for his exemplary and generous help, including access to his meticulous original notebooks.

5 *MI6: the History of the Secret Intelligence Service 1909–1949*, by Keith Jeffery (Bloomsbury, 2010).

6 A microfilmed copy of the agency's records was kept in the basement of Stig Synnergren, later head of the Swedish defence forces, in his home at Tullinge outside Stockholm, and was returned to defence ministry custody in 1997. As the researcher Jonas Öhman notes, this could be 'perceived as symbolic in terms of the official attitude in Sweden to its post-war history'. See 'A Review of Western Intelligence Reports Regarding the Lithuanian Resistance', published as an afterword in a revised and updated edition of *Forest Brothers, an Account of an Anti-Soviet Freedom Fighter*, by Juozas Lukša (Central European University Press, Budapest, 2009), p. 393.

7 The original suggestion was for it to be headquartered in Oslo or Stockholm. The Swedish capital would remain important for SIS but proved too far from the action. Jeffery, p. 135.

8 *Churchill's Man of Mystery: Desmond Morton and the World of Intelligence* (Government Official History Series) by Gill Bennett (Routledge, 2006) p. 42. She also notes the development of the SIS doctrine that spying is best done from a neighbouring country to the one being spied on.

9 See *Die Geschichte der baltischen Staaten* (Deutsche Taschenbuch Verlag, 1990) by Georg von Rauch; in English as *The Baltic States: The Years of Independence: Estonia, Latvia, Lithuania, 1917–1940* (St Martin's Press, 1995). Another warring party in Estonia and Latvia was a powerful German army marooned in the east by the collapse of the Kaiser's empire at the end of the war, which was trying to create a 'Teutonic superstate' in the east, in which German feudal hegemony over the region would survive. Though the northern Baltic provinces had been part of the Russian empire, they had been ruled by a powerful caste of Baltic German barons, the distant descendants of the medieval Teutonic Knights. Their rule and riches were deeply resented and they were soon to suffer the expropriation of much of their property in land reforms. The feudal era ended only in the mid nineteenth century; for Estonia and Latvia the era when serfs had to struggle even for literacy and the right to a surname was a bitter living memory. In Lithuania, books and newspapers in the Latin alphabet were forbidden under Tsarist Russification policies.

Adding a further dimension of complexity (and vulnerability) was a fierce conflict between Poland and Lithuania over the ancient city of Vilnius

(Wilno in Polish). Once the historical capital of the old Grand Duchy of Lithuania, it had become predominantly Polish in the intervening centuries. Barely had Lithuania declared independence than in 1920 a Polish military force seized Vilnius. The two countries froze relations for twenty years, and the issue plagues their ties to this day.

10 In 2005 Mr Putin, answering a question from an Estonian journalist about Russia's unwillingness to apologise for the Soviet occupation of the Baltic states, referred to it thus:

> As I see it, in 1918, Russia and Germany did a deal . . . under which Russia handed over part of its territories to German control. This marked the beginning of Estonian statehood. In 1939, Russia and Germany did another deal and Germany handed these territories back to Russia. In 1939, they were absorbed into the Soviet Union. Let us not talk now about whether this was good or bad. This is part of history. I think that this was a deal, and small countries and small nations were the bargaining chips in this deal. Regrettably, such was the reality of those times, just as there was the reality of European countries' colonial past, or the use of slave labour in the United States [. . .] If the Baltic states had already been absorbed into the Soviet Union in 1939, then the Soviet Union could not occupy them in 1945 because they had already become part of its territory.

The video of the press conference, after the EU–Russia summit on 10 May 2005, where he responds to the Estonian journalist Astrid Kannel, can be seen here http://www.youtube.com/watch?v=32X_FxR4KZg. An English transcript can be found here http://archive.kremlin.ru/eng/ speeches/2005/05/10/2030_type82914type82915_88025.shtml. I have slightly amended the translation.

11 'From being accessories to military operations in 1914, they had become major players in the survival and destruction of states.' From *Dances in Deep Shadow* by Michael Occleshaw (Constable, 2006) p. 309.

12 Ibid, p. 7.

13 *The Eyes of the Navy* by Admiral Sir William James (Methuen & Co., 1955) p. 177.

14 *The Quest for C* by Alan Judd (Harper Press paperback edn, 2000) p. 434.

15 The 'intervention', as it is known, involved fourteen foreign countries in all. An Anglo-American force, with French, Canadian and White Russian elements, attacked from Archangel. A French-led force, with Polish and Greek soldiers, supported General Deniken in southern Russia. Japanese,

American, Czechoslovak and other troops fought alongside the Admiral Kolchak's forces in Siberia. 'Dunsterforce' comprising Australian, British, and Canadian troops under General Lionel Dunsterville (the original 'Stalky' from Kipling's 'Stalky & Co.') pushed north from Persia and occupied Baku. See among other works *The Adventures of Dunsterforce* (London, 1920) by Major-General L. C. Dunsterville C.B.

16 I first saw this poster in the excellent Civil War exhibition in the municipal history museum in Khabarovsk. The transliterated Russian reads as follows

Moi russkie druzya! Ya Anglichanin. Vo imya nashevo obshago soyuznago dela, proshu vas, eshche nemnogo proderzhites takimi molodtsami, kakimi vyi byili vsegda. Ya dostavlyal i eshche bezgranichno dostavlyu vse, chto vam budet nuzhno, i samoye glavnoye, dostavlyu vam noviye oruzhie, kotoroye istrebit etikh otvratitelnykh krovozhadnyikh krasnykh chudovisch.

17 *Iron Maze* by the former British intelligence officer Gordon Brook-Shepherd (Pan paperback edn, 1998), p. 103. The author draws heavily on Orlov's then unpublished memoir. Orlov had earlier compiled an in-house history of the affair for the NKVD. Brook-Shepherd also had access to the early part of the private memoirs of Harry Carr. These are still classified and in the hands of SIS. Orlov's book was subsequently published as *The March of Time*, edited by Philip Knightley (St Ermin's Press, 2004). The same material quoted by Brook-Shepherd is found on p. 124 onwards. Orlov's reliability has been questioned by, among others, Boris Volodarsky. But I do not find it plausible that he would have invented the entire affair.

18 *Memoirs of a British Agent* by Robert Bruce Lockhart (Putnam, 1932), p. 314. In accounts at the time his surname (depending on who is writing it) was given variously as Šmithens (in Latvian); Shmegkhen or Shmidkhen (in Russian transliteration, the former probably garbled) or 'Smidchen'. Had he written it in Latvian, his real name was probably Jānis Buikis. At any rate, he was to play a vital role in the first big British intelligence fiasco of post-imperial Russia. Lockhart was a notorious frequenter of nightclubs. During a later stint in Prague, he even had a cocktail named after him, involving hefty slugs of brandy and champagne. Sadly, by the time I moved to Prague in 1989, all memory of this heroic drink had been lost.

19 Bennett, p. 48.

20 *The March of Time*, p. 129. Orlov notes: 'Reilly fell into two major errors, ignorance and wishful thinking, which if combined with reckless courage, spell tragedy.'

21 Brook-Shepherd, p.107.

22 Judd, p. 426.

23 *Red Dusk and the Morrow. Adventures and Investigations in Red Russia*, by Sir Paul Dukes KBE (Doubleday, 1922). Downloadable at http://www.archive. org/stream/redduskandmorroo1dukegoog#page/n8/mode/2up, p. 7.

24 Jeffery, p. 175.

25 Brook-Shepherd, p. 133.

26 A lively account of Dukes's mission can be found in *Operation Kronstadt* (Arrow, 2010) by the pseudonymous former SIS officer Harry Ferguson.

27 Brook-Shepherd, p. 135.

28 *The Last Englishman* by Roland Chambers (paperback edn, Faber & Faber, 2010), p. 287. Shortly after Ransome returned, the Red Army defeated the 'White' forces under General Nikolai Yudenich. British destroyers evacuated them to a life in exile; Estonia and Soviet Russia opened talks on a peace treaty, signed in Tartu in 1920. Admiral Cowan's squadron went home, basking in Estonian gratitude that was still heartfelt seventy years later. Ransome noted that this result represented a rare instance of being thanked for meddling in other countries' affairs. He left with thirty-five diamonds and three strings of pearls of questionable provenance.

29 Bennett, p. 46.

30 Jeffery, p. 181.

31 Bennett, p. 51.

32 Brook-Shepherd, p. 255.

33 Ibid, p. 288.

34 Ibid, p. 291; the author spells his name Deribass.

35 Bennett, pp. 43–4.

36 Jeffery, p. 186.

37 Ibid, p. 185.

38 Ibid, p. 218.

39 For a thorough treatment of this remarkable and still puzzling affair, I recommend Gill Bennett's monograph, 'A most extraordinary and mysterious business: The Zinoviev Letter of 1924' http://www.fco.gov.uk/resources/ en/pdf/pdf5/fco_pdf_zinovievletter1 It draws heavily on the unpublished work of Millicent Bagot, the MI5 expert on communism who was the real-life model for Connie Sachs in le Carré's *Tinker, Tailor, Soldier, Spy*. http:// www.guardian.co.uk/news/2006/jun/17/guardianobituaries.mainsection

40 Jeffery, p. 312. In fact, the agent had the information from close friends in the East Prussian aristocracy, who had met the German negotiators on a social visit, during which they had spoken freely.

41 Jeffery, pp. 372–3.

42 Jeffery, pp. 192–3.

9 BETWEEN THE HAMMER AND THE ANVIL

1 It involved tens of thousands of fighters, pitched battles, networks of underground bunkers, elaborate command structures, education and welfare
   systems, propaganda newspapers and a parallel justice system. The historian
   Joseph Pajaujis-Javis lists the Lithuanian partisans' goals as: (1) To prevent
   Sovietisation of the country by annihilating communist activists and the
   KGB forces in the countryside; (2) to safeguard the public order, to protect
   the population from robberies, either by civilians, or by Red soldiers; (3)
   to free political prisoners from detention wherever circumstances allowed
   it; (4) to enforce the boycott of the 'elections' to the Supreme Soviet of
   the USSR or to the leadership of the puppet state, and thus to prevent the
   falsification of the will of the Lithuanian nation and the creation of a false
   base for the legality of the Soviet-imposed regime; (5) to disrupt the draft of
   Lithuanian youth into the Red Army; (6) to obstruct the nationalisation of
   landed property and collectivisation of agriculture; (7) to prevent the settling
   of Russian colonists on the land and in the homesteads of the Lithuanian
   farmers deported to Siberia. From *Soviet Genocide in Lithuania* (Manyland
   Books, New York, 1980), p. 95, quoted (p. 24) in 'Forest Brothers from
   the West' by Darius Razgaitis (Boston University thesis 2002) available at
   http://www.mrdarius.com/fb/wfd.pdf

2 *A Tangled Web: The memoirs of an Estonian who fell into the clutches of MI6 and
   the KGB* by Mart Männik, translated and introduced by the Earl of Carlisle
   (Greif Grenader Publishing, Tallinn, 2008) p. 50. http://www.scribd.com/
   doc/50728582/Mart-Mannik-A-Tangled-Web

3 Quoted in *The Last Ambassador* by Tina Tamman (Rodopi, 2011), p. 176.

4 See *The War in the Woods* by Mart Laar (Compass Press, 1992), p. 207.

5 The partisan leader was Algirdas Vokietaitis; the intermediary was the
   Lithuanian diplomat and later SIS agent Vladas 'Walter' Žilinskas. See
   Pavargęs herojus, Jonas Deksnys trijų žvalgybų tarnyboje (*The Weary Hero: Jonas
   Deksnys in the Service of Three Intelligence Agencies*) by Liūtas Mockūnas (Baltos
   Lankos, Vilnius, 1997), p. 138. See also Razgaitis, p. 17. This is earlier than
   the 1947 date given by Jeffery. Mart Laar's book states (p. 208) that contact
   was re-established between SIS and the Lithuanian partisan movement in
   the 'spring of 1945'. A lengthy KGB history written by Lukaševičs in 1986
   gives the date as March 1943.

6 See *Toomas Hellat ja KGB* (*Toomas Hellat and the KGB*) by Tõnis Ritson
   http://riigi.arhiiv.ee/public/TUNA/Artiklid_Biblio/RitsonTonis_
   Toomas_Hellat_1_TUNA1998_1.pdf

7 Having originally felt themselves buttressed by a British naval presence in the Baltic Sea and by the League of Nations' pledge to protect small countries, the Baltic states found they had to look out for themselves. France and America were far away; Britain, having pulled out of the Baltic under a deal with Germany in 1935, was no longer to be trusted. The three small countries tried permutations of friendship with Poland, Sweden, Germany and the Soviet Union, as well as an abortive Baltic entente. None of it worked.

8 Timothy Snyder's book *Bloodlands: Europe between Hitler and Stalin* (Basic Books/Bodley Head, 2010) is an incomparable account of the wider picture of mass murder: www.bloodlandsbook.com

9 A shortlived Estonian government under the lawyer Otto Tief, for example, took power as the Nazis withdrew in 1944. Those of its members who could not escape were jailed. One, Arnold Susi, befriended Aleksandr Solzhenitsyn in a prison camp. In *The Gulag Archipelago*, Solzhenitsyn wrote:

> [Susi] breathed a completely different sort of air. And he would tell me passionately about his own interests, and these were Estonia and democracy. And although I had never expected to become interested in Estonia, much less bourgeois democracy, I nevertheless kept listening to his loving stories of twenty free years in that modest, work-loving, small nation of big men whose ways were slow and set. I listened to the principles of the Estonian constitution, which had been borrowed from the best of European experience, and to how their hundred-member, one-house parliament had worked. And, though the 'why' of it wasn't clear, I began to like it all and store it all away in my experience.
>
> I listened willingly to their fatal history: the tiny Estonian anvil had, from way, way back, been caught between two hammers, the Teutons and the Slavs. Blows showered on it from East and West in turn; there was no end to it, and there still isn't. (Harper & Row edition, 1974, p. 242.)

10 *Laiškai Mylimosioms* (*Letters to Loved Ones*) (American Foundation for Lithuanian Research, 1993), p. 10; quoted in Razgaitis, p. 20. Some had until recently been in German uniform: many Estonians and Latvians had joined (or were conscripted into) the Third Reich's military. In a perverse bit of branding (non-Germans were not allowed to join the 'real' German army, the *Wehrmacht*), these were enlisted under the Waffen-SS logo. Though some had previously been in police and other units involved in the Holocaust, others were guilty only of being on the wrong side of history.

The units have been confused with Hitler's gruesome *Schutzstaffel*, originally the paramilitary wing of the Nazi Party. The US Displaced Persons Commission in September 1950 declared that 'The Baltic Waffen SS Units (Baltic Legions) are to be considered as separate and distinct in purpose, ideology, activities, and qualifications for membership from the German SS, and therefore the Commission holds them not to be a movement hostile to the Government of the United States.'

As the post-war Stalinist terror intensified, the regime's tactics became ever more cynical and brutal. The authorities repeatedly offered amnesties, but those who tried to take advantage of them were imprisoned, tortured, deported or forced to fight on the other side. Staying on the sidelines was all but impossible. Those who refused to inform on their colleagues, families and friends were themselves suspect. Taking up arms offered at least the chance of a more glorious death.

11 Bower, p. 59–60. The later cover for the operation was the British Baltic Fishery Protection Service, based in Kiel in the British zone of Germany, and using two souped-up German Lursen E-Boats. The crew were German; the captain, Hans Helmut Klose, later became the commander-in-chief of the West German navy.

12 The genuine movement was called VLIK – *Vyriausiasis Lietuvos išlaisvinimo komitetas* (Supreme Committee for the Liberation of Lithuania). The Soviet-sponsored one was VLAK – *Vyriausiasis Lietuvos atstatymo komitetas* (Supreme Committee for the Restoration of Lithuania). Many working for VLAK initially did not realise that it was bogus. The KGB provided flawless forged papers for its unwitting emissaries when they visited the West. Genuine partisans later made three attempts to kill the VLAK leader Markulis, until the KGB took him to a safe house in Leningrad.

13 *Partizanai Apie Pasaulį, Politiką ir Save (Partisans on the World, Politics and Themselves)*, ed. Nijolė Gaškaitė-Žemaitienė (Genocide and Resistance Studies Center, Vilnius, 1998), p. 95, quoted in Razgaitis, p. 30. The men and women involved in the struggle displayed a determination and optimism that can seem almost delusional to the outsider. Perhaps naively, few in the region imagined the West and the Kremlin would let the countries snuffed out by the dictators' pact of 1939 be the biggest losers of the post-war settlement. They took at face value the words of the Atlantic Charter: self-determination for all, and that 'territorial adjustments must be in accord with the wishes of the peoples concerned' http://www.archives.gov/education/lessons/fdr-churchill/images/atlantic-charter.gif

14 'Management of Covert Actions in the Truman Presidency' http://www. globalsecurity.org/intell/ops/covert-action-truman.htm

15 According to a fragment of declassified material, CIA operations in the region included:

- AEBALCONY (1960–62) was designed to use US citizens with Baltic language fluency in 'mounted' and 'piggy-back' legal traveller operations into Soviet-occupied Estonia, Latvia, and Lithuania.

- AECOB, approved in 1950, was a vehicle for foreign intelligence operations into and within Soviet Latvia and involved infiltration and exfiltration of black agents and the recruitment of legally resident agents in the USSR, especially Latvia.

- AEASTER was a program in near east areas to spot, recruit, and train Circassians and other Russian émigrés and send them back into the USSR.

- AEFREEMAN (1953–64), which included AEBASIN/AEROOT (1953–60), AEFLAG (1955–62), and AEPOLE (formerly AECHAMP) (1949–59), was designed to strengthen resistance to communism and harass the Soviet regime in the Baltic countries.

- AEBASIN/AEROOT supported Estonian émigrés and émigré activities against the Estonian SSR.

- AEFLAG was aimed at people of the Latvian SSR.

- AEMARSH (1953–9) involved collecting foreign intelligence on the Soviet regime in Latvia through sources residing in the Latvian SSR, legal travellers, and all possible legal means.

- The Institute for Latvian Culture (AEMINX) was established as a cover facility engaged in the preservation and development of Latvian national culture, collection of information on Latvian national life, and the safeguarding and preserving of physical, spiritual, and moral conditions of Latvians who were separated from their homeland.

- AEPOLE (formerly AECHAMP, formerly BGLAPIN) targeted the Lithuanian SSR. These projects provided intelligence and operational data from Baltic countries through radio broadcasts, mailing operations, liaison with émigré organizations, political and psychological briefings for legal travellers and exploitation of other media such as demonstrations.

- AEGEAN (formerly CAPSTAN) provided FI (foreign intelligence) from the Baltic States and USSR using support bases developed in the Lithuanian SSR as transit points.

- AEGEAN/CAPSTAN work continued under Project AECHAMP. AEMANNER (1955–8) was an operation to collect intelligence on the Lithuanian SSR by spotting, recruiting, and training Lithuanians who planned to return to Lithuania; spotting, recruiting, and training Lithuanian merchant seamen who would be on vessels calling at Lithuanian SSR ports; exploiting existing postal channels between Lithuanian SSR and the West; and interrogating persons coming out of the Lithuanian SSR.
- ZRLYNCH was approved in 1950 for use of the Latvian Resistance Movement, which had been formed in 1944, as a vehicle for clandestine activities within the USSR. ZRLYNCH was renewed in 1952 as a part of AECOB, which then provided both FI and political and psychological activities.

See http://www.archives.gov/iwg/declassified-records/rg-263-cia-records/second-release-lexicon.pdf and http://www.globalsecurity.org/intell/ops/ussr-redsox.htm (both accessed July 2011).

16 'How to be a spy' by Anthony Cavendish, *Sydney Morning Herald*, 17 December 1988. A broadly similar account appears in a book by the same author, *Inside Intelligence*, published amidst intense official disapproval by Palu in 1987.

17 *My Silent War* by Kim Philby (Panther, 1969), p. 146.

18 Freds Launags, in the film *Red Web*.

19 *The CIA's Secret Operations* by Harry Rositzke (Reader's Digest Press, 1977), p. 20.

20 Ibid, p.17.

21 Recruited in Operation Bloodstone. For details see *Blowback* by Christopher Simpson (Collier Books/Macmillan, August 1989).

22 Bower, p. 153.

23 *Lithuania: The Outposts of Freedom* by Constantine Jurgela (The National Guard of Lithuania in Exile and Valkyrie Press, 1976), p. 232. Quoted in Razgaitis, p. 40.

24 Männik, p. 57.

25 'A Review of Western Intelligence Reports Regarding The Lithuanian Resistance', by Jonas Öhman, published as an afterword (p. 393) in a revised and updated edition of *Forest Brothers, an Account of an Anti-Soviet Freedom Fighter* by Juozas Lukša (Central European University Press, Budapest, 2009). 'Swedish espionage in the Baltics 1943–1957: A study of a fiasco?' by Peteris Ininbergs http://kau.diva-portal.org/smash/get/diva2:5494/

FULLTEXT01 (accessed July 2011). It includes an abstract in English; the rest is in Swedish.

26 Linksmakalnis was the last Russian military installation to be decommissioned in Lithuania. Construction started in 1946, with, according to Lukša's report, the use of Italian or Hungarian POWs (he noted that they spoke a 'language that the local visitors did not understand'.) It included deep bunkers and a huge array of antennae, with a colossal satellite dish towering over the village. Access to outsiders was strictly forbidden. Staff there joked to locals, in its dying days, that they could connect a telephone to Fidel Castro's private line. Pictures of the ruins can be found here http://www.urbanexploration.lt/irasai/KGB-radiozvalgybos-kompleksas-linksmakalnyje/

27 I draw heavily here on Bower, pp. 158ff., who gives an excellent account of this.

28 Bower, p. 164.

29 Readers may wish to seek out a copy of the haunting and neglected *Russian Hide and Seek* by Kingsley Amis (Hutchinson, 1980) for an idea of what Britain would be like after decades of Soviet occupation and 'denationing'. Pages 49–53 in the Penguin edition are strongly recommended. I am indebted to my friend Peter Hitchens for this suggestion. An excellent fictional treatment of the psychological torment caused by the failure of the resistance can be found in *Purge*, a novel by the Finnish–Estonian writer Sofi Oksanen (Atlantic Books, 2011).

30 Remeikis, p. 278.

31 *The Unknown War: Armed Anti-Soviet Resistance in Lithuania in 1944–1953* by Dalia Kuodytė and Rokas Tracevskis, (Genocide and Resistance Museum, Lithuania, 2004).

32 He died in 2002. '*Pēdējā pasaules kara pēdējais mežabrālis*' (*Last Forest Brother of the Last World War*) by Māra Grīnberga, published in *Diena* (Riga, Latvia) 18 May 1995.

33 I am indebted to Ritvars Jansons of the Occupation Museum in Riga for this information, based on Latvian émigrés' unpublished correspondence.

34 Tamman, p. 182. I would be delighted to hear from any of Capt. Nelberg's surviving relatives.

35 Hans Toomla and Kaljo Kukk were parachuted into Estonia on 7 May 1954. They carried, according to a KGB report:

> a machine gun with ammunition, four revolvers, two portable transmitters, ciphers and codes ... topographical maps, cameras, blank Soviet passports, military identity cards and certificates, counterfeit seals of

Soviet institutions, Swedish and Norwegian crowns and 80,000 roubles.

A KGB statement reported in the Soviet media gives details of their capture and can be accessed in English (for a fee) here http://dlib.eastview.com/browse/doc/13847060

36 *A Secret Life* by Benjamin Weiser (Public Affairs, 2004). See also www. kuklinski.us

37 He was interviewed by Bower in the *Red Web* documentary. Algirdas Vokietaitis, the Lithuanian émigré who made the first contact with the Western secret services in Stockholm in 1943, moved to America, where he was a notable instructor in photography.

38 Two lengthy KGB archive documents (in Estonian) give a thorough picture of the activities of American, British, French, German and Swedish espionage in the Baltics. Dated 4 January 1956 http://www.esm.ee/public/projektid/5/2.osak55.html and 20 February 1957 http://www.esm.ee/public/projektid/5/dokumendid/doko454.html

39 'Spies caught and exposed', *Izvestia*, 7 March 1957 https://dlib.eastview.com/browse/doc/13972020

40 This link (in Swedish) gives an account of the story and of a filmed version of Hallisk's life. http://www.expressen.se/nyheter/1.3727/verklighetens-ramona

41 Ininbergs gives an excellent account of this little-known history.

42 The mission was dogged by bad luck. The three men were dropped a hundred miles from their supposed destination. One of their supply containers was found by a peasant who gave it to what he thought were real partisans, but who were in fact a phoney group run by the KGB (what happened to the peasant is not known, but can be imagined). 'Broken promises reward Lithuania's forgotten heroes' by Edward Lucas, *Independent*, 9 September 1991.

43 Interviewed in the *Red Web* documentary.

44 Interviewed by Tom Bower, *Independent* Saturday Magazine, 22 September 1990.

45 A partial account of this remarkable story (in Czech) is in *Československobritské Zpravodajské Soupeřen* (Czechoslovak–British Intelligence Rivalry) by Dr Prokop Tomek, *Úřad dokumentace a vyšetřování zločinů komunismu* (Institute for the Documentation and Research of the Crimes of Communism, 2006. http://aplikace.mvcr.cz/archiv2008/policie/udv/securita/sbornik14/sbornik14.pdf

46 Along with Hallisk, van Jung and others, they featured in an Estonian documentary, *Külalised* (*The Visitors*) in 2002. I am

grateful to the producers for providing me with a copy of their film, which deserved a wider audience. http://www.allfilm.ee/web/index. php?lang=en&page_id=111&file_id=1052&cat_id=116

10 THE UPSIDE DOWN WORLD

1 I draw heavily here on *The Main Enemy: the Inside Story of the CIA's Final Showdown with the KGB* by Milt Bearden and James Risen (Random House, 2003). The 'Gavrilov' backchannel is discussed on p. 184.

2 *Battleground Berlin: CIA vs. KGB in the Cold War* by David Murphy and Sergei Kondrashev (Yale University Press, 1999).

3 'Death of a Perfect Spy' by Elaine Shannon, *Time*, 24 June 2001 http:// www.time.com/time/magazine/printout/0,8816,164863,00.html

4 This article gives a good indication of what the West was trying to buy – and by implication what it would obtain by other means if necessary. 'US Is Shopping as Soviets Offer To Sell Once-Secret Technology' by William Broad, *New York Times*, 4 November 1991 http://www.nytimes. com/1991/11/04/world/us-is-shopping-as-soviets-offer-to-sell-once- secret-technology.html

5 The KGB cannily tried to revive the story of 'Red Web' to derail the Baltic independence movements in the late 1980s. The aim was to contrast the frankness of Gorbachev's approach to history with the silence of the West about its use of fascist collaborators in the post-war era, and the cynical and incompetent behaviour of the CIA and SIS. In November 1987 the KGB brought its greatest trophy, Kim Philby, to Riga, and filmed him in a meet- ing with Lukaševičs, purportedly (and quite possibly truly) the first time that the two men had met. Philby's lizard-like face lights up as he discusses Operation Jungle with his host (who spoke fluent English, having been posted to London, under a pseudonym, as a reward for his efforts). The initial aim was to demoralise the Baltic independence movements by high- lighting the past. The Soviet authorities then made the material, and former KGB officers, and surviving partisans, available to Mr Bower. In the West, SIS – never before the subject of an unauthorised and unflattering exposé – was furious, telling retired officers that they risked their pensions if they talked to Mr Bower. He short-circuited the ban by talking to CIA veterans and pensionless émigrés. But the tide of history was running too strongly, and Estonians, Latvians and Lithuanians were in no mood to believe Soviet propaganda of any kind, even when it was true. Mr Bower, quite unfairly, was assumed to be a Kremlin stooge.

An early example of KGB propaganda is *Polymany s polichnim: sbornik faktov spionazhom protiv SSSR (Caught red-handed: a collection of facts about espionage against the USSR)*, State Publishing House for Political Literature, Moscow, 1963. See also *KGB, Stasi ja Eesti luureajalugu (KGB, Stasi and Estonian intelligence history)* by Ivo Juurvee http://rahvusarhiiv.ra.ee/public/ TUNA/Artiklid_Biblio/JuurveeIvo_KGB_Stasi_TUNA2008_2.pdf

6 *The Friends: Britain's post-war secret intelligence operations* by Nigel West (Weidenfeld and Nicolson, 1988).

7 A gripping account of his defection comes in his autobiographical *Tower of Secrets* (Naval Institute Press, 1993).

8 The journalist David Satter, then the Moscow correspondent of the *Financial Times*, gives a vivid account of his attempt to meet dissidents in Estonia in 1977.

> 'So,' I said, 'you are trying to tell me that someone arranged for you to meet me in Tallinn?' Several of them nodded their heads yes. 'Show me some identification,' I said. 'No, we don't show any identification,' said the sandy-haired man, shaking his head firmly. 'I'm glad to hear that,' I said, 'because for a moment it occurred to me that you might actually be the dissidents, but if you won't identify yourselves, it only proves to me that you're the KGB.' The superficial politeness that had prevailed up until that point disappeared. The tall, solemn member of the group leaned over the table. 'I spent twelve years in the camps,' he said. 'My friends have spent six, seven, and eight years in the camps. You're not going to treat us like a bunch of niggers.'

Stung by the rebuke, Satter resolved to trust his hosts, who gave every appearance of being terrified by KGB surveillance and of making elaborate precautions to avoid it. Only when he returned to Moscow did he find out that the entire meeting had indeed been a charade staged to find out more about his own views and contacts. The real Estonian dissidents had waited in vain for their visitor. 'Never Speak to Strangers: A memoir of journalism, the Cold War, and the KGB' by David Satter, *The Weekly Standard*, 6 August 2007 (vol. 12, no. 44) http://www.weeklystandard.com/Content/ Public/Articles/000/000/013/932plsuu.asp. Satter's article 'The Ghost in the Machine' in the *Financial Times* on 5 April 1977 was none the less a remarkable event, which not only shocked Western Sovietologists who thought the Baltic struggle for independence was over, but also boosted spirits in the region.

9 See https://www.cia.gov/news-information/featured-story-archive/2010-featured-story-archive/colonel-penkovsky.html Penkovsky passed his messages in a park to a British diplomat's wife wheeling a pram.

10 *Next Stop Execution* (Macmillan, 1995) is one of Mr Gordievsky's many books.

11 'Cold War Spy Tale Came to Life on the Streets of Moscow' by Matt Schudel, *Washington Post*, 20 April 2008 http://www.washingtonpost.com/wp-dyn/content/article/2008/04/19/AR2008041902071_pf.html

12 Bearden/Risen, p. 382.

13 Paul Goble, then at the CIA, deserves special mention here. His blog has been essential reading http://windowoneurasia2.blogspot.com

14 'Transitional Justice in the Former Yugoslavia' http://ictj.org/sites/default/files/ICTJ-FormerYugoslavia-Justice-Facts-2009-English.pdf

15 Entitled *Lähtealused Eesti eriteenistuste väljaarendamiseks* (*Guidelines on the development of Estonia's special services*), it is still classified and my requests to view it have been politely rejected. See *Eesti nähtamatud mehed* (*Estonia's invisible men*) by Toomas Sildam and Kaarel Tarand, *Postimees*, 20 January 1997 http://www.postimees.ee/luup/97/02/top.htm

16 Interview with the author, March 2011.

17 '*Riigikogu* (Estonian Parliament) Committee of Investigation to Ascertain the Circumstances Related to the Export of Military Equipment from the Territory of the Republic of Estonia on the Ferry *Estonia* in 1994, Final Report.' Available at http://www.riigikogu.ee/public/Riigikogu/Dokumendid/estcom_eng.pdf

18 See 'Death in the Baltic, the MI6 Connection' by Stephen Davis, *New Statesman*, 23 May 2005 http://www.newstatesman.com/200505230019 and this report (in Swedish) by the judge Johan Hirschfeldt 'Transport of military material on the *MV Estonia* in September 1994' http://www.estoniasamlingen.se/textfiles/Fo_2004_06.pdf

19 '*In der Bermuda Dreieck der Ostsea*' ('In the Bermuda Triangle of the Baltic Sea'), *Der Spiegel*, 23 December 1999 http://www.spiegel.de/panorama/0,1518,57520,00.html I am grateful to Jutta Rabe for her help.

20 I was the managing editor and major shareholder of the *Baltic Independent*, which in late 1994 merged with the *Baltic Observer* to become the *Baltic Times* www.baltictimes.com

21 A particular puzzle concerns the fate of the captain, Arvo Piht, and several other survivors. They include Lembit Leiger (chief engineer), Viktor Bogdanov (ship's doctor), Kaimar Kikas (navigation officer), Agur Targama (fourth engineer), Tiina Müür (manager of the duty-free shop) and Hannely Veid and

Hanka-Hannika Veide (dancers). All eight were seen by multiple witnesses leaving the vessel on the same life raft and were recorded as rescued in multiple lists compiled on shore. In several cases (including Captain Piht and the twins) their families received phone calls informing them that their relatives were safe – in the twins' case using a nickname known only to close friends and family. The twins' parents say they have received phone calls from their daughters; they believe they were until recently living in San Diego. Captain Piht's rescue was also reported in the *New York Times*, in an article by Richard Stevenson on 1 October 1994 http://www.nytimes.com/1994/10/01/world/investigators-cite-bow-door-in-estonian-ferry-s-sinking.html

In the confusing aftermath of a disaster, many mistakes happen, not least in record-keeping; bereaved parents' grief can render them delusional. The idea that eight people could be abducted from Sweden as part of an international cover-up of a botched smuggling operation will strike many as outrageously implausible. I am not endorsing any particular theory and I am aware that some people speculating about the 'real' story of the *Estonia* are bigots and nutcases. Among the many sites dealing with the tragedy are http://members.tripod.com/mv_estonia http://www.elaestonia.org/eng/index.php and http://www.estoniaferrydisaster.net Interviews with the Veide parents (in Estonian) can be found here http://www.epl.ee/artikkel/22560 (in which one of the supposedly dead twin daughters is said to have phoned) and http://www.parnupostimees.ee/?id=268822 (with the San Diego reference).

11 THE TRAITOR'S TALE

1 I cannot find independent confirmation of this but Bo Kragh, a banker and government adviser at the time, terms the claim 'very plausible'. Suitcases of cash crossing the Baltic Sea in those days were not unusual.

2 This and some other quotes come from *Riigereetur* (*State Traitor*) a film about the Simm case, originally in Estonian. It is available with English subtitles here as *The Spy Inside* http://www.javafilms.fr/spip.php?article427

3 In the 1990s, even Russian course members (from the GRU) took part in courses there. However this has ceased due to some clumsy attempts by those invited to spy. The museum at Chicksands is well worth visiting. http://www.army.mod.uk/intelligence/about/default.aspx

4 Its full name is the *Kaitsepolitseiamet*. www.kapo.ee/eng

5 A brief account of Scott's meetings with Simm comes in *Spionimängud* (*Spy Games*) by Virkko Lepassalu (Pegasus, Tallinn, 2009), pp.106–109.

6 These and other details come from discussions with serving officials who prefer not to be mentioned in print.

7 Interview with Mr Savisaar, March 2010.

8 http://www.mod.gov.ee/en/1252 Other documents such as www.mod. gov.ee/files/kmin/img/File/palgad_2003.xls give his 2003 annual salary of 233715.95 Estonian kroons (in those days about £10,000); another shows him as one of the participants on the 'Higher National Defence Course' http://www.mod.gov.ee/et/i-krkk

9 He has been bankrupted by a lawsuit brought by the Estonian state to recover some of the costs of his betrayal. The sum involved, €1.28m (around $1.8m at the then exchange rate), is to pay for new cryptographic equipment and other security fittings. After some haggling, I agreed to pay his wife €2,000 for the exclusive rights to her side of the story. My original plan was to use this as a personal appendix to a book wholly devoted to her husband's betrayal and arrest. In the event, I decided that her story was not sufficiently distinctive to deserve special treatment and that the Simm case was best covered in a wider geographical and historical context. But I have paid her none the less.

10 'New Documents Reveal Truth on NATO's "Most Damaging" Spy' by Fidelius Schmid and Andreas Ulrich, *Der Spiegel*, 30 April 2010 http://www.spiegel.de/international/europe/0,1518,691817-3,00.html

11 Details of this base, and another one in Poland, were leaked in 2009, with the accusation that they had been secret prisons for terrorism suspects. In 2002 America did press all three Baltic states to cooperate in the extraordinary rendition of terrorists, saying that their NATO chances would be blighted if they declined. Estonia said no, arguing that the torture, deportation and illegal imprisonment in its own history made it impossible to compromise in such a way. Estonian officials also worried, in retrospect rightly, that any such cooperation would not remain secret for long. The American presence in Lithuania, which dated from 2004, was remarkably conspicuous. The location was known to Vilnius taxi drivers and the supposedly secret building had been rewired at 110 volts. http://abcnews.go.com/Blotter/cia-secret-prison-found/story?id=9115978

12 This is by Simm's account: I presume it is a detail he gleaned during his interrogation.

13 http://www.rferl.org/content/NATO_Expels_Two_Russians_Over_Estonia_Spy_Scandal/1619004.html

14 See for example 'Russian top spy was paid also by the BND', *Der Spiegel*, 12 December 2008. http://www.spiegel.de/spiegel/print/d-62603838.

html; and '*Spion für Russland: Es ist ein Dauerritt auf Messers Schneide*' ('A Spy for Russia: It is a Long Ride on a Knife-Edge'); http://www.spiegel.de/politik/ausland/0,1518,704117,00.html; and *Weisser Ritter* (White Knight) http://www.spiegel.de/spiegel/print/d-70228790.html

15 '*Poteyevi shpionili vsei semyei*' ('The whole family spied on Poteyev'), 16 November 2010 http://www.rosbalt.ru/moscow/2010/11/16/790436.html

16 See '*Deshevniy predatel*' ('Cheap Traitor'), 4 May 2011, by Yelena Ovcharenko and Basil Voropaev, originally from *Izvestiya*, but available at http://www.chekist.ru/article/3650

17 A lively account of his life and defection comes in *Comrade J: The Untold Secrets of Russia's Master Spy in America After the End of the Cold War* (Penguin, 2007). Like all defectors' books, it should be taken with a degree of scepticism.

CONCLUSION

1 Quoted in *The United States and Germany in the era of the Cold War, 1945 to 1990, A Handbook: Volume 1: 1945–1968*, ed. Detlef Junker (Cambridge University Press, 2004), p. 98; Dulles' book *War or Peace* (1950) is available online http://www.questia.com/PM.qst?a=o&d=34046074

2 Committee on Banking and Financial Services, Hearing on Russian Money Laundering, 21 September 1999, testimony by R. James Woolsey http://www.cdi.org/russia/johnson/3516.html##2

3 'No more Western hugs for Russia's rulers' by Mikhail Kasyanov, Vladimir Milov, Boris Nemtsov and Vladimir Ryzhkov, *Washington Post*, 20 February 2011; http://www.washingtonpost.com/wp-dyn/content/article/2011/02/20/AR2011022002548.html

4 Cohen and Jensen, 'Reset regret'.

Acknowledgements

Meelis Saueauk of Estonia's Institute for Historical Memory kindly helped me find KGB documents about Operation Jungle from Estonian and Latvian archives. Ivo Juurvee also provided important examples of Soviet-era propaganda. Ritvars Jansons at the Occupation Museum in Riga generously shared his insights. Māra Grīnberga helped me find her article about the remarkable Mr Pīnups. Prokop Tomek in Prague shared his research on Miloslav Kroča and his daughter. Tom Bower effortlessly unearthed his twenty-year-old notebooks and lent me his unique copy of the film *Red Web*. Tina Tamman helped me track down Alexander Koppel, whose daughter Catherine and son-in-law Michael Breslin provided kind hospitality. Juho and Janno Kiik readily shared their memories of Voldemar. Ben Judah provided excellent research on Anna Chapman's life in Russia. Sam Donaldson in Dublin investigated the mysteries of Rossmore Grove. I am grateful to all of them, and to the people I have quoted. Bill Swainson at Bloomsbury deftly untangled the book's structure and helped me signpost it for a wider audience. Zoe Waldie at Rogers, Coleridge and Wright calmed my jitters.

My children Johnny, Hugo and Izzy uncomplainingly put up with my physical and mental absences. My wife Cristina Odone's critique was invaluable, as were her love and patience from beginning to end. In 1970s Oxford, my father J.R. Lucas's thoughts on espionage and communism inspired this book; it is dedicated to him and my mother Morar, who have been my unfailing support for fifty years. I am grateful to my editors at the *Economist* for giving me a sabbatical, and to my colleagues, particularly Ludwig Siegele, John Peet, Tom Nuttall and Bruce Clark, for uncomplainingly covering for my absences. However, the views, and mistakes, in this book are mine alone.

I owe a great debt to people who must remain nameless. They know who they are.

No government agency has sponsored or censored this book.

Index